A G-MAN'S LIFE

THE FBI,

BEING "DEEP THROAT,"

AND THE STRUGGLE FOR HONOR

IN WASHINGTON

———

MARK FELT

and John O'Connor

First published in hardcover in 2006
in the United States by PublicAffairs™, a member of
the Perseus Books Group. First published in paperback in
2006 by PublicAffairs™.

Book design and composition by Mark McGarry, Texas Type & Book Works
Set in Monotype Dante

Library of Congress Cataloging-in-Publication Data
Felt, W. Mark, 1913–
A G-man's life : the FBI, being "Deep Throat",
and the struggle for honor in Washington /
Mark Felt and John O'Connor.— 1st ed.
p. cm.
Includes index.
ISBN-13: 978-1-58648-377-7
ISBN-10: 1-58648-377-3
1. Felt, W. Mark, 1913- 2. United States. Federal Bureau of Investigation—
Officials and employees—Biography. 3. Watergate Affair, 1972–1974.
4. United States. Federal Bureau of Investigation.
I. O'Connor, John, 1946 Dec. 29– II. Title.
HV7911.F446 2006
973.924092—dc22
2005056521

FIRST EDITION
10 9 8 7 6 5 4 3 2 1

Mark Felt dedicates this book to the stalwart Special Agents of the modern FBI, present and former, whose skill, dedication, and integrity have served our country so well for over eight decades. When permitted to do their jobs, these Agents have evenly enforced our laws without regard to power or privilege, protecting both our civil liberties against unnecessary governmental incursion and our lives against criminal and terrorist assault. Mark hopes that by telling his story, those who have criticized these Agents will reevaluate, and come to view them as the principled protectors of society that they are.

John O'Connor dedicates his work to his late father and former (1940–43) FBI Agent, John C. O'Connor. The senior O'Connor taught his son, by example, the FBI technique for picking up used beverage glasses without compromising the latent fingerprints, always loudly announcing "FBI John!" when so doing. Although this was the sole FBI technique he taught his son, he always practiced the core FBI values of fairness, loyalty, and honesty, thus proving himself truly worthy of the sobriquet "FBI John."

CONTENTS

I

It was one of those events that divide history. Before dawn on the morning of June 17, 1972, five intruders wearing surgical gloves and business suits were found hiding in a small office at the Watergate, a luxury complex located along the Potomac River in Washington. The crime itself was a curiosity; there didn't seem to be much worth bugging or stealing in the office, part of a suite occupied by the Democratic National Committee. But within two days, agents of the Federal Bureau of Investigation had linked the intruders to the White House. The investigation intensified into a war of wills between FBI agents determined to follow these links and senior officials of the Nixon administration determined to hide them. Over the next two years, the confrontation shook our government to its constitutional foundations.

As the scandal developed, the headlines grew bigger and darker. Nixon's men had subverted the democratic electoral process and obstructed the criminal justice system. The Internal Revenue Service, the Federal Communications Commission, and other government offices were manipulated to punish political enemies and harass opponents. White House agents committed burglaries and conducted illegal electronic surveillance. The investigation spread from the FBI to the courts to Congress. On August 8, 1974, President Richard M. Nixon resigned in disgrace.

American politics still can be classified as either Before Watergate or After Watergate. In the end, the "national nightmare" led to the destruction of a presidency and criminal cases against dozens of government officials. But what survives from that era is the series of reforms that came in the aftermath. Today, Washington operates by new standards of openness and accountability. Presidents face stronger scrutiny by Congress and the press. Since Nixon's time, the use of presidential power has been examined microscopically, and any scandal worth its salt has become a "gate," from "Iran-Contragate" to "Monicagate." But "Watergate" above all has entered the political lexicon, standing for abuses of epic proportions—and for the forces that worked against those crimes.

The phenomenon we now call Watergate began to take shape years earlier, in the first months of the Nixon presidency. It was a time of war in Vietnam and confrontation at home, pitting the children of a growing counterculture against their parents in the "silent majority." Nixon came to office in 1969 on a promise to withdraw from Vietnam honorably, yet his first move was to expand the war, targeting enemy sanctuaries in neighboring Cambodia. When news of the administration's secret bombing campaign leaked out, the antiwar movement exploded—and so did Nixon's staffers, enraged by the unauthorized disclosure. On White House orders, the FBI tapped the phones of administration officials and journalists in search of the leaker. When the leaks continued, Nixon's men ordered up a more aggressive program of break-ins, bugging, mail opening, and other measures. The FBI and other intelligence agencies resisted them. So the White House organized its own

"Plumbers," a group of extralegal operatives tasked to stop the leaks.

Once the Plumbers had set up shop, it was all but inevitable that they would delve into politics. Nixon's men called on their services to gather intelligence and disrupt the plans of the administration's opponents. Much of this work proceeded in the netherworld of political competition until that June night in 1972 when a security guard discovered the break-in at the Watergate—and a *Washington Post* editor assigned junior reporter Bob Woodward to the story.

When we think of Watergate, we think of Woodward and Carl Bernstein, the reporters who pursued the case, and the force they unleashed: the tremendous power of modern investigative journalism. Today's era of adversarial reporting, for better or worse, offers financial rewards and critical acclaim to journalists who make sensational, politically charged investigative breakthroughs.

Watergate also established the rights and duties of whistleblowers—government and business employees who report illegal activities in the workplace. In 2002 three whistleblowers, Coleen Rowley of the FBI, Cynthia Cooper of WorldCom, and Sherron Watkins of Enron, were named Persons of the Year by *Time* magazine. The deference we afford these truth tellers today and the various whistleblowing statutes that protect them testify to the power of Watergate's most mysterious figure and one of the most sensational secret agents of all time, Woodward's confidential source, the man dubbed Deep Throat by a *Post* editor.

As Woodward and Bernstein made clear in their book, *All the President's Men*, Deep Throat essentially created the Watergate story, steering Woodward to the major issues of crime and corruption that went far beyond the "third-rate burglary" of the Democratic National Committee headquarters in Washington's Watergate complex. From the moment the book was published, guessing the identity of Deep Throat became a high-level parlor game. Deep Throat is the model for the modern whistleblower. Deep Throat introduced the era of anonymous sources that have become a staple of journalism today. Deep Throat helped reinvent the profession of investigative journalism. And Deep Throat set the high standards of government transparency that we have come to expect.

The question is not simply, Who is Deep Throat? but, Why did he do it? What motivated "my friend," as Woodward identified him, "a source in the Executive Branch who had access to information at [Nixon's Committee to Reelect the President] as well as at the White House"? Was he a man of honor willing to risk his career for the truth, or a man with a grudge? Why did Deep Throat remain anonymous for so many years, in spite of the fame and fortune to be gained through his notoriety?

The main question was answered on May 31, 2005, when I identified Deep Throat in a press release announcing my article on the subject in the magazine *Vanity Fair.* That person is my client, William Mark Felt, ninety-two years old at this writing, formerly the number two man in the Federal Bureau of Investigation. With his consent and the encouragement of his family, Deep Throat finally went public almost thirty-three years after the Watergate break-in.

The *Vanity Fair* article told of how we identified W. Mark Felt and how his family persuaded him to reveal the secret he had intended to keep until death. Much of the article recapitulated the Watergate story for the benefit of younger readers. But what of Mark himself, his personality, moral background, and motives? How did he work his way through a time of tension and isolation, taking on not only a corrupt administration but the new, compliant FBI leadership that the Nixon administration had installed? How did this rational careerist become the nervous agent recorded by Woodward, the secret source pacing in a darkened parking garage, his jaw quivering, as he issued the warning that Woodward later relayed to Bernstein: "Everyone's life is in danger"?

The purpose of this book is to allow Mark Felt to answer these questions in his own words. For more than three decades, the world has known him only through the work of Woodward. Woodward used only Mark's newsroom nickname, taken from the title of a popular pornographic movie of the 1970s. "Deep Throat" was an irreverent honorific at the *Washington Post*—describing an impressive source with a prodigious ability to open his mouth. If this book does nothing else, let it destroy that caricature. Deep Throat was a journalistic joke; Mark Felt never accepted the name. After Woodward revealed that he had a senior source in the executive branch, thereby breaking his agreement with Mark, and after the journalist identified his confidant as "Deep Throat," the retired FBI man was furious—slamming down the phone when Woodward called for his reaction.

Mark has never seen himself as a chatterbox who gave up secrets. Nor would he concede that he was a "leaker," as journalists label those sources who impart confidential information, although Mark did pass a few tidbits to Woodward and other reporters. Mark Felt was a classic G-man (a shortened form of "government man" and a popular nickname for federal agents since the 1930s). Above all, he was a protector, a man willing to shoulder responsibility alone, if need be, to guard his family and his Bureau. In Watergate, facing immense odds, he stood alone to guard the FBI's integrity. When the Nixon administration tried to subvert the Bureau as it had other government agencies, Mark met with Woodward to shed light on the abundant misuses of power. Woodward used Felt effectively. But Felt used Woodward brilliantly, guiding the young reporter one step at a time toward the biggest story of his life. "I suspect he did not consider that he was 'leaking' information—he was only supposed to confirm what I had and steer me," Woodward wrote in his book, *The Secret Man.* "But the sum of all the confirmations and guidance added up to more than a leak. It was a road map."

In compiling this volume, we have drawn from Mark Felt's own writings—including his 1979 memoir as well as a manuscript prepared with his son in the 1980s, his FBI memos, Mark's private reminiscences, and many comments he made to his family, his caretaker, and me from early 2002 to late 2005. Though the debilitations of age caused Mark to lose most of his memories, he had moments when associations and attitudes came back to him (in some instances after we prodded him with his old memos), and we recorded as many of his recollections as we could. I supplemented Mark's observations on his trial, which concluded after he had published his memoir, and to a lesser extent on Watergate, but the central analysis is his, drawn from his own writings. My introduction and epilogue are designed to provide a context for his story and to fill in gaps from the perspective of family, friends, and former associates.

His memoir, *The FBI Pyramid from the Inside*, gives us a narrative account of his rise through the FBI ranks from adventure-seeking agent to J. Edgar Hoover's right-hand man. It was written at the nadir of his career, as he faced conviction for authorizing what were said to be illegal break-ins against a domestic terrorist group, the Weather Underground Organization (WUO). He lashed out at his accusers and denied leaking Watergate stories to Woodward and Bernstein (without quite denying that he had been Woodward's source).

In a subsequent manuscript, completed after he cleared his name, Felt recounted happier times as a counterspy and crime-busting G-man (including stories that had been left out of his published book). A more relaxed author edged closer to his Deep Throat identity, providing his rationale for steering Woodward toward the Watergate story (never "leaking" information not known to Woodward, Mark claimed). During the most pressure-filled moments, as the full weight of the White House, Justice Department, and even the new Bureau leadership seemed to be closing on him, Felt saw himself as one man alone fighting for the integrity of the FBI. "I really can't describe adequately how bad it was," he wrote. "What we needed was a 'Lone Ranger' who could derail the White House cover-up." The image is compatible with his public persona. The world came to see Mark Felt as the shadowy figure in the parking garage, pushing a young reporter to pursue justice; Felt saw himself as the masked lawman, riding alone in pursuit of justice.

Now in his nineties, Mark Felt remains alert and articulate, with a strong handshake, a lively sense of humor, and a leader's way of making his guests feel comfortable. The important people in his life remain clear in his mind: his late wife, Audrey; his stern boss, J. Edgar Hoover; and, yes, Bob Woodward, among others. Though memories of his Deep Throat operations—arranging the clandestine meetings with Woodward, deciding how to direct the story, covering his tracks—have faded, the record as it exists gives us a compelling account of the making of the world's most famous secret source. We have combined and edited the manuscripts to chronicle the events and influences that helped shape Felt's hidden identity, from his days tracking Nazi and Soviet spies to his battles against the Kansas City mob to his role as protector of Hoover's ideals at the FBI. This book adds to what has already been told about Mark Felt, his work, and his motives.

II

Mark Felt always had style. He was six feet tall, a good athlete, and kept himself trim and fit with regular exercise. He had a head of unusually thick, sandy hair that had turned handsomely silver by the early 1960s, fitting well with his clear blue eyes. His strong jaw line was accented by a lip always slightly upturned on the left side, giving the impression of thoughtfulness, which could, with slight adjustment, morph into either a scowl or an inviting smile.

His blue eyes were framed by black horn-rimmed glasses. Always impeccably tailored at work, he favored crisp blue or gray pinstriped suits with starched white shirts and Italian ties. He stood and sat ramrod straight. He commanded respect.

Mark Felt was a listener, not a talker, always observing, assessing, sensing the psychology of the speaker. When he did speak, the words were succinct. This spare style allowed him to present different personalities to different audiences. To a field agent he was questioning in his role as a high-level official with the Inspection Division, Mark could be an imposing, icy disciplinarian. To the wives of other FBI agents he encountered socially, he was a charming, attentive gentleman. To White House adversaries, he was an inscrutable bureaucrat playing his cards close to the vest. And to his superiors, he was an industrious if serene subordinate. "He reminded me of a quiet Baptist minister," said Cartha "Deke" DeLoach, a senior FBI official who retired in 1970. "He seemed not to be a leader, but simply a fellow who was doing his job."

Mark Felt carefully developed this ability to modulate his image. He was an early student of body language, a novel concept in the 1960s. Felt was intensely curious about the psychology of sales, said longtime friend and neighbor Bea Reade Burke, a marketing consultant, often making suggestions to her about sales psychology, choice of words, and presentation. His astuteness always impressed Burke. "He saw into the trick, through the trick. You didn't fool Mark Felt," Burke said.

These characteristics made Felt an effective subordinate to the legendary Hoover. That Felt knew how to manipulate Hoover is beyond dispute. Felt, a great listener, prided himself on knowing how to make Hoover, an avid talker, feel that any decision was Hoover's idea. But Hoover had captivated Felt as well. Mark bought the image of the FBI that Hoover had so masterfully sold prior to Watergate: an incorruptible law enforcement organization, pursuing the highest American ideals and values, with the best and most honorable agents the world had known.

Mark Felt took responsibility for protecting the image of the FBI. He saw the Bureau as the primary guardian of America's rule of law and its solid middle-class values. To his way of thinking, protecting the FBI from political corruption was the same as protecting the country. He showed his instincts before Watergate developed. In early 1972, muckraking columnist Jack Anderson came up with a memo from lobbyist Dita Beard, suggesting that Nixon's Justice Department would dismiss a serious antitrust case against ITT in exchange for a $400,000 political contribution from the corporation. The White House wanted the FBI to declare the memo a forgery, but Felt stood by his lab's conclusion that it was probably authentic.

At times, Felt had to protect the FBI from itself. He engaged in a multiyear bureaucratic war with the associate director for counterintelligence, William Sullivan, who was as abrasive and scruffy as Felt was smooth and well groomed. Sullivan had risen to power within the FBI on the strength of his anticommunist investigations, which Hoover used astutely on Capitol Hill to bolster the Bureau's image and budget. As a counterintelligence official, Sullivan had amassed power in the secret world of electronic surveillance and other spook-like operations, rarely dealing with the rank-and-file agents who represented the FBI to the public. Felt, on the other hand, had risen to power in the Inspection Division after distinguished service as a field agent and supervisor, and as such was the chief enforcer of correct behavior throughout the Bureau.

No two Bureau officials could have been more different, and their conflicts came to a head when Sullivan supported (and likely coauthored anonymously) a massive constitutional incursion known as the Huston plan. This White House initiative called for the CIA, FBI, Defense Intelligence Agency, and National Security Agency, among other services, to undertake a massive campaign of electronic surveillance, wiretaps, mail openings, and warrantless entries, an effort that would have served Nixon's political strategy more than legitimate national security needs.

It was Felt's ultimate victory in derailing this plan that led Nixon to form the so-called Plumber's Unit to perform outlaw operations, now that the White House could not count on governmental agencies to perform the skullduggery. Although the defeat of the Huston plan was a major blow for Sullivan and ultimately helped force him from the Bureau, it also pushed Sullivan deeper into the Nixon camp, where he not only helped the White House fight the *Washington Post* but also probably fingered Mark Felt early in the Watergate probe as the *Post*'s key source.

By the time Hoover died suddenly on May 2, 1972, Felt had become a bogey on the White House radar screen. Determined to tame the FBI, Nixon bypassed the logical inside candidate to succeed Hoover—Felt—and appointed L. Patrick Gray, an undistinguished political loyalist, as the new director. Many analysts have speculated that Felt's resentment at being passed over prompted him to attack the Nixon administration as Deep Throat. Felt admits he was disappointed not to get the top job, but insists that he worked to make a smooth transition. Gray kept Felt as number two and delegated most decisions to the established pro. Gray came to his office at headquarters so rarely that he was known as "Three-Day Gray," and Felt was happy to run the Bureau on a routine basis. Before the Watergate burglary, Felt kept the FBI machinery running efficiently, controlling all the major FBI cases and decisions. He also guarded the Bureau's integrity against a chain of command that now included an ethically challenged White House. The Lone Ranger was in the saddle.

Felt quickly showed that he understood the uses of the press in his new role. Less than a month after Hoover's death, the new FBI team had to contend with the attempted assassination of Alabama governor George Wallace, who was shot and paralyzed while campaigning for the Democratic presidential nomination in Laurel, Maryland. Felt sensed that the incident could blow into a violent political storm, fanned by conspiracy theories on both the left and the right, each side claiming the other had reason to eliminate the conservative Democrat for political advantage. Then the results of the hard-charging FBI investigation were leaked to Bob Woodward of the *Washington Post*, whose lengthy report dispelled both notions, casting would-be assassin Arthur Bremer as a crazed loner. Felt had protected the Bureau and the country before a gathering threat could gain momentum.

Years after Watergate, Felt was still in this protective mode. By the mid-1970s, the massive crackdown on government abuses unleashed by Watergate—and in large measure by Deep Throat— had turned on the FBI itself. For Felt, the climax came in August 1976. He showed up voluntarily to testify before a Washington grand jury investigating charges against numerous lower-level FBI agents for warrantless break-ins conducted in 1972 and 1973 against friends and relatives of the Weather Underground Organization. The WUO had bombed fifty government buildings and had received training in North Vietnam and Cuba, both active enemies of the United States. By stepping in front of the grand jury and national press and accepting responsibility for ordering these break-ins, Mark Felt ruined the government's cases against these field agents and made himself the prosecutor's bull's-eye, a target who was later indicted and found guilty. Mark Felt shouldered this responsibility to defend what he saw as the FBI's lawful battle against foreign-inspired terrorism.

His trial followed years of governmental harassment. Mark Felt endured long stints as a witness or potential target in the investigations inspired by the post-Watergate catharsis. He remained emotionally strong and defended his actions and those of the Bureau firmly and coolly. He refused to break, refused to turn on Gray and

others in exchange for soft treatment, and ultimately refused a
sweetheart, no-jail misdemeanor plea that would have extricated
him from the stress of the WUO trial. Mark Felt would never
admit that his FBI had acted inappropriately. During trial, Felt
watched impassively as his actions were defended by witness
Richard M. Nixon, who, as Felt knew, hurt the defendant in front
of an urban jury clearly dismissive of the disgraced ex-president.

Felt looked forward to a peaceful retirement with his beautiful
wife. Audrey Felt, however, was deteriorating emotionally from the
stress of the investigations and prosecutions involving her husband.
Even after President Reagan pardoned Mark in 1981 and thus ended
his legal problems, Audrey's decline continued. In 1984, while her
husband was running errands, she walked into the guest bathroom
in their apartment near Washington and shot herself in the temple
with his .38 service revolver. Mark came home and found the body.
Their son, Mark Jr., lived nearby and was there to console his
father. For years, Felt kept Audrey's suicide secret, even from his
daughter, Joan, explaining that her mother had died of heart failure. As he had protected the Bureau from Watergate, he now
wanted to protect family and friends from unnecessary trauma and
shouldered the personal burden, as he had his political burdens,
mostly alone.

III

I first met Mark Felt in late April 2002, in the modest Santa Rosa,
California, home he shared with his daughter Joan, a busy single
mother of three scratching out a modest living as a college Spanish
instructor. I found a man with an enviable shock of white hair, a
firm handshake, and a welcoming smile, making steady eye contact.
He spent most of his hours in an apartment converted from an
attached garage, a comfortable arrangement that gave him access to

the yard without the burden of stairs. He moved about with the aid of his metal walker, assisted by his gentle Fijian caregiver.

I had long suspected that Mark Felt was Deep Throat. I had spent the summer of 1970 working as an intern in the Justice Department, and from 1974 through 1979 I was an assistant United States attorney in San Francisco, working mainly with FBI investigators. Consequently I understood the flow of investigative information within the Justice Department. Based on Woodward and Bernstein's best-selling book and my knowledge of the federal criminal process, I had concluded that Felt alone had the motive, means, and opportunity to be Deep Throat. While I had come to believe this in the late 1970s, my law practice and family life kept me too busy to take the time to prove my thesis.

As I wrote in *Vanity Fair*, my hobby became an obsession in early 2002. One spring evening, my wife, Jan, and I served a meal of pasta and grilled chicken to our daughter, Christy, and seven of her friends from Stanford University. Some of the students had just come back from a sabbatical in South America, and traded adventure stories in the serene setting of our home in Marin County, overlooking the San Rafael Hills. I told them about my father, an attorney who had served in Rio during World War II as an undercover agent for the FBI. One of Christy's friends, Nick Jones, said his grandfather, also an attorney, had joined the Bureau at about the same time—in the early 1940s—and had made his career there.

"What's his name?" I asked.

"You may have heard of him," Nick said. "He was a pretty senior guy in the FBI . . . Mark Felt."

I couldn't believe it. I had known Nick for three years—a bright, hardworking kid who was going to make something of his life. In many ways he reminded me of myself as a young man; I was even encouraging him to follow in my footsteps and study the law. And now here he was telling me for the first time that his grandfather was the top FBI man I had singled out as Woodward's key source.

"Mark Felt!" I said. "You're kidding me. Your granddad is Deep Throat! Did you know that?"

"You know, Big John, I've heard that for a long time," Nick answered calmly. "Just recently we've started to think maybe it's him."

I spoke with Nick about why his grandfather may have been clinging to his anonymity, worried about what his former colleagues might think of his meetings with Woodward. As a sympathetic former prosecutor, I suggested, I could help dispel his concerns. We let the subject drop after a few moments and rejoined the group. But several days later, Nick called me, saying his mother thought I should talk to Mark. I agreed to drive up to the Felts' home in Santa Rosa that Sunday.

There I met Joan Felt, an attractive former actress working hard at two teaching jobs—and Mark, a relaxed and congenial man approaching ninety. As far as I knew, Mark had never told his family of his secret identity. I launched into a discussion of Deep Throat's contributions, hoping to elicit some kind of reaction. When I mentioned that young prosecutors of my acquaintance admired Deep Throat for helping protect the integrity of the justice system, I could see his eyes soften, as if I were offering him absolution. Nonetheless, he held firm against revealing his secret: "I'll think about what you have said, and let you know of my decision."

About ten days later, Nick called again and asked me to make a second visit. He said his grandfather now was inclined to admit that he was Deep Throat. I could see why the family might be getting anxious. A reporter for the *Globe* tabloid, Dawna Kaufmann, had called Joan and asked whether her father was the source. Joan mentioned that Woodward had shown up at the Felt home unannounced three years earlier and visited with her father. Kaufmann then wrote an article headlined "Deep Throat Exposed!" She quoted a young man, Chase Culeman-Beckman, who claimed that while he was attending summer camp in 1988, his friend Jacob Bernstein—the son of Carl Bernstein and writer Nora Ephron—said his father had told him that a man named Mark Felt was Deep Throat. Ephron and Bernstein, long divorced by 2002, both denied that Bernstein had disclosed the secret; they said their son was merely repeating his mother's guess that Felt was the secret source.

Soon after the *Globe* article appeared, in late April 2002, Joan received a call from Yvette La Garde, who became her father's friend and companion after the death of her mother. "Why is he announcing it now?" La Garde asked. "I thought he wouldn't be revealed until he was dead."

"Announcing what?" Joan asked.

La Garde hesitated but finally gave up the secret she had kept for years: Felt had told her he was Woodward's source but had sworn her to silence.

Joan went straight to her father and told him of her conversation with La Garde. "I know now that you're Deep Throat," she said.

"Since that's the case, well, yes, I am," Mark replied.

Joan urged her father to give up his secret immediately, so that he could have some closure—and accept the praise that was his due. Felt agreed, then changed his mind.

But Yvette La Garde had already shared the secret with others. In 1987 or 1988, she had told her son Mickey and his wife Dee of Mark's identity. Mickey, who had a top secret clearance and worked as an army lieutenant colonel in Europe, said he had kept quiet about the disclosure ever since.

We later learned from Woodward's most recent book that at least one other person knew: Stan Pottinger, an assistant attorney general in the mid-1970s, had stumbled onto Mark's secret. As Pottinger later related the incident to us, Mark arrived with his usual imposing swagger to testify before a grand jury investigating the FBI's break-ins against the Weather Underground. During his testimony, Mark jokingly mentioned that some people in the White House thought he was Deep Throat. Then a juror raised his hand and called Mark's bluff, asking directly, "Were you Deep Throat?" Mark turned pale and denied it, said Pottinger, who was in charge of the proceeding. At that point, Pottinger went off the record, got up from the prosecutor's table, walked over to the witness chair, and quietly reminded Mark that he was under oath. Deeming the question to be irrelevant, Pottinger offered to withdraw it if Mark preferred. The flushed witness snapped: "Withdraw the question."

Three decades later, his secretiveness finally was fading, at least among family and friends, and Mark began to come to terms with the prospect of the whole world knowing his hidden identity. One afternoon, he took his usual car ride with Atama Batisaresare, an assisted-living aide. This time, however, instead of enjoying the outing Felt obsessed over his past. "He did tell me, 'An FBI man should have loyalty to the department,'" Batisaresare told Joan and me. "He talked about loyalty. He didn't mention he was Deep Throat. He told me he didn't want to do it, but 'it was my duty to do it, regarding Nixon.'"

On the Sunday I talked to Mark Felt, he was debating with himself about whether or not his former Bureau colleagues would see him as a decent man. I told him that agents and prosecutors now thought Deep Throat was a patriot, and he now had an opportunity to tell his story his way. Felt later told Joan that he also worried "what the judge would think." If his secret came out, in other words, could he be prosecuted for his actions as Deep Throat? We continued to reason with Mark, and the more we talked the more comfortable he became with the idea of revealing his role. He seemed to be disputing the implication of the nickname he was saddled with—the idea that he blabbed a lot of secrets—while conceding that the nickname was his. On several occasions he told me, "I'm not Deep Throat," but then added the admission that *Vanity*

Fair used for its headline: "I'm the guy they used to call Deep Throat."

Once we were certain that Mark was admitting his identity, the family asked me to negotiate a deal to publish his story. Joan did not want her father's life history consigned to the subsidiary role it would have if it were told posthumously by Bob Woodward. The family wanted a story about Mark while Mark was still alive, and not another story about Bob Woodward after Mark's death. The family wanted Mark to take pride in his role as a hero and be recognized as such by the public.

Even after admitting his identity, however, Mark stoutly refused to publish his secret. Joan could not win him over with visions of family glory, so she tried a new tack: she had gone into debt paying school bills for her three sons, and perhaps his book would bring some modest financial relief. Ever the caring father and doting grandfather, Mark finally agreed, but only if his friend Woodward collaborated. Although Mark's memory had become impaired with age, he was still in firm control of his decision making, and obviously respected by Joan and family.

I first called Woodward in May 2002, telling him that Mark had revealed himself to me and the family and asking if he would collaborate with us on a "coming out" book. I followed up with several more phone calls, and Joan and Mark Jr. also talked with Woodward.

Woodward refused to confirm Mark's identity but asked to talk to him to confirm that he was competent and willing to reveal his secret. Woodward scheduled two visits to the Felt home but canceled them. Then, after Joan confided to Woodward that Mark would not reveal himself without Woodward's cooperation, Woodward cut off further discussion of the project.

After some time passed, Woodward contacted Joan by e-mail, generally inquiring about Mark's health and exchanging niceties but avoiding further talk of collaborating on a book with the family. Woodward still hesitated to identify Deep Throat while Mark Felt was alive, worrying that his source had not given his permission knowingly and willingly. When I earlier had suggested publishing a collaboration posthumously, Woodward adamantly refused. I tried to change his mind, arguing that if he agreed to our scenario, the family would not reveal the story without him. When I emphasized that we were certain without a doubt that Mark was Deep Throat, Woodward twice warned me, "There will be some surprises." The family took his response as proof of something Woodward was hinting to us: that Deep Throat was a composite character, not an individual. Although this suggestion alarmed Joan—and Mark Jr. even more so—I never put much stock in it. I assumed that Woodward must have other reasons for refusing to cooperate.

I could see the commercial sense in Woodward's position. In talking to the journalist as an FBI insider, Mark Felt had no intention of promoting himself. The name we all knew him by, Deep Throat, was a play on the fact that Mark spoke to Woodward on "deep background," meaning that any information Mark provided could be used, but only without any reference to the source. The very existence of the source was to be kept secret. Nonetheless, Woodward partially exposed Mark's identity in 1974 by revealing, in *All the President's Men*, the role of Deep Throat. The tantalizing tidbits about Deep Throat's knowledge and motives in that book helped convince me—among others—that Mark Felt was Woodward's source.

I also knew from the book that Woodward and his source were friends. So I assumed that the journalist would not reveal Deep Throat's existence (thereby creating a sensation that would enhance book sales) without Mark's release. Mark ethically could have given this release after his retirement in 1973, presumably for a share of the book's proceeds. That would explain Woodward's reluctance to pay Mark a second time for another release, as I was proposing.

Given these assumptions, I was stunned to learn from Woodward's recent work, *The Secret Man*, that no deal releasing Woodward had been struck. Woodward admitted that his original deal with Mark included a promise never to reveal in print that he had an important source like Deep Throat. Since millions, if not billions, of people had heard of Deep Throat by May 2002, obviously this part of the deal had been breached.

In their historic collaboration over Watergate, Felt and Woodward used each other, each to his own ends. The difference between them is that Mark always kept his word. The Felt family understands, though, that Woodward was under no obligation to collaborate with them. The Felts got to know Bob well in recent years, and they regard him as a good friend.

Whatever Woodward's reasons, the fact that he would not be involved in a joint project allowed the Felts to tell Mark's tale from his and their perspective. Mark Felt, the family knew, loved the FBI, upheld its integrity, and protected its honor, priorities not shared by Woodward. Mark Felt, they knew, had been a hardworking public servant, a highly intelligent, capable man who could have made a lot of money in private industry. But he believed in what he and the FBI had done to protect America. He was proud of J. Edgar Hoover and proud of his career. He was hurt by the FBI's tarnished image after Watergate. Perhaps a book by Mark and his family could help restore the FBI's lost honor.

Mark's book, *The FBI Pyramid from the Inside*, was poorly published. It received little promotion and indifferent editing. It lacked an index and even a contents page. Mark's decision to hide his identity as Deep Throat cost the book headlines. And his staunch defense of J. Edgar Hoover played poorly at a time when the Watergate scandal had produced a backlash against overreaching by government institutions across the board, including the FBI. Mark's warnings against foreign and domestic terrorists struck many as an attempt to justify FBI civil rights abuses, although in the light of

9/11, his warnings appear tragically prophetic. In short, the book was a failure of timing and tone, although it provided a vivid portrait of FBI culture.

Mark Felt and other FBI leaders were prosecuted for approving warrantless entries against people suspected of supporting terrorists, the so-called black bag jobs named for the satchels that contained break-in tools. Today, when we have learned to take antiterrorist measures more seriously, it is time to acknowledge Mark Felt's wrongful 1980 conviction by a kangaroo court. His FBI was part of the solution to society's challenges, not part of the problem. In retrospect, he took the appropriate, tough approach to foreign-inspired terrorism.

Mark's emergence also gives perspective on a form of public discussion that Watergate elevated: investigative reporting. The work of Woodward and Bernstein was a watershed, destroying the old tacit agreement by which the press kept quiet about "sensitive" information like the sexual peccadilloes of John F. Kennedy and the unethical dealings of Lyndon Johnson. But the *Washington Post* reporters were not working alone. Mark Felt's collaboration with Bob Woodward demonstrates that modern investigative reporting was not invented primarily by two energetic journalists, but by an experienced government investigator who married traditional, headline-grabbing journalism with the rigor of sophisticated professional investigative techniques. Watergate and Deep Throat raised the bar for the media, introducing the standards of vigorous investigation and reporting a complex political narrative, not just isolated stories. No better practitioner of this new field of in-depth reporting now exists than Woodward, exemplified by his many significant post-Watergate works. This form of journalism can greatly influence public attitudes and can keep government and business officials accountable.

And just as Deep Throat's anonymous collaboration with the media protected his Bureau from political corruption, so too did the publication of his exploits embolden other lower-level governmental and business employees to publicize wrongdoing and withstand pressure and threats. Had it not been for the *Post*'s Watergate reporting, the Nixon administration would have finished its second term bathed in glory, our transparent institutions would be considerably more opaque, and honest employees would be paralyzed by intimidation.

Mark Felt's actions during Watergate are best explained not by his bureaucratic infighting in 1972 but by values he embraced in 1922. Mark calmly and assuredly risked his job and his family's security because it was the right thing to do. Why he was so strongly motivated by conscience boils down to the things that mattered most to this young man growing up in small-town, pretelevision America: his mother, his moral training, and his dog.

IV

In the early 1900s, life in Twin Falls, Idaho, reflected the common values of small-town America. Mark's father, Earl Felt, a product of the University of Chicago, was a general contractor who built a home for his family on several acres just outside Twin Falls. Mark's mother, Rose Dygert Felt, was unusually well educated for a woman of the time, especially a middle-class woman in a western state. She graduated from Drake University, an excellent religiously affiliated liberal arts college in Des Moines, Iowa.

In family reminiscences written for posterity, Mark's younger sister and only sibling, Janet (now deceased), recalled catching bees in mason jars among the apple, cherry, and pear trees her father planted. Mark and a friend dug a swimming hole beside a shed. In winter, the Christmas tree was lit by real candles. "March winds and kites," Janet wrote, "April Fool's Day and May Day (we danced the May Pole dance) with baskets of flowers and candy. Lovely June,

XXX INTRODUCTION BY JOHN O'CONNOR

staying up late playing Kick the Can, Hide and Seek and Kidnapping. The Fourth of July was the greatest. We kids would get a dime each to spend and this actually was plenty! Always some politician would talk long and loud from the bandstand. We had a Ferris Wheel and a Merry-Go-Round."

Both sides of the Felt family could trace Welsh, Scottish, and German ancestors almost as far back as the *Mayflower*.* The extended family had Presbyterian roots but included Quakers, Puritans, Baptists, and Congregationalists. Earl Felt and later his son avoided the rituals of formal religion, but their values were cemented in the gentler Presbyterian ideals of generosity and social justice. Mark and Janet regularly attended church dances as preteens and teens. Theirs apparently was not a revival-style evangelical congregation, but a cooler and more cerebral institution in the mainline Presbyterian tradition. Self-control is emblematic of Presbyterianism, as well as sensitivity to the needs of others, considerate behavior, and a deep sense of responsibility for one's actions. From the age of six, Mark was responsible for cutting and bailing hay in the summer and rising early in the winter to feed the horses.

Although Earl Felt administered the occasional whipping to young Mark, his mother was the dominant disciplinary force. Mark in his middle age often related that he "would rather be beaten ten times by my dad than hear my mother say once that she was disappointed in me." Rose Felt, always cerebral and level-headed, imposed a high standard of conduct on young Mark.

That message required repetition. Always something of a dare-

---

* George Felt (originally "Feltch," meaning "field," likely of Dutch or Flemish origin), a stonemason from Wales, came to Massachusetts in 1628 with a Puritan group headed by Winthrop and Endicott. The ancestors of Mark's mother also came to the New World to escape religious discrimination. Charles Dygert, a devout member of the Reformed German Church living in Strasbourg, immigrated from Alsace in the early 1700s after France conquered the territory and imposed Roman Catholicism.

devil, Mark boasted to his grandsons that several times as a boy he had climbed the towering arches of the Twin Falls bridge, perhaps 400 feet above the water. Later, when he was an FBI trainee learning to fly, an instructor offered him the controls for a routine maneuver and hung on as Mark executed a loop-de-loop.

In a quiet but firm voice, Rose stressed self-discipline and self-control. During the Watergate and post-Watergate years, Mark confided to friends how difficult it was for him to learn self-control as a rambunctious young boy, but how important it was to his success as an FBI agent.

Mark showed leadership talent in high school, where he won election to student offices. From his teenage years through his pivotal role at the FBI, his leadership skills evolved from the mission his mother gave him, not a quest for power. "You have a responsibility to others," Rose taught him. "Fulfill it."

The organized religion of his youth did not play a major role in his adult life. Perhaps that separation came in childhood, after his father brought home a puppy with curly brown hair that the family named Mickey. "We were both in ecstasy over this adorable dog," Janet wrote. In the course of three years, the dog became an indispensable part of family life. After someone poisoned Mickey, "we all were devastated," Janet wrote, "especially Mark [ten years old at the time]. For one whole day, Mark could be heard praying aloud. He would go from one room to another, upstairs and downstairs, and then back to the kitchen where Mickey lay on the floor beside the range. As sick as he was, Mickey always wagged his tail when Mark would lie down beside him." After the dog died, Janet wrote, "Mark lost all faith in God right at this time, and nothing Dad or Mother would say helped any."

Mark Felt achieved a sense of serenity in a vigilant sensitivity to others and hard work. He worked methodically throughout his career, never complaining about long hours. Yet virtually no one describes Mark Felt at any time in his life as overwrought, depressed, anxious, or burned out. "He was never the edgy, nervous guy Woodward portrays in *All the President's Men*," said Mark Jr. "When he made a decision, no matter how difficult, he carried it out without worry."

During Mark's prosecution, his attorneys remember, he was stronger and more emotionally stable than they were. "When the verdict came down against him, he made great efforts to comfort me, as if I were the one who should be upset," said Mark Cummings, then a young counsel on his team and now an experienced white-collar defense lawyer in the Washington, D.C., area.

Larry Callahan, a San Francisco lawyer who represented a key witness, described Felt's calm. "He was amazingly unfazed by the trial," said Callahan, a former federal prosecutor and now a defense lawyer who has been through his share of trials. "He seemed more interested in talking about his daughter Joan and her problems than his own."

Mark worked his way through the University of Idaho in the 1930s, during the Depression. He fed and stoked the frat house boilers daily and washed dishes at a sorority house. He still managed to get good grades and be elected president of his fraternity. The same pattern emerged in his early days in Washington, where he worked his way through George Washington University Law School while employed at the office of Sen. James P. Pope. (After Pope was defeated in 1938, the new senator, D. Worth Clark, kept Felt on.) In addition to a full-time job and law studies, Felt became the first person to be elected head of the Idaho Society (Idahoans living in Washington) who was not a congressman or senator. A coworker, Dr. Edward Hill, now a retired physician in San Francisco, described Mark Felt as a meticulous worker who handled the high volume of correspondence and constituent requests with great diligence, even though he attended law school and then studied for the bar while working in the office. "He was something of a prankster and played several practical jokes on me," related Hill. In one case, Hill arrived

at work to find his desk bare. He worried that he had been fired until
he discovered that Mark had swept the desktop contents into a bag
and hung it from a ceiling pipe in the corner.

Mark Felt's ambition was directed, as his mother would have
wanted, toward the common good. He and two other young
lawyers in the senator's office began reading and discussing communist literature, still an acceptable intellectual pursuit in Depression
era America, years before Stalinist repression became widely understood. Mark seemed to be interested in communism because it cri-
tiqued self-seeking behavior, supposedly exacerbated by the
capitalist system. The utopian ideal expressed as "from each according to his ability, to each according to his need" was an accurate ren-
dering of Rose Felt's loving but stern prescription for her son's
conduct. Mark was no ideologue, but his views differed from those
of the Senate isolationists who frequented Clark's chambers. They
often justified their soft stance toward Nazism by evoking fears of
Soviet communism. As always, Mark Felt looked evenly at both sides
of the ideological spectrum.

Felt's fascination with communism gave way to a more practical
outlet for his social idealism, and he applied for employment with
the Federal Trade Commission (FTC) after graduating from law
school. The FTC's mission was to ameliorate the wrongs of the capitalist system by ridding it of unfair or misleading commercial practices, a goal Mark found worthy. The reality differed from the
promise, however, as the young lawyer soon discovered that his
work often centered on commercial battles in which neither com-
plainer nor target was free of covetousness. Moreover, the work was
boring. And Mark's early assignment—to ask people about their
uses of and attitudes toward toilet paper—was a less than ideal
introduction to the agency's work.

When Mark passed the D.C. bar exam in 1940, he became eligible
to apply to the FBI. The disenchanted young lawyer saw the oppor-

tunity to move to an organization that was truly effective and enjoyed wide public support, if not adulation. Director J. Edgar Hoover, using the media skillfully, had created a clean-cut, square-jawed image of FBI agents as vanquishers of all American enemies: mobsters like John Dillinger, Nazi spies, communists, violent criminals, the Lindbergh kidnapper.

Mark, like so many agents who worked for Hoover, respected what he saw as Hoover's well-conceived, efficient system, and made its preservation an end in itself. Mark appreciated the practical uses of Hoover's spectacular public relations efforts. Universal respect for the FBI simplified the individual agent's job of obtaining cooperation from citizens and local law enforcement officers. "Our job was half done before we closed the car door," said longtime agent Phil Basher.

Mark Felt became a true believer in this system. His people skills, his penchant for hard work, his meticulousness, and his unflappable demeanor made him a model agent, one with the savvy for career advancement. But he never let himself appear too eager for promotion as he moved up the ranks. "He never wore his ambition on his sleeve," said coworker Joe Ponder. As Mark once told his daughter, "Finesse was my strong suit."

In the early 1940s he began his FBI career in a field that required great finesse and strong analytical ability: counterintelligence. During these years, Mark learned the cloak-and-dagger techniques that would be so important in his secret contacts with Woodward: how to shake off a tail, how to pass messages without detection, how to avoid raising suspicion in his group. He quickly made a name for himself by uncovering a key Nazi spy who had slipped the notice of more seasoned investigators. Throughout his career, Mark supervised counterintelligence agents and worked with undercover operatives. Joan recalled coming home once to find a scruffy "radical" sitting in her living room—an FBI man briefing her father on a leftist group the agent had penetrated. As the head of curriculum at the

FBI Academy at Quantico, Virginia, Mark was responsible for educating the new agents in basic counterintelligence tactics. As he rose to the top of the hierarchy, he became intimately familiar with the FBI's infamous counterintelligence program (COINTELPRO) run by Sullivan, which coordinated informants and agents who infiltrated radical organizations.

In sum, Mark Felt knew more than most FBI people about spycraft. Part of this craft was to create a "legend" for an agent who sought infiltration to disguise his law enforcement status. Creating a legend often involved building "credentials," for example, a prison record, to bolster the agent's radical bona fides. It also could involve erasing personal history. Before Mark Felt became Bob Woodward's secret source, Felt hid the fact that they had been friends for two years. Woodward was just as discreet. During his Watergate reporting, and indeed during the thirty-year search for Deep Throat, no one ever determined that the reporter and the FBI official had a personal connection.

In the FBI, agents learned to keep secrets and compartmentalize, and nobody built more compartments than Mark Felt. He isolated his family life from his Bureau life, hid aspects of his personal life and aspects of his professional life, and of course walled off his secret identity from his public identity. When Woodward contacted Felt out of the blue by telephone early in 2000 and said, "I wish I could persuade you to remember and talk more," his old source hesitated, Woodward related in *The Secret Man*. Then Felt said, "Let's just . . . I'll hang up. And this closet door can be a closed door."

As associate director in charge of the Inspection Division, Mark Felt had access to sensitive information about every agent in the Bureau, and he was known for his discretion. But he was kept in the dark at first about such operations as the Kissinger wiretaps, which the White House ordered installed to eavesdrop on national security officials and reporters.

Discretion was an important qualification for rising to the top in Hoover's FBI. Another was an ability to get along with the director. Hoover's first rule was clear: Don't embarrass the Bureau. FBI trainers and supervisors pounded rule number one into new recruits, supervisors enforced it, and inspectors punished violators. The mandate covered every aspect of an agent's life, from the way he dressed in the morning (business suit and tie) to the hours he devoted to his work (many and long). An ambitious agent had to move his family every two or three years to get the broad experience that Hoover required for promotion. It was a proud feature of Hoover's vaunted system that an agent could move from one office to any other without skipping a beat. But the families of these agents experienced profound stress as they pulled up stakes and moved again and again to new homes and new schools, frequently in the absence of the man of the house. Several wives committed suicide. Even then the mandate to avoid embarrassing the Bureau applied. One wife, it was said, made sure to can all her fruit for the winter and write a neat explanatory note before taking her life.

Throughout Mark Felt's career, his wife, Audrey, encouraged his ambition. A Phi Beta Kappa graduate of the University of Idaho, Audrey Felt, like many women of her generation, merged her life into her husband's, helping pick out his natty attire, selecting his ties, and decorating his office. When Mark became the Bureau's number two official, Audrey installed small spotlights to shine on his desk and made sure the desk itself was slightly elevated.

But the stresses of Mark's FBI career also weighed on Audrey, who had a high-strung personality. After a dozen years of six-day workweeks, frequent moves, and a social life that did not stray far beyond the uptight FBI culture, Audrey collapsed of nervous exhaustion in 1954, when the family was living in Seattle. She recovered but remained fragile, and as young Joan developed into a strong-willed and beautiful woman, Audrey and her daughter clashed constantly. Mark had to work hard as an FBI agent during the day and just as hard as a family mediator at night.

In the 1960s, toward the end of Mark's career, American society was changing rapidly. When Joan moved to a California farm, took up the alternative lifestyle, and joined a religious community, the Felts could see this happening in their own family. Across the country, opposition to the Vietnam War was growing, lifestyle issues—sex, drugs, and rock and roll—were dividing generations, cities were burning, and radical political ideas were catching hold.

The FBI could not avoid these social storms, and many of its actions later put its agents in the political and legal spotlight. On orders from the Kennedy administration, the Bureau bugged the rooms of Martin Luther King, Jr., attempting to monitor the influence of two advisers with communist links. Never straying far from Hoover's policy, Felt supported the King operation but not the efforts of Felt's rival, counterintelligence chief Sullivan, to harass and threaten the civil rights leader.

Felt backed away from the Nixon administration's plan for an intelligence war against its enemies—the so-called Huston plan, which Sullivan helped create and Hoover ultimately rejected. Felt's quiet war with Sullivan was not just a squabble over policy but a showdown over the future of the FBI. The White House staff pushed the Huston plan as a key tool in its efforts to control political enemies, especially those opposing the administration's strategy in Vietnam. As an architect of the plan, Sullivan's political aim was to win White House support in his power struggle with Hoover. Felt sided with Hoover, and understood that if the Huston plan were approved, a White House functionary would be coordinating and directing the FBI's most sensitive missions, many of doubtful legality, while robbing the Bureau of its cherished independence.

Sullivan broke with Hoover publicly in October 1970. Sullivan remarked after a speech that the New Left was a threat to America, but the day of the old, Soviet-style Communist Party USA was over. Hoover, who had evoked the Soviet threat for years as a way to scare money out of Congress—largely using intelligence gathered by Sullivan—went ballistic. But Sullivan's aim was clear. He likely was speaking at the behest of the White House, which was seeking to calm anticommunist fears at a time when the president was negotiating U.S.-Soviet arms agreements and laying the groundwork for his 1972 trip to China. In August 1971, Sullivan wrote a letter to Hoover boldly suggesting that the director retire. But Sullivan played his hand too soon: Hoover fired him, leaving Felt as the unchallenged inside candidate to succeed the director.

That didn't ease the way for Felt. Eight months later, after Hoover died, the White House installed outsider Gray as FBI director. A month later, a security guard caught the Watergate intruders. The case could not have come at a more sensitive time for the FBI—or for Mark Felt. He and the Bureau's Hooverite old guard no longer had their director to stand up to the politicians, not to mention Hoover's famous personal files, which supposedly contained embarrassments to use against any politician who crossed the FBI. Felt takes the doctrinaire Hooverite position—no files were used to blackmail politicians, although the personal files that did not end up in the control of Gray and Felt were destroyed after Hoover's death. In short, Hoover's intimidation factor died with him, leaving the FBI vulnerable to political assaults on its independence.

Mark Felt's actions that summer as Deep Throat, he suggests in this book, were intended to throw a spotlight on the White House so that it could not impede the FBI investigation. Such motives are common in Washington. What began as garden-variety leaking, though, soon evolved into something much riskier. In October 1972, Felt and Woodward began the daring, courageous collaboration that became a crucial element in the toppling of a presidency.

Until now, Watergate has been popularly understood as a story about the heroics of two aggressive, savvy young reporters, and that version is true as far as it goes. But at the heart of the Watergate story is the senior FBI source who had worked more than thirty years as, in effect, an investigative reporter for prosecutors and grand juries.

The most difficult part of Mark Felt's role as Deep Throat was not avoiding detection at his meetings with Woodward, but evading suspicion as he worked with colleagues searching for the leaker. In the summer of 1972, he and Gray ordered subordinate agents to be grilled under oath. Later he convinced Gray that Attorney General Richard Kleindienst's suspicions of Felt were absurd. In the first version of his book, Mark quoted himself telling Gray, "Pat, I haven't leaked anything to anybody. They are wrong."

"I believe you," Gray answered, "but the White House doesn't. Kleindienst has told me on three or four occasions to get rid of you, but I refused. He didn't say this came from higher up but I am convinced it did."

In that version of his story, Mark appealed directly to his readers: "I never leaked information to Woodward and Bernstein or anyone else!"

Mark's supporters argue that he was not lying, even if he was playing games with the truth. (After all, he met with Woodward only, never with Bernstein.) And in his own mind, he did not see himself as lying at all. In Mark Felt's way of compartmentalizing his various roles, it was perfectly logical to hunt down leakers as an FBI official by day, then to help Woodward interpret those leaks as an unofficial source by night.

In the end, credit Deep Throat with guiding Woodward toward the larger story of Watergate—the complex web of criminality that went far beyond the burglary itself. After a long night in the parking garage, Woodward emerged with the key elements of the story that he and Bernstein produced on October 10, 1972, elevating the tale of a strange little burglary into a national political crisis. They set the tone in their first paragraph on page 1:

> FBI agents have established that the Watergate bugging incident stemmed from a massive campaign of political spying and sabotage conducted on behalf of President Nixon's re-election and directed by officials of the White House and the Committee for the Re-election of the President.

V

Mark Felt could not anticipate that the FBI's reputation would become a collateral victim of Watergate. This was largely the work of forces beyond anyone's control. Late in his reign, Hoover had lost his PR magic. The old rules of cooperation with the administration in power had led him to investigate Reverend King and place wiretaps on government officials and journalists. But after Nixon fell, these old rules came crashing down on the FBI, and past investigations became damaging liabilities. The Bureau was also hurt by the 1971 break-in at the FBI office in Media, Pennsylvania, where the radical Berrigan brothers liberated documents uncovering the secret counterintelligence program against leftist radicals. And in 1973, the FBI's sloppy handling of an Indian takeover at Wounded Knee, South Dakota, added to complaints about Bureau "abuses," though Mark blamed Justice Department planners for contravening FBI procedures.

Watergate was the catalyst for the FBI's new problems. Woodward and Bernstein's reporting from October 1972 through February 1973—much of it guided by Deep Throat—helped provoke the Ervin Committee's Senate Watergate hearings and the Rodino Committee's House impeachment hearings. These dramas in turn led to the explosive 1975 hearings of the Church Committee on intelligence abuses by the CIA and FBI.

The Watergate-inspired hearings gave the media fodder for reams of anti-FBI reporting, not all of it fair. These proceedings, in which Mark Felt was a key witness, became a public relations disaster for the FBI, casting it as a thuggish, discriminatory organization that held itself above the law. In the virulently antiestablishment atmosphere of those days, White House political crimes like the break-in at the office of the psychiatrist treating Daniel Ellsberg (who leaked the Pentagon papers on the Vietnam War) were denounced, but so were valid FBI operations that could be justified on legitimate national security grounds. Radical leftists like those of the Weather Underground were traveling to Cuba for training, calling for revolution, and staging violent attacks. In response, the FBI did its job: it went after the WUO, with Mark Felt leading the charge—an operation that brought him years of legal troubles.

Early intimations of his personal problems appeared in late February 1973. Just before L. Patrick Gray commenced his doomed hearings to be confirmed as permanent director of the FBI, *Time* magazine reported the existence of the Kissinger wiretaps—based on a leak by Felt (who also informed Bob Woodward of the taps). These leaks were likely intended to embarrass Sullivan, a key FBI operative in the Kissinger case, scuttling any possibility that Sullivan would succeed Gray. Yet Gray ended up embarrassing himself. Asked about the taps at his hearing, he responded that "there is no record of any such business here of bugging news reporters and White House people." His answer was too clever by half. There was "no record" in official files simply because Sullivan had secreted the Kissinger records in his own office, as Gray well knew.

As a result of Gray's clumsiness, prosecutors later pressured Felt to testify against Gray in a perjury investigation. Felt, never easily bullied, refused to give the prosecutors the testimony they wanted and Gray slipped off the hook for the time being. Next the prosecutors shone their spotlight directly on Felt. A *New York Times* correspondent, John Crewdson, reportedly had received numerous FBI investigative files on the activities of Donald Segretti, an agent of the White House "dirty tricks" operations that attempted to disrupt the Democrats during the 1972 campaign. Likely spurred on by the Nixon White House, the special prosecutor began a leak investigation that centered on Felt—though he denied ever meeting Crewdson. But if Felt was Deep Throat, as Nixon and his men suspected, the likelihood increased that he was capable of leaking the Segretti documents to Crewdson. Woodward's description of Deep Throat had stoked book sales, but in the process he had also increased the criminal jeopardy of his key source.

After Felt fought off those charges, he confronted accusations that he had approved break-ins against the Weather Underground radicals. The ensuing ordeal lasted almost five years, a prosecution that ravaged Felt's reputation and undermined Audrey's tenuous hold on mental health. Felt, indicted with Edward Miller (associate director for counterintelligence) and Gray for the break-ins, steered the defense. The witnesses included five former attorneys general as well as former president Nixon; all except Ramsey Clark, attorney general for President Johnson, agreed with Felt's claim that such break-ins were justified by the interests of national security.

Most of us reading this testimony today—after 9/11 and after court decisions approving "sneak and peek" antiterrorist activities reminiscent of the old black bag jobs—would say that the two strongest witnesses, Felt and Nixon, carried the day. Charges against Gray were dropped for lack of evidence. But jury members were publicly disdainful of the disgraced Nixon and, in those highly charged times, the FBI. The inexperienced judge, recently appointed by President Jimmy Carter, instructed the jury in such a way that the outcome was inevitable. On November 6, 1980, Felt and Miller were convicted in the proverbial New York minute.

A few months later, the newly elected president, Ronald Reagan, pardoned both men, but Felt's honor had been tarnished by the conviction. He continued to push his case to clear his name completely, until the court of appeals dismissed the appeal in 1983 as moot in light of the pardon.

With the prosecutions and investigations behind him, Mark Felt tried to salvage what was left of his crumbling personal life. He continued to worry about Joan, who eluded her disapproving mother by leaving home for a remote mountain farm. Her father quickly found her and reestablished communication but continued to worry about her wellbeing into the 1980s. Audrey deteriorated as a result of the stress, and after her suicide Felt privately unleashed his invective against the government he served so long and so well, charging it with killing his wife.

Later Mark struck up a romantic friendship with Yvette La Garde, a beautiful French-born widow ten years his junior. As their relationship deepened, so too did Mark's concern for Joan as a single mother of three boys in California. As he realized he would need to leave Washington and his lady friend to be with Joan, one romantic night he gave Yvette something he had given to no one else: his secret identity. Years later, as he sat in his easy chair suffering from memory loss, Yvette would help Joan unlock his secret.

Mark sometimes bristled when asked about the persistent rumor that he was Deep Throat. He would unleash a tight-jawed, principled denunciation of Deep Throat's disloyalty. But at other times, especially later in life, he would respond with winking, nondenial denials. Uncharacteristically, Mark Felt was not of one mind about Deep Throat. He defended the secret source as good for the country, but he insisted that a loyal FBI agent would never violate rule number one.

Over time, the bitterness began to ease for Mark Felt. As an architect of the Watergate story, he had upheld the principles of fairness, transparency, and honesty. The experience had cost him a peaceful retirement with his wife, yet in his later years he experienced enduring love from his family and Yvette. Starting in 2002, when Mark's secret became known to his family and me, his legacy began to redeem his honor.

His grandsons Nick, Will, and Rob told Mark what a "cool guy" Deep Throat was. Joan, his loving daughter and ex-flower child, and Mark Jr., a retired military officer and airline pilot, each validated Deep Throat's heroism. I chimed in, having some credibility as a former Justice Department prosecutor. Each of us, experiencing Watergate in a different way, regarded Deep Throat as a hero.

The purpose of this introduction is to prepare you to hear Mark's voice as a balanced man, one who does not try to collapse the tension inherent in a free society by viscerally moving left or right on any issue. I expect you will see him as a kind man who tried to act generously toward each human being he encountered and to follow his conscience in his work. More importantly, you will see a public official who tried passionately to protect the civil liberties of all Americans, while refusing to view our Constitution as a suicide pact benefiting terrorists.

Whatever you think about Mark Felt's actions, you will recognize him as an honest and above all honorable man.

A G-MAN'S LIFE

ONE

HOOVER'S ACOLYTE

IN THE SPRING OF 1954, I received the invitation I had awaited for a dozen years. I was shown into an imposing conference room in the heart of the U.S. Justice Department headquarters in Washington. Portraits and other artwork adorned the fifty-foot walls. The center of the room was occupied by a massive table and beyond it stood a ceremonial executive desk. My destination was a spartan private office in the rear, dominated by a well-worn desk piled high with papers and files. As my host rose to greet me, I sensed his great power. After a long apprenticeship in the Federal Bureau of Investigation—all of it spent preparing for this moment— I was about to have my first private meeting with J. Edgar Hoover.

I had seen Hoover face-to-face once before and experienced his intimidating presence. During the final week of my basic FBI training in 1942, a reception was held for the young agents of Class 15 at the Mayflower Hotel in Washington. Before the director arrived, we were carefully instructed how to handle ourselves. We must not crowd around him. We were to form a line and march by to shake his hand, with no unnecessary conversation. Our handshake had to be firm but not too firm. Hoover disliked a "bone crusher" as well as a limp grip. He detested moist palms, and we were told to have a dry handkerchief ready to wipe off any sweat before the crucial handclasp.

Hoover arrived at precisely 6:30 P.M. He strode into the room briskly with Clyde Tolson, associate director, trailing, as always, a few steps behind. Hoover was vigorous and alert, dignified but friendly, and in complete control. He was forty-seven years old and at the peak of his physical capacities. Perhaps more than anything else, I noticed his immaculate appearance. He looked as if he had shaved, showered, and put on a freshly pressed suit for the occasion. Through the years, I never saw him looking otherwise.

The handshaking ceremony took less than fifteen minutes. Each of us received a quick, tight smile from the director. As the last member of the class passed by, Tolson, who had scrutinized each new agent, approached the director and whispered in his ear. A few seconds later, they were on their way out of the room, Tolson again a few steps behind.

Now, in 1954, I was one-on-one with the director, trying to keep my palms warm and dry. Hoover held out his hand and said, "It's nice to see you, Mr. Felt." His square face was accentuated by a jutting jaw. His piercing eyes bore into mine, sizing me up. He was stocky but not fat. He carried himself with a military bearing that made him appear taller than his 5 feet 10. His voice was strong and cultivated, with a trace of southern accent. His clothes were as immaculate as ever. I particularly remember his bright necktie.

Hoover was cordial and gracious as he took a seat behind the desk he had used from his first day as director (and would use until the day he died). I did not feel intimidated or uncomfortable as I launched into my presentation. I had a message to get across. It was common knowledge that Hoover promoted only those who had a demonstrated commitment to the Bureau and a "burning desire" to rise in its hierarchy. I wanted to convey those qualities to him.

"Mr. Hoover," I said, "I feel ready for more responsibility. My ambition is to be a special agent in charge. I feel confident I can handle the job whenever you feel I am ready for it."

Hoover looked pleased. "Mr. Felt, I am glad to hear that," he said. "We need ambitious, hardworking young men. You can be sure I will give you consideration when promotions are being made."

He began to discuss problems facing the FBI. In his forceful, staccato style, he spoke of the demands that Congress and the Atomic Energy Commission were making on the Bureau, requiring time-consuming background clearances for AEC employees. I took copious notes, but after ten minutes I wondered if I was being tested. It was not easy to interrupt J. Edgar Hoover, but when he paused for breath, I pointed out that this was a very real problem in the Seattle office, where I was stationed. "We conduct thousands of these investigations," I said. "Most of them are routine and could be handled by the Civil Service Commission. The FBI has more important things to do and we should be responsible for only the top positions."

Hoover thought for a minute and then agreed. "You are probably right. We'll have to take a long, hard look at this problem." He did, and my career may have turned on this exchange. From that point on, I injected myself into the conversation whenever possible. We talked for about thirty minutes and then he rose, holding out his hand. "Mr. Felt, I enjoyed this conversation," he said. "You can be sure you will be kept in mind for a promotion."

Six days later, back in Seattle, I received a letter from Hoover transferring me to Washington—the "seat of government" (SOG) as he called it. I was now an inspector's aide, the next step up on the promotion ladder.

Washington was the center of the world in those postwar years, and Hoover's FBI was one of the capital's most respected institutions. As I rose to the top ranks of the FBI hierarchy under Hoover, I had the FBI career kids dreamed of in those days: a counterspy against the Nazis, a crime buster arresting dangerous felons, and finally a top official in Washington taking on domestic terrorists and political corruption.

Toward the end of my three decades in the Bureau, however, this service was turned against me. Critics in the Nixon administration and the Justice Department denounced me as a "Hooverite," someone overly attached to the director's secretive leadership style. Yes, I was a Hoover loyalist and remained so. Hoover was a political operative par excellence, a genius at manipulating Congress and the press. But he used these skills to protect the standing of the FBI as an incorruptible institution, as the paragon of science and criminology that "always gets its man." After his passing, our first challenge was to maintain those standards against an administration determined to make the FBI into a political tool for its own use.

Unquestionably, Hoover put his stamp on the men who served him. His ideal agent was tall, slim, and rock-jawed, like Efrem Zimbalist, Jr. on television's *The F.B.I.*, an actor approved by Hoover personally. His agents were expected to handle a prodigious number of cases, and they prospered by solving high-profile crimes, making the bureau look invincible in the public eye. Hoover's G-men always comported themselves with an aura of professionalism in public. Maintaining appearances was key to winning Hoover's good graces. Working within his strict organizational scheme and thinking clearly were just as important.

After being transferred to SOG, I had to learn the tricks of the trade. I quickly found out, for example, that Hoover would not accept a long memorandum. Getting his favorable response depended on a succinct presentation. I also learned the importance of the abstract—a three-by-five typed slip with the title of the document, the date, to whom addressed, the name of the writer, and a one- or two-sentence description of the content of the document. Hoover went through a tremendous volume of reports and letters each day, and he usually read only the abstract. If that piqued his interest, he read the document itself. Unlike many agents, I took special care to write a good abstract. Careful wording was often enough to point Hoover in the desired direction.

Under no circumstances would Hoover tolerate a lapse of discipline. His seat of government was the nerve center of a tightly controlled and responsive organization. SOG occupied 40 percent of the imposing Justice Department building on Pennsylvania Avenue, and from there it directed all field operations. The special agent in charge (SAC) of every field office across the country conducted his own local operations, but he was kept under constant supervision through correspondence, carefully reviewed reports, and a system of annual inspections. In turn, SOG was scrutinized by Hoover, who kept his finger on everything and made all the decisions from the apex of the pyramid.

Headquarters operations at the time consisted of eight divisions.* They competed with each other to extract the maximum amount of work from the field. The SACs had to juggle operations in a way that kept the power centers happy. Politics permeated everything in Washington, and sound political skills were required to climb the FBI pyramid. Every field agent had a chance to learn the ropes at SOG during in-service training, a two-week session held at regular intervals in Washington and at the FBI Academy in Quantico, Virginia.

Some disagreed, but I thought this training was valuable for passing on the benefit of other agents' experience and sharing new investigative techniques. The first week in Washington consisted entirely of lectures by Bureau supervisors, each an expert in his field. For

* The administrative side included the Identification Division, the Administrative Division, the Crime Records Division, the Training and Inspection Division, and Files and Communications. The investigative side was made up of the General Investigative Division, the Domestic Intelligence Division, and the laboratory.

example, we would hear from someone on the bank robbery desk, where eight or ten supervisors divided up responsibility for investigating crimes in various regions of the country. In addition to these lectures, there were two full days of firearms training at Quantico, and hours devoted to solving hypothetical arrest problems.

Making it in Hoover's FBI meant staying on top of the latest techniques in criminal justice—and looking professional while doing it. J. Edgar Hoover always insisted that his agents dress like the lawyers and accountants most of them were and avoid any hint of slacking off—not even taking a public coffee break. Agents who were short in stature had to work extra hard to prove themselves, and agents who were noted as overweight on their annual physical soon found "fat" letters in their mailboxes.

Hoover was obsessed with fighting the battle of the bulge. He had studied life insurance charts that suggested "minimum," "desirable," and "maximum" weights for each height and frame. He arbitrarily decided that each agent must fall into the "desirable" category. This standard made sense for most agents, and in my case they meant bringing down my weight from 181 pounds to a healthier 171. Hoover himself gained weight over the years, eventually reaching over 200 pounds. But, full of enthusiasm for his new program, he plunged into a four-month regimen of diet and exercise, losing thirty-three pounds. He achieved the desirable bracket but couldn't maintain it. At death he was sixteen pounds over the standard he demanded of others.

Most agents adjusted to the weight standards without much difficulty, but some could not. The penalty was "limited duty" status, which excluded them from dangerous assignments or strenuous physical exertion, with an added forfeiture of overtime pay. Here agent ingenuity came into play. A sympathetic physician could be talked into listing an agent with a medium frame as having a heavy frame, a difference of fourteen pounds in allowable weight. Or he might add an inch to an agent's height, which added five pounds to the allowable weight. I did nothing to stop these practices in my jurisdictions. But as pressure from SOG increased, the Bureau instructed each office to obtain scales and measuring tapes. Agents who had a weight problem were to be weighed and measured every thirty days until they achieved the desired bracket. One of my agents spent hours in the steam room and took no liquids for days before the weigh-in. An agent with an unusually heavy bone structure took on a skeletal appearance, and I ordered him to gain ten pounds.

Despite the excessive aspects, we appreciated Hoover's goal: to fashion the FBI into a model of public service in action and appearance, an organization that criminals would fear and good citizens would adulate. This was the vision that drew children to become "Junior G-men" and persuaded qualified young men to join the Bureau in spite of the modest pay, long hours, and family disruptions that characterized an FBI career. I personally felt privileged to join this indispensable American institution. I could not foresee the social and political forces that would assault the FBI while I served it, and the anguish that would mark the end of my career.

TWO

THE G-MAN CULTURE

T HEY SAY AN FBI agent is born, not made. Perhaps so. I always nurtured an ambition for adventure and advancement. I had a pleasant boyhood in Twin Falls, Idaho, where my father was a moderately successful building contractor until the 1929 crash. I was a student who did "not live up to his potential," as a high school teacher put it. I always felt attracted to adventure and advancement and saw myself as a leader. I worked my way through the University of Idaho waiting tables and stoking furnaces. I was elected president of my fraternity, Beta Theta Pi, and after earning a bachelor of arts degree in 1935 I set my sights on Washington, D.C. I wanted to become a lawyer and had heard that a government job would give me time to go to law school at night. I appealed to Senator James P. Pope for help, and to my great good fortune he found an opening for me in his office as a correspondence clerk.

At 4:45 each afternoon I would leave the office and dash off to George Washington University Law School to attend classes from 5:00 P.M. to 7:00 P.M. and then return to Capitol Hill to finish my duties. I worked for Senator Pope and then for his successor,

D. Worth Clark, who arranged my schedule so that it would not interfere with my education. I thrived on the pressure. Around this time I began dating a beautiful and intelligent girl, Audrey Robinson, who had attended the University of Idaho with me and was working for the Internal Revenue Service. In June 1938 we were married by Rev. Sheara Montgomery, chaplain of the House of Representatives.

I received my bachelor of law degree in 1940. After passing the D.C. bar examination, I applied for a legal position with the Federal Trade Commission and was accepted. I could hardly wait to get my first assignment, but wait I did. Finally I asked my supervisor for an assignment. He gave me a complaint the FTC had received and asked me to prepare a report on it.

Skipping lunch and working at night, I completed the report in short order. But there was a penalty for completing an assignment rapidly—going without another one for a long time, several weeks in this case. And when it came, it was hardly one to set my heart pounding. I was to determine whether people using Red Cross brand toilet tissue did so because they thought it had some connection with the American Red Cross. My research, which required days of travel and hundreds of interviews, produced two definitive conclusions:

1. Most people did use toilet tissue.
2. Most people did not appreciate being asked about it.

That was when I started looking for other employment.

Two friends who worked for the FBI urged me to consider applying. I was aware that J. Edgar Hoover was a tough disciplinarian, that the work was demanding, and that the Bureau imposed strict conformity. But the salary was a munificent $3,200 a year, and I had the impression that FBI agents led a life of daily excitement tracking down bank robbers or engaging in gun battles with desperados.

In November 1941, I applied for a position as a special agent with the FBI. The screening process was demanding and thorough. The primary requirement was a law degree or an accounting degree with three years of experience. In addition, I filled out a detailed application form with questions covering every aspect of my life. Some ten days later I was interviewed at FBI headquarters in Washington. The interviewer, an official of the Administrative Division, went over my application question by question and probed my experiences. Why was I applying? Did I intend to make the FBI a career or was I looking for a way to avoid military service at a time when war was spreading in Europe?

My answers must have been satisfactory, since I was sent on to the next step, a law exam. Most of the questions described a factual situation, cited the law, and asked if the facts constituted a violation. If so, what investigative steps would I pursue to establish the evidence needed for prosecution? Next I was subjected to a rigorous physical examination. Then I waited for weeks while FBI agents checked out my educational and employment background and interviewed friends, neighbors, teachers, and associates. Finally, on January 19, 1942, two months after I filed my application, I received a letter of acceptance.

The letter, imprinted with J. Edgar Hoover's signature, instructed me to report to Room 5231 in the Justice Department Building at 9:00 A.M. on Monday, January 26, 1942. I arrived lugging a suitcase with enough clothing to last me for three weeks of training at the Marine base in Quantico. This would be followed by another thirteen weeks of training in Washington. (I learned later that the FBI was undergoing the greatest expansion in its history, from fewer than 600 agents before the war to more than 4,000 by the end of World War II.)

We had probationary status for one year, Hugh H. Clegg, assistant director of the Training and Inspection Division, told us. If we didn't measure up to FBI standards, we would be dropped. The passing grade in all courses was eighty-five, and a failing grade was cause for dismissal. On weekdays, classes would be held from 9:00 A.M. until 9:00 P.M. with one hour each for lunch and dinner. On Saturday, classes would end at 6:00 P.M., and Sunday, with only five hours of afternoon classes, would be our day of rest.

Clegg laid down the rules. There must be extreme moderation in the use of alcohol. There was no consumption of alcoholic beverages on assignment, regardless of the hour of day or night, and no excessive drinking off duty because an agent could never know when an emergency would call him back to the office. "Violation of these rules will result in dismissal with prejudice," Clegg said, meaning that the trainee would lose not only his FBI job but any chance of employment elsewhere in the federal government.

Finally Clegg said, "Gentlemen, if any of you has any doubts about it, now is the time to withdraw before I administer the oath of office." After a long silence he told us to stand up, raise our right hand, and repeat after him, very solemnly, our promise to defend the Constitution and protect the nation from all enemies, foreign and domestic.

We were issued briefcases containing a .38-caliber police revolver, a holster, and a badge. There were also two large looseleaf books—a manual of rules and regulations and a manual of instructions focusing on the investigative methods and reporting procedures in the one hundred types of cases handled by the FBI at that time. (When I retired, the number of categories had increased to more than 150 as Congress added to the FBI's responsibilities.)

For the next two weeks, ten hours each weekday, we were drilled on rules and regulations at the new FBI Academy in Quantico. The only break in this instruction was a daily session in the gymnasium doing calisthenics and learning judo and disarming tactics. We learned the kinds of moves a skilled adversary might use and what to expect when making arrests. At the end of the second week, we sweated out an examination on rules and regulations. They were not unduly complicated, but there were thousands of them.

I was more concerned about the next week's training on the firearms range. I had no experience with guns, and I knew that the FBI considered marksmanship as important as academic training. Agents rarely engaged in gun battles, partly because early G-men had shown a willingness and an ability to shoot it out with criminals. Agents were to use their weapons only in self-defense, but they shot to kill.

FBI firearms training was calculated to weed out the unfit. The FBI taught agents to fire the .38-caliber police revolver, the standard weapon; the .30-caliber rifle, needed where the target lies beyond the fifty-yard effective range of the pistol; the .45-caliber machine gun; the 12-gauge shotgun; and the 37-millimeter "cannon," which was occasionally used for lobbing tear gas projectiles into a room occupied by fugitives resisting arrest. Trainees also had a chance to fire the .357 Magnum revolver, which was powerful enough to stop an automobile by penetrating the motor block.

We spent hours learning how to strip and assemble these weapons, how to care for them, how to fire them, and how to handle them safely. Before we went to the range, we had a session of "dry firing" (without ammunition) to teach us the essentials of marksmanship: squeezing the trigger slowly and smoothly, learning not to anticipate the weapon's recoil. Because I had no previous experience with firearms, I was ahead of some of the men who had to unlearn bad habits.

I never had to fire a weapon in my career with the Bureau, but the knowledge of firearms I acquired was of tremendous value. They were drawn and ready during many raid and arrest situations. I knew how dangerous a firearm was and appreciated the rigid discipline necessary to protect others from injury.

After completing our three weeks at Quantico, we returned to Washington to learn the routine of FBI work. We studied the various laws over which the FBI had jurisdiction and the essential elements of each violation. We were taught how to develop evidence and how to write various reports. We saw the extraordinary capabilities of the FBI lab and learned how evidence was prepared for examination. We observed the work of the Identification Division and became adept at taking fingerprints and dusting for latent prints. I even learned how to pick locks.

During project training, we worked on simulated cases, interviewed "suspects" and "witnesses," wrote reports, and testified in Moot Court. We spent the last week of training at the Washington field office (WFO), where we were supposed to work on actual cases under the guidance of experienced agents. But the WFO was being reorganized, and we spent our time moving office equipment. The only cases I worked on were the cases of files I pushed from one location to another.

Finally I could look forward to my first assignment. Hoover wanted every agent to fit into any field office at any time. It was FBI policy to assign new agents for three months to their first office, six months to the second, and three years to the third. Agents could expect to remain in their fourth assigned office from seven to ten years. Hoover himself was a single man and had never been transferred, so he had no idea of the financial and personal hardships these transfers entailed.

Ross Prescott, one of my instructors at Quantico, was a Texan. If he liked you, he would say, "This man needs roughening up. Send him to a Texas office." Perhaps this was the reason my first assignment was to Houston. Audrey and I elected to drive from Washington to Houston and, in the one day allotted to us, managed to find a pleasant furnished apartment.

I left the job of settling in to Audrey and plunged into my new assignment. The Houston FBI office was located in the center of the downtown area and was crowded with three times the number of people it had been designed for. The territory we had to cover was, like everything else in Texas, very large. It encompassed forty-five counties, from the Louisiana border to Beaumont and south almost to the Mexican border. The special agent in charge (SAC), Ray Abbaticchio, was a kindly man who was thoroughly intimidated by J. Edgar Hoover. As a result, he made the office ground rules one notch tighter than the Bureau required.

Exceeding Bureau policy, the Houston office required each agent to wear his revolver at all times while working. For an agent doing little but interviewing friends, neighbors, and references of applicants for government jobs, carrying a three-pound revolver in a heavy leather holster in the Houston heat was more than a little burdensome. It also precluded removing your coat to cool off.

In addition, the SAC excluded all agents from the office during regular working hours except to dictate their correspondence. Organizing your work, reviewing files, preparing dictation, and sorting through notes had to be done during overtime hours. Hoover would not have objected to any legitimate activity in the office, and Abbaticchio's rule created more problems than it solved. New agents frequently left the office without enough investigative leads to keep them busy during the day, but they were afraid to return to their desks. Not knowing what to do, some just wandered through the streets.

My solution was to carry all my papers and documents in my briefcase and visit the public library, where I could organize my work for the following day. As a result, my reports were what Hoover wanted—terse, succinct, and relevant. One particular report, on a wartime plant protection program, was detailed and innovative enough to bring me Bureau commendation.

Three months to the day after my assignment to Houston, I was transferred to San Antonio. Although Audrey had to give up her job with the IRS in Houston, we were pleased. The San Antonio office was responsible for sixty counties, and the special agent in charge kept most of us out of the city covering the vast territory. My new SAC, Maurice W. Acers, was always cordial and considerate to me, but he was not popular in the office. Agents resented some of his management techniques, particularly the pressure he exerted to keep San Antonio's voluntary overtime, or VOT, the highest of any FBI office. Acers compiled a list showing where every man stood on the VOT totem pole. The four low men were given weekend duty during the ensuing month to "assist" them in moving up the list. This meant a "voluntary" eight-hour shift every Sunday of that month. Acers augmented his overtime by claiming as VOT the time he spent on overnight train rides to and from his frequent engagements out of the city. I was pleased when Hoover subsequently disallowed credit for travel time.

After I settled in, Acers gave me a "very important" assignment—the Waco road trip. Each Monday morning, I started out from San Antonio loaded with leads to be covered in the territory between Austin and Waco, mostly on the Fort Hood military reservation, a battle training area for an army tank corps. My job was to track down and interview tank trainees who had been listed as references by people applying for positions in the FBI, the Justice Department, or the Office of Strategic Services (the wartime predecessor of the CIA). It was grueling work that required long hours on the road and the rough tank trails. I had almost no time at home, and when I managed a few hours with Audrey I was too tired to do anything except fall into bed. It was good news for us when I was transferred again, this time to a war-fighting job in Washington.

THREE

SPY V. COUNTERSPY

W HEN I CAME TO Washington in late 1942, the nation was heading into a war, and the seat of government was the place to be. I was promoted to the rank of Bureau supervisor, though I received no increase in pay and no indication of what job I would be given. As part of my in-service training I was interviewed by Harry Kimball, chief of the Espionage Section. He congratulated me on my promotion but ruled out any chance that I was bound for a frontline assignment protecting America from German spies. Because of my lack of experience, he said, he was sure I would not be assigned to the Espionage Section.

Two weeks after my interview with Kimball, I found myself reporting to him. He informed me that my new boss was the assistant director in charge of the Domestic Intelligence Division, D. Milton (Mickey) Ladd, who deserved great credit for the Bureau's success in combating German espionage and sabotage and was known for sticking up for the supervisors under him. When the director criticized the division for some shortcoming, Ladd took the heat and never passed it down.

I was assigned to help three other supervisors at the general desk, where the thousands of unimportant cases were handled. With war fever running high, concerned citizens passed on to us every suspicion in regard to possible saboteurs or espionage agents. Relatively inexperienced in such matters, the FBI opened an investigation of nearly every tip. Wiretaps, microphones, and physical surveillance were reserved for the major cases. In minor cases, we kept in touch with neighbors and employers of the suspect and made spot checks on their activities. All of this created a heavy volume of work for the general desk.

The four-man team I joined handled thousands of these cases, and I had to review fifty or more files a day. New to the work, we tended to resolve doubts in favor of continuing the investigations. In time, we realized that 98 percent of the cases could be closed immediately and we made substantial reductions in the case load. The work I did was routine, but I was familiar with the major cases, sharing in the excitement. I also learned about German espionage techniques, from invisible ink to secret codes to dead drops.

In April 1944, a four-volume file involving a Nazi sympathizer was routed to me. The subject, Maximilian Gerhard Waldemar Othmer, was born in Germany, immigrated to the United States in 1919, and was naturalized in New Jersey in April 1935. The very next day he joined the German-American Bund and became the local führer before the year was out. He made no secret of his Nazi sympathies and returned to Germany several times. On one of these trips, he received an espionage assignment from the Abwehr, Germany's military intelligence service. Subsequently he obtained a job at Camp Pendleton (near Norfolk, Virginia) as an electrician and part-time stevedore. In 1942, the army relocated him to Knoxville, Tennessee, under its wartime powers.

The investigation of Othmer had been inconclusive and he was not suspected of being a Nazi agent. As I studied Othmer's file, how-

ever, several details aroused my interest. The wide mouth of Chesa-
peake Bay between Norfolk and Hampton, where he had lived in
Virginia, was the staging area for convoys bound for England. The
German submarine command seemed to have an uncanny knowledge of this activity.

I noted too that Othmer had received $500 from Shanghai through
the Chase National Bank. The amount was insignificant, but the
Abwehr funneled money to its agents in this manner. And a Trenton
dentist once mentioned receiving a letter from Othmer pleading for a
prescription for Pyramidon, a commonly used painkiller in Europe.
(The dentist told Othmer to use aspirin.) This last fact was the real tip-
off for me. Abwehr agents used Pyramidon to make invisible ink. A
tablet was dissolved in water and the solution was used to write a
message between the lines of a seemingly innocuous letter. The
receiving agent heated the letter and the secret message appeared.

Convinced that Othmer was a spy, I prepared a carefully worded
memorandum recommending that the case be reopened and that
Othmer be interviewed again as soon as possible. To make sure that
the agents asked the right questions, I created a detailed summary
and outlined what he should be asked. Finally word came that Othmer had confessed. He told his questioners that he had sent secret
messages to his German superiors in 1940 and 1941 via a letter drop
in Milan, Italy. These were radioed to the German high command,
which in turn passed them on to German U-boats preying on Allied
shipping. Because it took days for the convoys to be assembled and
then reach submarine hunting grounds, Nazi raiders had sufficient
time to sink many Allied vessels.

Othmer was charged with violations of the federal espionage
statutes. But he denied sending messages after Pearl Harbor and
refused to implicate other German agents. When I questioned
him—arguing, pleading, and even threatening him with a maximum
prison sentence—he refused to budge but identified his mail drop as

R. A. Homburg, 46 Via Gran Sassa, Milan. A file search disclosed two other suspects using the same drop.

Eventually Othmer was convicted and given twenty years, the maximum sentence for espionage committed before we entered the war. Though Othmer claimed to be a minor agent, his dossier suggested that he was one of the most valuable Abwehr spies in the United States, furnishing reports on damaged British warships being repaired in Norfolk, the details of departing convoys, and tank production. He helped the Abwehr piece together a picture of naval aid to Great Britain and America's growing preparedness at sea.

While Othmer was on his way to the federal penitentiary in Atlanta, he wrote to David Scruggs, an agent who had interviewed him, and asked him to handle some personal matters. Scruggs agreed, and a few weeks later Othmer requested permission to see him. "You have been kind to me," the spy told the FBI agent, "and now I want to do something for you." Othmer directed Scruggs to a steamer trunk full of books in storage at the YMCA in Knoxville. He identified one in particular: a volume entitled *Weiers Taschenbuch der Kriegsflotten* (1940).

When the FBI lab examined the book, technicians found a frame of microfilm concealed in the binding, the negative of a photo of a typewritten page. Othmer had given us a code used for writing in open text, as opposed to secret ink. A message in this code would appear to be innocuous. For example, "Mrs." meant a convoy. If the proper name started with an A, it would indicate a convoy of under ten ships. B would indicate ten to twenty ships, C from twenty to thirty, and so on. "Suitcase" meant a destroyer. Any date was ten days earlier than stated. We found the code exactly as it had been placed there by the authorities at Nest Bremen, one of the Abwehr subdivisions. This was a valuable find because the same code, prepared on the same typewriter, had been used by other German agents and proved to be an important link to other Nazi espionage cases.

My role in the Othmer case created opportunities for me. When a vacancy on the major case desk occurred, I was promoted from the general desk (still with no increase in pay). My involvement in the case had made me something of an expert on Nest Bremen and I was assigned to coordinate all information on this operation and familiarize myself with the personnel. As we learned later, Nest Bremen had primary responsibility for Abwehr operations directed against the United States.

Information about Nest Bremen was routed to me for study and indexing. Much of our knowledge came from MI-5, the British counterpart to the FBI, which had caught and debriefed a number of German agents trained at Nest Bremen. I used this information, along with what the FBI had gathered, to prepare brief dossiers on each staff member, which were furnished to MI-5 so that they could complete their records. Eventually I developed the ability to identify other German agents just by reviewing our accumulated files.

This was not my only assignment. The agent I replaced on the major case desk had been handling the Mexican microdot case, one of the great breakthroughs in our counterintelligence efforts. German agents in Mexico, abusing that country's neutrality, accumulated vast amounts of information about the United States—far too much to send by radio. So the Germans devised a process of photographic reduction—prints small enough to be disguised as a period on a typewritten page. The surface of the microdot looked smooth even when magnified a hundred times.

This mode of transmitting information might have gone undetected but for an alert examiner at the British censorship station in Bermuda. He had opened and examined a letter and detected nothing at first. But as he put it aside, he noticed a shiny spot. Examining the letter more carefully, he saw that what seemed to be a typewritten period was actually a microdot glued to the paper.

The letter and the problem it posed were turned over to the FBI.

It was imperative not to let the enemy know that this process had been discovered, yet we could not allow vital information to reach Germany. As a general rule, it is best to contain and control a foreign agent. With containment, you can learn much about enemy agents and intelligence operations. With control, you can feed false information through the agent, misleading and confusing the enemy.

Ultimately we decided to let the letter go through. The information on the microdot had come from various American publications sold openly in Mexico. As the end of the war approached, more than three hundred microdots had been intercepted, and many were cleared to go to the enemy. At that point data on our capabilities did more to discourage than to help the German high command. If the information was too sensitive to be passed on, the microdot was rubbed off so that it appeared to have come loose in transit.

My work in the microdot case introduced me to the art of misinformation. My next case, code-named Peasant, was a double agent operation designed to mislead the Japanese military. It was part of a bigger misinformation program. What we transmitted to the Japanese made it possible for Gen. Douglas MacArthur to land almost without opposition in the Philippines toward the end of the war.

In another German case, we created our own enemy spy. Early in 1944, Nest Bremen had trained an espionage agent, Helmut Gold, for assignment in the United States and instructed him to send his messages by Morse code. Since each person's touch on the wireless key is unique—telegraphers call it his "fist"—Nest Bremen had made a tape recording of Gold's transmitting style to serve as his signature. The agent had left Germany with $5,000 in cash. In Lisbon, on his way to Washington, he defected to the Allies, revealing his whole operation to the British embassy. At first the British planned to make Gold a double agent. But he was unreliable and chased women, so they turned him over to us.

What to do with Gold? Because he had been trained at Nest Bremen, the question was referred to me. I recommended that we take the case but leave Gold in England, in protective custody. We would create a fictitious Gold who would come to Washington and set up an espionage operation. Thus we would control what information went to the Nazis and use the bogus Gold to ferret out the spies he was to work with. Hoover agreed. The critical point—and most of my memorandum to Hoover addressed this—was the ability of an FBI radio specialist to duplicate Gold's "fist" at the Morse key.

The case gave us a glimpse into the minds of the German leadership as the Allies closed in. We got corroboration of the German military's growing confusion and despair over the magnitude of America's war effort. On one occasion, the Abwehr asked Gold to procure the production figures for two-engine transport planes in the United States. Knowing the impact the true figures would have, the Joint Security Council decided to supply them. The Abwehr radioed back to Gold that his source obviously did not have access to the facts and he was instructed not to use it any more.

Most of the information "volunteered" to "Gold" by his "high-level contacts" was designed to be of more interest to Japan than to Germany. We prepared fragmentary data that we knew would be given to the Japanese by the Germans. "Gold" was only one channel. Pieces of the jigsaw puzzle were leaked to Japan from many sources. In Tokyo, they would be pieced together into one erroneous picture. We could monitor the progress of our work. A message to Gold's superiors in Bremen would contain a small amount of valid information and a great deal of misinformation relating to U.S. military operations in the Pacific. A few days later, the Signal Security Service (later merged into the National Security Agency), which had broken the Japanese diplomatic code before the outbreak of hostilities, would intercept a message from the Japanese embassy in Berlin to Tokyo. Its substance would be what Gold had transmitted to Nest Bremen.

My career as a counterspy ended on May 7, 1945, when the Third Reich surrendered to the Allies. Hoover disbanded the Espionage Section and allowed me and the eleven other supervisory agents in that section to choose our next station. I chose the Seattle office, in my native Northwest, where my counterespionage skills came in handy. Our wartime alliance with the Soviet Union had opened up the United States to Kremlin spies, and the FBI was busy learning to cope with a new adversary: Russian agents and their underground American supporters.

FOUR

ON THE FBI ROLLER COASTER

M Y WORK against the Nazis familiarized me with the tricks spies used to arrange secret meetings and pass documents. In Seattle I needed all my skills to keep track of Nikolai Reddin, a Russian naval liaison officer stationed in the city. Reddin had bribed a technician at the naval shipyard in Bremerton (a ferry ride across Puget Sound from Seattle) to furnish him with information about our ships. The technician contacted the FBI and was told to continue his meetings with the Soviet intelligence agent.

As a trained agent, Reddin knew all the tricks, including how to avoid surveillance. Driving around town in his car, he made left turns where they were prohibited and we either had to follow or lose him. He slowed down when approaching an intersection, and as the light turned red, he would drive through. He rode up and down elevators to spot those who were following him. We were ordered not to arrest him unless he boarded a Russian freighter. This was precisely what he tried to do and was subsequently tried on charges of espionage. But he was acquitted, in part because the government could prove only minor violations of the espionage statutes, and in part because the Russians were still considered allies.

But those spy-conscious times created drudgery as well as excitement. The Atomic Energy Act transferred supervision for the production of atomic warheads from the military, which had successfully supervised the Manhattan Project, to the new Atomic Energy Commission. The FBI was charged with screening AEC employees and guarding against the theft of atomic secrets. As the supervisor of this process in Seattle, I found myself overseeing as many as 2,500 pending cases at a time—a burden that diverted me from more important FBI priorities, as I later pointed out to Hoover in our private meeting.

Preventing the theft of nuclear materials was one such priority. The major U.S. plutonium production facility was at Hanford, Washington, which fell within the jurisdiction of the Seattle office. One day we received a breathless report that eleven ounces of plutonium were missing. These consisted of minute machine filings, the by-product of lathing down raw plutonium into the shapes necessary for an atomic explosion. The scientists at Hanford were worried because the chemical composition of the filings could disclose to a Russian chemist the processes used in refining the plutonium.

To investigate the alleged theft, I took a squad of agents to the Hanford lab and examined its operation. We realized almost at once that stealing the plutonium would have been virtually impossible. We therefore checked the cleanup and accountability procedures. The lab floors were covered with brown wrapping paper. If a technician detected signs of radiation during periodic sweeps of the area, the paper was rolled up, sealed in a large cardboard box, and buried under tons of dirt. The floor covering was discarded at the end of the day, whether or not radiation was detected. Eventually we concluded that the missing plutonium was a result of these rigorous cleanup measures rather than Soviet espionage. Some of the scientists, I suspect, were not entirely convinced.

Seattle was a great assignment, but it was a long way from the seat of government. That's where one man would decide whether I fulfilled my modest ambition to become a special agent in charge. In May 1951, when I was scheduled for another round of in-service training in D.C., Seattle SAC Richard Auerbach called me into his office for some friendly advice.

"You've got to call yourself to Hoover's attention," he said. "Clyde Tolson is a good friend of mine. Ask to see him and say it was my idea. Explain that you want to be a SAC and feel you're ready for the responsibility. Ask him to help you."

I decided to try that strategy and put in for a meeting with Tolson. On the last day of my training, the supervisor who was lecturing us announced, "Mr. Felt, Mr. Tolson wants to see you right away." This was my first real encounter with Hoover's number two, the close confidant who trailed behind the director, vacationed with him, and dined with him. There were whispers that Tolson had an intimate private relationship with Hoover, though I never saw any evidence of this.

"Hello, Mr. Felt," Tolson said and motioned me to the long couch on his right. I had not seen him since the reception for new agents more than eight years before. He looked thin, drawn, and tired, and smiling seemed an effort. He appeared much older than the director. When I outlined my Bureau experience and expressed my desire for an SAC assignment, he appeared remote and impersonal. "I am glad to know that you are interested," he said. "Your record is good. I will make a note of your visit."

Whatever note he made had no effect. The next time I was scheduled for in-service training, in 1954, I decided to contact Hoover. Our private meeting went very well indeed. In the next few years I was sent on a roller coaster ride of five different jobs—in Washington, New Orleans, Los Angeles, Salt Lake City, and Kansas City—each one a step toward a senior leadership position. My first assignments went by so quickly that I often felt I was punching my ticket on the way through—though I couldn't complain about a lack of action.

WASHINGTON

My job as an inspector's aide in D.C. was less than ideal. I served on what agents called the "goon squad," charged with monitoring the performance of field offices around the country, acting as Hoover's eyes and ears. After a couple of months, I was transferred to New Orleans as the assistant special agent in charge. It was a tough move for my family, as we had just settled into Washington, but it wouldn't be the last. Audrey and I had survived seventeen moves by the time I finally retired.

NEW ORLEANS

The FBI office in New Orleans had an average-size staff of fifty-one agents and twenty-six clerical employees. It was the nerve center for FBI activities in Louisiana, with suboffices in Baton Rouge, Shreveport, Monroe, Alexandria, and Lake Charles. The SAC, Morton P. Chiles, supervised most of the major cases and had overall responsibility for the office. As assistant SAC, I handled the other cases in the criminal field and supervised the Criminal Informant Program, which was very active in sinful New Orleans.

The Bureau trained new assistant SACS by placing them under the tutelage of an experienced SAC. This was tough for me because I had no background in the day-to-day management of an FBI field office. And, unlike the average agent, I had spent no time tracking criminals, a job that constituted more than 80 percent of the Bureau's work. Lacking experience with bank robbery investigations, apprehending criminals, and the justice system, I quickly earned five censure letters, the bane of an agent's existence. These letters, which were sent out over Hoover's signature, contained doomsday language and typically began, "I am amazed and astounded," and so on. Censure letters were more than a slap on the wrist, for they could hold up a prospective raise for as long as six months. Agents resented them, feeling that minor transgressions were better overlooked. But if Hoover was quick to blame, he was even quicker to praise; letters of commendation, often accompanied by a cash incentive award, outnumbered censure letters by 3 to 1. The censure letters I received did not hurt my FBI career.

New Orleans, or NOLA as we liked to call it, featured a diverse culture—the French Quarter, Mardi Gras, gambling, and a wide variety of people, some of whom attracted our interest. I spent many evenings on Bourbon Street combing the bars and strip joints tracking down fugitives from justice. Try telling your wife you have to spend another evening at a strip joint to apprehend a bank robber who is dating one of the girls. As they say, somebody has to do it.

NOLA offered some sort of FBI action every night. Sometimes we had to find the bad guys and sometimes they came to us. Harold Pauley, a man in his early twenties living in Seattle, wanted to go to California. He answered an advertisement in the *Seattle Times* placed by an elderly couple looking for someone to drive them to Los Angeles. They hired Pauley, probably because of his clean-cut appearance.

On the road both nagged Pauley incessantly about his driving. A short distance south of Fresno, Pauley had to pull over to fix a flat tire, which the couple also blamed on him. While removing the spare from the trunk, Pauley noticed a hatchet. He concealed the tool in a road map and placed it under the driver's seat, resolving, as he told me later, to kill the man and his wife the next time they nagged him. He didn't have long to wait. They passed Bakersfield and started over the Tehachapie Mountains on the long grapevine grade, known for the many large trucks slowly grinding their way up to the top. The nagging started again. Pauley took the next turnoff, drove a short distance from the main road, and parked. He took out the hatchet and hacked the couple to pieces, deaf to their horrific screams.

The California Highway Patrol was responsible for the murder investigation. The couple's car was found abandoned at Los Angeles International Airport, and Pauley's fingerprints were all over the driver's seat. After interviewing hundreds of airport personnel and passengers, officers determined that Pauley was a passenger on a recent flight to Dallas, Texas. This brought the FBI into the case, and a federal warrant was issued charging him with unlawful flight to avoid prosecution. We were too late to stop him in Dallas, but FBI agents determined that Pauley then boarded a bus to New Orleans. The Dallas FBI field office informed me that Pauley was headed my way and I should consider the suspect armed and dangerous.

The special agent in charge was out of town, so I took the case. The call from the Dallas field office came only twenty minutes before the bus was scheduled to arrive in New Orleans, so I instructed two agents to meet me at the bus station and then hurried downtown, arriving at the station just as the bus pulled in. One of the agents also pulled up, and we decided to board the bus before our man had a chance to melt into the crowd in the terminal.

We had his general description and his seat number. As I stepped onto the Greyhound, I put my right hand inside my coat, unsnapped my shoulder holster, and held the grip of my .38-caliber police special. I had ugly visions of Pauley taking hostages or opening fire and killing innocent passengers. We had to take him before he had a chance to react. The first thing I saw was a couple of women in the front row showing off their long legs and ample cleavage. Their clothing and heavy makeup suggested that I would run into them again on Bourbon Street. Pauley was still in his seat, but he started to rise as we moved slowly toward him. Since the aisle was narrow, we had to go one at a time, and the agent behind me was climbing up my back. I introduced Pauley to my .38-caliber companion pointed at the ceiling and said, "FBI, Pauley. Freeze." He readily admitted his identity and I took him off the bus and put him in the backseat of the car with the other agent. Once handcuffed, he was docile. I retrieved Pauley's suitcase from the baggage claim and headed for the office.

Pauley could not have been more cooperative under questioning, though his eyes shifted constantly and seemed devoid of life. The victims' constant nagging had reminded him of his parents, he said, and he couldn't stand to think about them. After his statement was reduced to writing, he signed without the slightest hesitation. He volunteered to help the cleaners move furniture from the evidence room, perhaps hoping for an opportunity to retrieve his suitcase, where we later found the murder weapon. It was wrapped in the road map and still encrusted with his victims' blood. Why he had not disposed of it was a mystery to me. Possibly the hatchet had some sentimental value for him, which was not uncommon in cases like this.

After we completed the statement and pictures, I called Bureau headquarters in Washington round 2:00 A.M. and briefed the night supervisor on all developments. He called me back in a few minutes with instructions from the director to issue a press release. While two other agents took Pauley to the lockup, I wrote the release and then read it to the various media outlets over the phone. I finished up at about 4:00 A.M. and drove home, hoping to get an hour or two of sleep before returning to the office. When I arrived at our apartment, however, Audrey told me the phone had been "ringing off the wall." She handed me messages to call nine different reporters, two in Los Angeles. I decided to shower and go back to the office, since it would be easier to handle the calls from there. While I was enjoying the hot shower, Audrey tugged at the shower curtain and said there was a reporter at the front door who wanted to talk to me immediately.

"Tell him I'm in the shower!" I said.

"I already did," she cried.

"Then tell him to jump in the lake."

She told him I would be out of the shower in a minute. When I finished dressing, he was waiting for me in the living room. He apologized for the early hour and said, "The news never sleeps." He explained that the story had created great interest in California and Washington State, and the wire services were demanding more details. I gave him what additional material I could but declined to let him use my phone to call in the story. A good thing for me, since I got four more calls from Bureau headquarters before I left.

Arriving back at work, I learned that the story had broken nationwide with my name prominently mentioned in a favorable light. One account said I had apprehended a ruthless ax murderer singlehandedly in the face of great personal risk and without a single injury to the many innocent bystanders on the bus. It went on to say that the community could breathe a sigh of relief now that the FBI had the vicious killer in custody. Those were the good old days.

At 8:15 A.M. I got another call from headquarters and was told to stand by for the director. "Felt, excellent job on the Pauley apprehension," Hoover said. "I've also read the news releases, and it seems you've managed to get back in the limelight again. Never mind, just keep up the good work. Good-bye."

"Yes sir," I replied as he hung up. He was definitely a charmer.

Pauley was extradited back to California, where he was tried and found guilty of second-degree murder. He was sentenced to life in the California state penitentiary.

I had finished taking more media calls on the hatchet murders and was looking forward to a New Orleans cruller and coffee. But then Sims Regard, our agent covering the oil fields near Morgan City, Louisiana, rushed into my office saying he had just located Henry Nolan, a fugitive from Texas. Nolan's crimes were rather low on the meter—passing bogus checks—but he was a high priority because he was a former professional wrestler, big and mean and considered highly dangerous. Since the special agent in charge was still out of town, I would have to handle this case also. A glance at the clock told me it was 8:35.

Sims had visited the drilling superintendents of several oil companies, asking them to keep an eye out for Nolan, and one of the supers had just called. The man said Nolan was in his office saying he wanted to quit his job and get his final paycheck. Sims told the superintendent to stall, but Nolan would be gone long before we could make the three-hour drive to Morgan City. Sims, however, had taken care of that. One of the oil companies agreed to lend us a vintage PBY military seaplane, and the pilots were on their way down to the old Lake Pontchartrain airport where the plane was based. We could be there in fifteen minutes. I strapped on my shoulder holster again, took the handcuffs out of my desk, and grabbed my coat. "Let's move," I said.

Exactly sixteen minutes later we were climbing into the old plane. We could take off on the old concrete runway, but at Morgan City we would have to land on the water. The pilots had already warmed up the engines, and we took off in a flurry of seagulls. Morgan City was sixty miles away by air, and we were there in thirty minutes. The pilot landed on the broad Atchafalaya River, which flows through Morgan City. As our big plane plowed through the water and slowed to a stop, I could see a motorboat speeding toward us from the shore. Sims smiled and said the boat was provided courtesy of the chief of police in Morgan City. A police cruiser and two officers were waiting for us when we reached the shore. This was back in the days when the local authorities thought the FBI was there to help them.

In minutes, we were walking into the oil company office where Nolan was patiently waiting for his check. He was an enormous man, seven feet tall and over three hundred pounds. His bulging muscles made him look every inch the professional wrestler. He could have thrown both of us around like rag dolls. Taken completely by surprise, however, Nolan just stood there and stared at us. Finally he must have decided that we were not good news, because he picked up the supervisor's desk and threw it at us. Fortunately there was a steel support pole between Nolan and us, so the desk splintered against the pole and came crashing down just short of where we were standing.

Nolan told us to back off before someone got hurt. I blurted out that we were FBI and he was under arrest. I doubt Nolan heard me, since he was busy crashing through a closed window to freedom. We took the door, ran around the building, and found Nolan limping away toward the swamp. We followed at a reasonable distance, and I told myself I would not shoot a man for writing bad checks. When he reached the edge of the swamp he turned and faced us.

"Nolan," I said, "this is the FBI. You are under arrest." It hadn't worked the first time, but I was willing to give it another shot. "You have nowhere to go. Put your hands over your head." He surrendered meekly and submitted to a body search. Then, without being asked, he held out his wrists for the handcuffs. His arms were so large that it took considerable pressure to force the cuffs into the last notch, and I could see they were cutting his wrists, but he didn't pull away. In those days most felons held the FBI in awe.

As we were getting back into the chief's car, it occurred to me that he deserved credit for the excellent support he had given us. So I asked him to stop by his office on the way back to the plane. We completed the paperwork and listed the chief as the arresting officer. I told him to take some mug shots of the prisoner and send one to the local paper along with a press release. The chief was gratified and launched into a long-winded history of his police experiences in the bayous. I told him he should write a book. Finally the chief drove Nolan and us back to the river where our speedboat was waiting.

LOS ANGELES

In New Orleans I showed Hoover that I could catch criminals and then handle myself in the glare of public attention. Within fifteen months he sent me to the much brighter lights of Los Angeles, a field office second in size only to New York's and another step to a SAC position. In a few months there I accumulated more on-the-job experience than I would have earned in three years at a smaller field office. I also received training in handling the "baggage detail" for Hoover himself.

To get away from official Washington, he and Tolson made several trips each year, and their favorite was their annual summer trip to Los Angeles and La Jolla. Preparations had to be made far in advance because Hoover insisted on the same seats in the plane, the same rooms in the same hotels, the same restaurants, the same haberdasher, and the same pleasure ride—each in the same sequence. My responsibility was to handle the luggage, a precision operation. When Hoover and Tolson departed from Washington, airline officials arranged for their suitcases to be loaded last into the forward baggage compartment. Numbers on the claim stubs were telephoned ahead. It was my job to get the luggage off the plane and deliver it to Hoover's hotel room exactly three minutes after he entered.

SALT LAKE CITY

I must have done it right because in 1956, almost two years to the day after I sat in Hoover's office, I was promoted to special agent in charge. My family pulled up stakes once again as we moved to Salt

Lake City. The FBI office was one of the smaller ones, but it included Las Vegas and Reno. Nevada gambling is a powerful lure to some of the world's biggest criminals, and consequently the Salt Lake City territory was a high-visibility FBI assignment.

Here I became a part of the FBI push against the Mafia. Critics have charged that Hoover did not move against organized crime until forced to by Attorney General Robert F. Kennedy. I happen to know differently. As SAC of a field office whose territory included Nevada, I was continuously pressured by the seat of government to move against Mafia infiltration of the gambling casinos in Reno and Las Vegas. But until Congress passed adequate laws in the 1960s, we could do little more than gather information through informants and electronic surveillance, and this is how we discovered that the underworld owners of the gambling casinos were skimming off profits without notifying state and federal authorities as required by law.

Beyond the glitz of the gambling cities, there was a frontier quality to the justice administered in much of the territory, and not always of the shoot-'em-up variety. In one case, we traced Hal and Pearl Butler, husband and wife bank robbers, to the quiet town of Blanding, Utah, in the four corners area where Utah, Colorado, New Mexico, and Arizona come together. We were positive that Hal had robbed the bank and Pearl had driven the getaway car. But in Blanding, by all accounts, they had settled down as quiet, likable members of the community.

I was taking no chances. Backed up by the three agents who were close but out of sight, I casually walked up to the Butler trailer in a remote construction camp. I had done away with my Hoover-regulation suit, including necktie and snap brimmed hat, and walked up to the Butlers' door wearing jeans and cowboy boots. I'm sure Butler thought I was just another construction worker. As I got closer, a large dog rushed out, barking wildly. I spoke to it in a friendly voice while walking slowly toward the door, and the dog seemed to relax. The door was open and I could see the suspects at a table, watching me. "May I come in?" I asked, opening the screen door as I spoke.

"Sure, come on in; we'll be through eating in a minute," Butler said after a short pause. "You hungry?" To my surprise there were four Butlers sitting at the table, two more than we were expecting. A child of about eighteen months was sitting in a high chair pounding the food in his dish with his spoon. Having casually closed her blouse as I came in, Pearl cradled in her arms a four-month-old infant.

"Mr. Butler," I said, "I am a special agent with the FBI. You and your wife are under arrest." One of my colleagues had just entered the trailer and the two other agents stood outside. Everything seemed frozen in time. The baby didn't cry and no one moved for what seemed like an eternity. Then Hal pushed his chair back abruptly. I moved my hand to my .38-special.

"Stay where you are, Hal, and don't try anything," I said. There was another long pause and then Hal slumped back into his chair.

"We knew you was coming sooner or later," he said. "I'm glad it's over." I drew a deep breath, relaxed a little, and advised the adult Butlers of their constitutional rights.

We took short statements, and both freely admitted what they had done. The four-month-old cried, and I began to consider the most difficult issue involved with this arrest. What were we going to do with the children? Pearl must have been pregnant when she drove the getaway car.

Had it not been for the young ones, both Hal and Pearl would have been taken to the federally approved jail in Monticello, Utah, some thirty miles away. But the sheriff's contract with the federal government for detention of federal prisoners made no provision for child care. The best place for these unfortunate young ones was with their mother at home in their trailer, and I asked Pearl what she thought about this. She gratefully accepted the idea. She had no money but believed Hal had wages coming from the drilling company where he had worked for almost two weeks. She said the bank robbery loot was meager and was spent long ago. I knew that was probably true, so I told Pearl we would see that she got Hal's check.

There was only one flaw in this solution: I had no legal authority to release Mrs. Butler. This had to be done in a judicial proceeding normally handled by a U.S. commissioner, and the nearest was in Salt Lake City. There was one other possibility, however. In the absence of a U.S. commissioner, the federal rules of criminal procedure provide that state judges and even local mayors can hold arraignments for federal prisoners, so I sent one of the agents to find the mayor of Blanding. I then directed two of the agents to take Hal Butler to the county jail at Monticello. Ken and I took Pearl to see the mayor, after finding a baby-sitter.

I asked the mayor to verify the identity of the prisoner and the probable cause for her arrest, as required.

"Pearl," the mayor said, "do you admit you are the person in this arrest warrant?

"Yes, I am that person."

"What do I do now, Mr. Felt?" the mayor asked.

"Mr. Mayor, in view of the two small children, I recommend this young lady be released on her own recognizance." The mayor's bewilderment was reflected on his face. "It means you will allow her to go free without bail if she promises to appear in the Salt Lake federal court to formally answer these charges when she is notified to do so."

"Young lady, do you promise to appear in the federal court in Salt Lake City when you are notified to do so?"

"I do, your honor," Pearl said with conviction.

"All right, Mr. Felt, this young lady is released on what you said."

"Thank you, Mr. Mayor," I replied. After we left the mayor's house, I insisted Pearl give me her parents' number and I called them. I listened as Pearl talked with her mother and explained her predicament. When she hung up the receiver, after receiving her mother's assurance of love and support, she told me they were on their way to help her. Then the tears started and flowed until we were back at the trailer. She wiped her eyes and stepped inside to relieve the baby-sitter. We left feeling pretty good about that situation. I am as tough on crime as anyone, but sometimes people need a break.

It was late when we arrived in Monticello after our unusual trip through stage one of federal criminal procedure. The next morning I thanked the sheriff for his assistance. As we were getting ready to start back to Salt Lake City, a deputy came by and unlocked the cellblock door. "Okay men, it's time for breakfast," he said. Six prisoners filed out and made their way toward the outside door. Hal was one of the six.

"Sheriff," I blurted, "where are they going?"

"They're going to eat breakfast at the Rainbow Café," he said. "It's down the street, about a block. It's the best darn eating in town."

"Prisoners go out to eat without a guard?" I said, trying not to sound surprised.

"Sure," he replied with a grin. "I ain't lost but three or four." Those odds were not good enough for me.

"Hal," I called out as he was about to step outside. "Come on back. We're going to take you to Salt Lake City today so you may as well eat with us." Much to my relief, Hal turned and came back. I asked him later what he thought about the unguarded breakfast plan for prisoners in the Monticello jail. He said he would have come back because he just wanted the whole thing over with.

Pearl Butler pleaded guilty to aiding in a bank robbery and received probation. Harold Butler pleaded guilty to bank robbery and was sentenced to three years in the federal penitentiary. He was released after serving two years as a model prisoner. I checked on

Pearl after Hal got out of prison and she told me that Hal had a new job, the kids were growing like weeds, and they were all doing okay.

If we sometimes looked like a local posse in action, we were backed by the FBI lab and Identification Division. They made the difference in a brutal Utah murder investigation I handled. On September 21, 1957, Sheriff Faye Gillette of Toole County, Utah, announced he had a "hot case" for us. A North American Van Lines driver, Thomas William Parsons, had dropped off a delivery in Oakland and had contacted his dispatcher twelve days earlier, saying he was on his way to Salt Lake City. Then he disappeared. On the day we were called in, another North American driver spotted Parsons's truck parked near the highway patrol weigh station on Highway 50 near Wendover, Utah.

"I don't suppose they found Parsons?" I asked Sheriff Gillette.

"No they haven't," he replied, "but it looks bad. The highway patrol found blood stains and a piece of denture in the cab."

Since Parsons's tractor had apparently been stolen and transported across state lines, a federal crime had been committed. Together, FBI agents from the Salt Lake office and a deputy from the Toole County sheriff's office searched the truck. Obviously someone had hurriedly cleaned the interior of the cab, but flecks of what appeared to be blood were smeared on the inside door of the cab, the dome light, the headliner, and the left window. The mattress in the sleeper had been turned over to hide large clots of blood. What appeared to be spots of blood were also found on maps and other papers in the driver's locker. Although many fingerprints were found, they could not be identified. After searching the outside of the vehicle without results, the deputy, a former truck driver, suggested that they tilt the cab forward to search underneath. After a painstaking effort, they found what turned out to be a key piece of evidence. Dangling in a crack where the brake pedal came through the floor of the cab, supported only by the flange around its rim, was a .22-caliber cartridge casing.

The moving van had been sitting by the side of the road in the hot desert sun for over a week, and investigators opened the rear doors to an overwhelming stench. A search of the interior revealed the badly decomposed body of a man with three bullet holes in his head lying face down on a cardboard carton under a pile of furniture pads. Another North American driver positively identified the body as Thomas William Parsons. No autopsy was conducted since we had a pretty good idea of what killed him.

Parsons had been a driver for North American Van Lines since 1945, and this would have been his last trip before retirement. On August 28, he said good-bye to his wife and child on their small farm in Jamaica, Iowa, and headed west to deliver furniture in Ely, Nevada, and Oakland. His helper, who usually accompanied Parsons on cross-country trips, was sick and did not make the trip. Parsons stopped at the North American office in Salt Lake City and mentioned that he would hire one of the roustabouts at a nearby truck stop as a helper. Witnesses at the Ely and Oakland unloading points confirmed that he had a helper with him.

Parsons's bloodstained and nearly illegible log was sent to the Document Section of the FBI lab. Experts reconstructed most of his itinerary and found that he had hired a helper named Steward. The last entry in the log indicated that on September 9, Parsons drove from San José, California, to Reno, Nevada, arriving at 9:00 A.M. FBI agents canvassing Nevada businesses along his route located a café operator in Fernley, Nevada, who knew Parsons, and she stated he was in her café about 9:00 P.M. on September 9. We suspected that was the murder date.

We interviewed the couple in Ely who received Parsons's first delivery, and they furnished a description of his helper and remembered that Parsons had called him Earl. Our investigators found two clear sets of fingerprints on a vanity mirror that had been part of the delivery. One set of prints belonged to Parsons, and the other set, found on the opposite side of the mirror, was most likely Earl Steward's. We also interviewed the Oakland customer, who remembered the helper stating that he had lived in Baltimore, Maryland, and was a machinist working his way across the country. This shipper had paid Parsons in cash, almost $1,400. Because the delivery day was a bank holiday in California and no money was found at the crime scene, we had a motive for the killing.

In the meantime, the FBI Identification Division matched the fingerprints from Ely to those of Earl L. Steward of Baltimore, Maryland. Steward had already been convicted of transporting a stolen motor vehicle across state lines. His record also listed numerous other minor offenses. Based on the information developed by the FBI, the Elko County prosecutor brought first-degree murder charges against Steward on September 29. On the same date, a federal warrant was obtained charging Steward with unlawful flight from Nevada to avoid prosecution for murder.

From interviewing relatives and friends, we learned that Steward visited the home of his sister and brother-in-law in Cumberland, Maryland. He was driving a 1951 Nash, which he told them he had purchased in Philadelphia. A check of Pennsylvania records revealed that on September 18, Earl L. Steward, of 5122 Walnut Street, Philadelphia, had purchased a 1951 Nash sedan from a used car dealer. A salesman at the dealership told FBI agents that Steward had just left the car lot after complaining about a bad generator in the car. Agents fanned out to check garages in the vicinity and within hours, Steward was located at a garage not far from his residence. I got the call and went to the scene.

Agents were covering all exits when I arrived, and Steward seemed unaware of our presence. Because there were several inno-

cent bystanders in the garage, I decided to go in, posing as a customer, to evaluate the situation. As I was waiting for customer service, Steward got up and went into the men's room. I noted that he
had not locked the door, and I decided that this was my chance to
move. I was extremely tense as I entered the bathroom with my .38-
caliber police special in hand. He was standing in front of the urinal
doing his business.

"Hey buddy, how about a little privacy," he said without looking around.

"FBI, Steward," I replied. "You are under arrest, and privacy is
the least of your problems."

We found a .22-caliber automatic pistol under the rear seat of
his car. Will wonders never cease? The gun was wrapped in a pil-
lowcase placed inside a paper shopping bag. When the gun was forwarded to the FBI lab, technicians determined that the cartridge
case found under the cab of Parsons's truck and the slugs recovered
from his body were fired from the pistol. This evidence was the
clincher, and the deputy sheriff who had the foresight to search
under the tractor cab deserves much of the credit for the successful
resolution of this case.

Steward was returned to Nevada for trial, found guilty of first-
degree murder, and executed in the Nevada state penitentiary at
8:25 A.M. on February 24, 1960. I could not help wondering why he
kept the murder weapon and why he didn't recover the missing cartridge casing. Steward said it never occurred to him that he would
get caught.

Like the double hatchet murders in California some years earlier,
this case generated positive publicity for the FBI and I was right in
the middle again. Hoover believed that good publicity was critical to
the FBI's continued success, so he liked to reward the agents responsible for it. But what he had in mind for me at first seemed less than
rewarding.

I liked Salt Lake City and hoped to remain there for at least three years. But in February 1958 I was informed that I was being transferred to Kansas City. For years the SAC there, Dwight Brantley, built a reputation as Hoover's roughest and toughest disciplinarian. An FBI man knew he was in Hoover's dog house if he was sent to work for Brantley, who ran what amounted to a reform school for fallen agents. In Kansas City, the rule was simple: either shape up or ship out. Now I had to be the new tough guy. The thought of pulling up stakes again was daunting, but orders were orders. Leaving my family behind until the end of the school year, I took off for the Siberia of field offices.

FIVE

KANSAS CITY AND THE MOB

S IBERIA TURNED out to be a beautiful place and an outstand-
ing community. And at the FBI field office, Brantley's methods
worked. He ran an excellent investigative machine, powered by a
staff that he had welded into an effective unit. Instead of the collection of misfits I had expected, I found a group of agents who had
been tried and passed with flying colors; those who had failed had
long since fallen by the wayside. Major cases abounded. Kansas City
was a transportation crossroads and the headquarters of an important Mafia family. There were more extortions, kidnappings, bombings, gangland slayings, and dangerous-fugitive apprehensions than
in several other large FBI offices combined. It was the kind of cops-
and-robbers work I had always craved, with plenty of the high-
profile cases that Hoover loved.

The Mafia leaders called themselves the Clique. They lived in an
enclave of fancy homes in North Kansas City. When we interviewed
them, they of course gave us no cooperation, and when summoned
to appear before federal grand juries, they usually invoked the Fifth
Amendment. Less important members known as "soldiers" were

arrogant, crude, and confident that any of their number who turned informer would end up in the Missouri River in concrete boots.

Washington pushed us hard to put the leaders behind bars. Though we knew where the Mafia hung out, physical surveillance was difficult and we were operating in the dark much of the time. Consequently we decided to plant microphones to eavesdrop on one of the Clique's meeting places, a technique that was legal under the standards of the time.

After securing Bureau approval, I assigned Max Richardson, our electronics specialist, or "sound man," to set up microphone coverage. He chose a meeting place in a very old building, and he rented a small apartment right above it. For three weeks, working late at night to avoid discovery, he slowly cut through the timbers of the old floor to the space above a false ceiling. To his chagrin, however, the members of the Clique congregated thirty feet from the spot where we had planned to lower a microphone. Undaunted, Richardson wired large fish hooks to an arrow. Then, hanging by his feet, he shot the arrow above the false ceiling toward the area where the Mafia types played cards. The hooks caught, and he used pulleys to maneuver the microphone so that it picked up the conversation below.

Unfortunately our effort netted us nothing but the conversation associated with a continuous high-stakes poker game and clinical descriptions of the sexual exploits of various Clique members. Later, when we placed a bug in the private office of a prominent second-echelon member, we captured only the squeaking of an old couch, the site of his daily fornications. In both instances, this microphone surveillance was discontinued. The FBI had more important matters to deal with.

When Robert F. Kennedy became attorney general in 1961, there was increased pressure to obtain probative evidence against leading figures in organized crime, and this meant more microphone installations. Later on, Kennedy would deny all knowledge of this activity. I have no way of knowing what he learned at other FBI field offices, but I do have direct knowledge of what he learned when he visited the Kansas City office. I gave him a guided tour and personally escorted him into the "plant"—the room where the microphones were being monitored. He was very busy shaking every hand in sight, but I find it difficult to believe that he did not hear what I explained to him.

Bobby Kennedy also knew that FBI efforts against the Mafia were hampered by the lack of federal legislation giving us jurisdiction. To his credit, he won congressional passage of federal gambling statutes that gave us a weapon to use against organized crime. Once Congress put teeth into the law, the Bureau developed so many cases that the federal criminal justice system was clogged with them.

Pressure from the seat of government was particularly fierce in extortion cases, and the Kansas City office handled more of them than either Los Angeles or New York. Because Hoover expected the special agent in charge to personally direct the stakeouts set up to catch extortionists, I learned a great deal about them. Unlike kidnapping or bank robbery, extortion requires little courage. With the exception of Mafia figures, the extortionist is usually unprepared physically or emotionally for violence, though he threatens it. And in case after case, as I learned after many freezing hours on stakeout duty, the extortionist is too frightened to come for the money he is attempting to extort.

Other cases did not rank as high as extortion, but Hoover put just as much emphasis on them. Shortly after I arrived in Kansas City, I received a phone call from the chief of the Deserter Section at FBI headquarters. "Mr. Felt," he began formally, "Mr. Hoover wants you to personally look into the case of Lloyd George Bell."

I had never heard of the guy. It turned out that Bell's was the oldest deserter case in our office, and one of the three oldest cases in the entire Bureau. As a crime it was small potatoes, but Hoover simply would not tolerate a case with that much dust on it.

I told the chief he could assure Hoover that I would wind up this case shortly. "You can tell him yourself," the Washington man said, and after a short pause, Hoover's staccato voice came on the line.

"Felt, you must clear up this matter immediately," the director said. (I knew I was rising in his esteem because he no longer called me "Mr. Felt.") "I will not tolerate an SAC that lets open cases build up in the inactive files." He recognized that I had done well in Salt Lake City, but "Kansas City is a whole different ball game. This assignment will make or break your chances for an assistant director's job and you had better start by finding this degenerate before he brings any further discredit on the Bureau."

"Consider it done, sir," was all I could say before the line went dead.

When I saw the file, I understood his concern. Lloyd Bell had deserted from the U.S. Army on October 24, 1952. Most deserter cases were solved within days or weeks, but Bell had eluded us for six years. Bell and his mother had objected to his being inducted into the army, claiming that he had an enlarged heart. But medical examiners could find nothing wrong and the induction process had gone ahead. Bell's mother then began a letter writing campaign all the way to President Eisenhower to get her son out of the army, all to no avail.

After induction, Bell showed little respect for the uniformed services, going AWOL to his mother's house on four separate occasions before his final departure from his post. This time he vanished without a trace. It seemed likely to me that Bell was again being harbored by his mother. I understood why agents were reluctant to pursue this particular deserter. Mrs. Bell was aggressive and belligerent, writing letters of complaint to Hoover and other government officials after each FBI visit.

I called in the latest agent on the case, Herb Cooper. "Bell's mother is nothing but trouble," Cooper said. "She won't tell you anything and when you go out there she slams the door in your face."

"Herb, I know all that," I said, "but this is the FBI. We can't keep letting her push us around."

Obviously we had to take a more aggressive approach. I took Cooper off all other cases and told him to put the Bell house under continuous surveillance.

After a few days, Cooper said he was positive the deserter was hiding with his mother. Each door had several locks, the curtains were always drawn, and at night the house was totally blacked out.

I told Cooper to find a relative who would tell us that Lloyd Bell was in the house. Finally he found a cousin willing to risk Mrs. Bell's wrath and tell us he had seen Lloyd there. That was enough to get us a search warrant. "It's still not going to be easy to get in," Cooper said. Only Mrs. Bell had the keys to all those locks, and not even her husband could get in unless she was home. There was also a second line of defense: a vicious German shepherd police dog.

We had to plan carefully. Mr. Bell went to work driving a taxi at 4:00 P.M., and Mrs. Bell worked at a department store until 6:00 P.M. So we decided to make our entry at 5:00 P.M.

We served the warrant on Mr. Bell at work. "The less we have to do with Mrs. Bell the better," I said. I had an ugly vision of her driving us off with an umbrella. As for the dog, I told the agents to fill toy water pistols with a solution of half water and half ammonia, hoping to distract the beast without hurting him.

Everything worked perfectly. We met Mr. Bell shortly after he arrived at work and showed him the search warrant. He wanted to call his wife, but we told him this would not be necessary. "But I can't get in without her," he said.

"You won't have to go in," I said. I decided to try the back entrance first. I pounded on the door and then waited. Nothing happened. Again, I pounded as hard as I could. Still nothing. After another full minute, I pounded again and announced in a loud voice, "This is the FBI. We have a search warrant." There was total silence in the house, not even barking from the dog. "Okay guys," I said, "we're going in."

I threw my weight against the door and it sagged but did not open. Paul Stoddard, the assistant agent in charge, stepped up and together we lunged at the door. The locks gave way and we burst into the kitchen. Other agents quickly followed, water pistols at the ready. The dog was nowhere to be seen, and the house was completely silent. We started a room-by-room search and found the dog in the master bedroom cowering in a corner. All that pounding had caused him to have an accident in the middle of the white bedroom carpet. I looked around and was struck by the sight of four FBI agents with water pistols standing around a big puddle of pee.

Bell, however, was nowhere to be found. We searched every room and then began looking for a secret compartment. We found a closet in the kitchen built under the stairs leading to the second floor. The closet was only two feet deep, but it appeared that there was more room under the stairs behind the closet's rear wall. The back of the closet had been wallpapered to match the kitchen, and some vacuum cleaner attachments were hung on it. I carefully took down the attachments and pushed against the wall. It appeared to give a little. A second harder push brought a response from behind the wall in a high-pitched voice.

"Momma is not gonna like this," it said.

"Come on out, Lloyd," I said, "and don't give us any trouble." The false wall moved forward and to one side. Lloyd George Bell crawled out of the secret compartment where he had been hiding and surrendered without resistance. Bell was promptly turned over to army authorities at Fort Leavenworth, Kansas. I called Bureau headquarters, glad to report that the case had been closed (and not mentioning the water pistols). Three days later I received a rare "eyes only" teletype from the director commending me on my timely resolution of the Bell matter. I still have it somewhere.

Not even Lloyd ranked above the main priority on the headquarter's agenda: the Top 10 fugitive program, the FBI's Most Wanted list. Conceived in 1950, it put dangerous criminals behind bars quickly, and it gave the Bureau great publicity. The idea was to put pressure on these fugitives by focusing media attention on them. Newspapers and television asked their readers and viewers to notify the nearest FBI office if they knew anything about a wanted man. On the day a new name was added to the list, FBI offices all over the country received hundreds of tips. These leads were checked immediately, and most Top 10 fugitives were caught soon after they achieved this dubious distinction.

Our Top 10 program was so successful that some critics charged we named only criminals we were sure of arresting, thus enhancing our image. But those critics didn't have to hunt down Frederick Grant Dunn.

Dunn looked like a bank president, but his interest in banks was limited to making withdrawals at gunpoint. Born in Iowa in 1905, he had established a reputation as a bandit by the time he was fourteen years old. At nineteen, he burglarized a jewelry story in Yankton, South Dakota, and earned his first stay behind bars. He was paroled three years later and promptly held up a bank in Slater, Iowa. This job put him in the slammer again until 1929, when he hit a bank in his native Sioux Falls. Apprehended again, Dunn escaped from jail, wounded a deputy sheriff, and was arrested the same day. This time he got twenty years.

Dunn had fastidious personal habits, and his mug shots always showed him wearing a tie. In prison he carried a red comb and a green toothbrush. Prisoners who are well groomed and well behaved have a greater chance of striking parole boards as "rehabilitated." In Dunn's case, his appearance, combined with his exemplary record as a prisoner, earned him a parole in 1941, after just ten years in prison. Within a year he joined two other robbers in taking almost $3,000 from the First Bank of Portis, Kansas. Two weeks later, the FBI apprehended him in Denver, Colorado, and this time he drew a fifteen-year sentence at Leavenworth penitentiary. He won a conditional release in 1952 but was picked up again two years later as a parole violator. Three years after that, in 1957, he was back on the streets again. We just couldn't hold this guy, and he just wouldn't give up.

In 1958 he was arrested in Russell, Kansas, for robbing a grocery store in nearby Sylvan Grove. He was taken to the Lincoln County jail to await prosecution. As always, Dunn exhibited model conduct, and soon the sheriff permitted him to do janitorial work around the jail. Dunn was the only inmate, and the sheriff thought nothing of leaving him alone. One day, when the sheriff forgot to snap the padlock shut, Dunn fashioned a hook from a clothes hanger and managed to lift the hanging padlock out of its clasp. An easy push on the steel door swung it open and Dunn was a free man once again.

The fugitive stole a pickup truck and got to Ellsworth, Kansas, where he tried to change a $100 bill. It was snowing heavily in Ellsworth as Dunn went into three different stores with no success. Finally he got change from the cashier at a movie theater, where he bought a sixty-cent ticket. But the cashier grew suspicious and called police. Patrolman Frank Kessler arrived in time to see Dunn slip out the side door of the theater. In the best Hollywood tradition, Kessler drew his revolver and shouted, "Stop or I'll shoot." Dunn wasn't about to go back to jail for the seventh time, so he took off as fast as his fifty-three-year-old legs would carry him. Kessler fired a warning shot, then emptied his revolver at the fleeing figure disappearing into the blinding snowstorm.

The search began, but Dunn evidently used his $99.40 to buy a magic carpet. He was reported in several Midwestern cities, often in two places at once, but no solid leads arose. Local authorities concluded that he had left the state. Since interstate flight to avoid prosecution is a federal offense, the case was handed to the FBI. I was put in charge but after months of investigative work got nowhere. Finally the Bureau put Dunn on the Most Wanted list, and the pressure on me increased considerably. J. Edgar Hoover expected the special agent in charge to become personally involved in Top 10 cases. He also expected favorable results within a reasonable period. But this time I could not produce. This case was making a mockery of the Top 10 program and, by association, me.

Finally we got a break. One day in October, a year after Dunn had escaped from the movie theater, a farmer found a human skull in an uncultivated corner of his property. A few days later he got around to reporting his find to the local sheriff, who notified me. He told me he thought we had found Dunn.

"Sheriff," I said, "I pray to God you are right."

Within an hour I had a carload of agents headed toward Ellsworth. There were no fingerprints left on the remains, and the skull was missing many teeth, so we anticipated major problems identifying the body. Fifteen agents, working shoulder to shoulder on hands and knees, conducted a systematic grid search of the two acres around the remains. (A local paper took a picture of the operation and labeled it "FBI pickin' with the chickens.") In addition to the skeleton, we found part of a green jacket that fit the description of the jacket Dunn was wearing at the time of his escape. We found a pair of shoes that were the same size that Dunn wore. The famous red comb and green toothbrush were also there amid the dirt and leaves. And we found a wad of moldy old greenbacks in the amount of $99. Most important of all, we found five teeth near the skeleton.

We sent our report to Washington, suggesting that Dunn be retired from the list, but I doubted that the evidence would satisfy Hoover. He reviewed all cases that reached the list and I knew he would not accept a "strong probability" that the criminal was dead. We needed a positive identification, so we boxed up the skeletal remains, including the teeth, and shipped them to the FBI lab in Washington. A Smithsonian Institution anthropologist examined the bones and concluded that they belonged to a male who was 5 feet 9, approximately Dunn's height. The expert also pointed out that the nose of the deceased had been broken. This was consistent with what we knew about Dunn, since he had been a boxer in prison. The lab took dried blood from the bone marrow of the remains and found that it matched Dunn's type. The final proof came from a dentist at Leavenworth. He remembered doing a particularly nasty root canal on Dunn's upper molar; his X ray of the work matched one of the teeth we had found near the skull.

That clinched it. We had our fugitive. We found no evidence that Dunn had been hit by any of the police bullets fired at him as he ran through the snowstorm; he may simply have died of a heart attack. In any case, Hoover was satisfied, and I was off the hook.

Taking one of the FBI's most wanted off the list was a big feather in my cap, but it did not guarantee me a promotion. Above all, I had to keep our Kansas City operation running at least as smoothly and efficiently as I had found it. J. Edgar Hoover was determined to make the FBI as perfect as humanly possible, pressing constantly to ferret out all mistakes, weaknesses, and indiscretions. Whatever the fault, the underperforming agent could expect to be dealt with summarily. This was what made the FBI such a finely tuned instrument.

But Hoover's mania for discipline lent itself to use in vendettas among Bureau members. He paid as much attention to anonymous letters from disgruntled employees as he did to signed communications. Any allegation against Bureau personnel had to be resolved to his satisfaction, regardless of the source.

In August 1959 someone sent Hoover an anonymous letter criticizing my operation. The writer was lethally clever in his approach. He marked the envelope "Personal," and anybody in the Bureau knew that such mail was sent, unopened, directly to Hoover. The author included allegations that were guaranteed to inflame the director. He reported seeing ten to fifteen agents drinking coffee in a Kansas City restaurant on government time—a mortal sin in the FBI. The second charge, equally damning, was that I had ordered agents not to complete pending cases in July in order to make our work load seem heavier, justifying a bigger staff. Had I actually doctored our docket that way, I would have been fired on the spot. In a twist of the dagger, the anonymous writer mentioned that these lackadaisical agents were talking about their cases loudly in public—also sure to bring down the wrath of the director. Washington sent a veteran inspector, W. W. "Smokey" Wood, to investigate the charges. Without notifying me in advance, he staked out the restaurant for three days and never saw an FBI coffee drinker. And a simple check of our files showed that we actually closed more cases than usual in July.

I knew which employee had written the spurious letter, but I could not prove it, and making an accusation would only disrupt the office. Surely Hoover realized that I was not afraid to discipline an employee if necessary. He could have found less painful ways to verify my administrative competence, but I did not let the incident rattle me. It was part of the job.

In the spring of 1962 I was expecting a promotion to the seat of government when a dramatic case shook my equilibrium. On May 22, Continental Airlines Flight 11 took off from Chicago's O'Hare Airport at 8:35 P.M. for Kansas City. Captain Fred Gray, a fifty-year-old veteran pilot from Pacific Palisades, California, who had been flying with the airline for twenty-three years, was in the cockpit. His crew included the copilot, flight engineer, and five flight attendants in the cabin to serve thirty-seven unsuspecting passengers.

Once they were airborne, Captain Gray kept in frequent radio contact with ground control concerning a storm and the best vectors to avoid it. At 9:15 he reported his position to the Kansas City center as thirty-five miles northeast of Kirksville, Missouri, at 39,000 feet. The flight recorder later showed that the plane moved out of the squall line into smooth air at 9:20. Captain Gray turned off the seat belt sign, and a man in the coach section made his way toward the rear lavatories carrying his briefcase. Approximately two minutes later, the jetliner went off the radar screens.

On the ground, motorist Jack Morris reported to police that he found scattered parts of an airplane on U.S. Highway 60, just outside of Centerville, Iowa. Other reports of wreckage began pouring into police headquarters. The Federal Aviation Administration in Kansas City said the plane might have disintegrated in midair due to violent wind shear in the heart of a thunderstorm. Other experts suggested that an electrical storm had disabled the aircraft. But several witnesses also reported seeing an explosion in the sky at about 9:20 P.M.

We later reconstructed what had happened. Within sixty seconds from the time the man went into the lavatory with his briefcase, a rending explosion blew through the right rear lavatory. The plane lurched violently and began shuddering and twisting from side to side. An explosive decompression occurred, and all loose objects in the plane were sucked out through a gaping hole in the rear of the fuselage. The air was also sucked out of the aircraft and out of people's lungs. Some of the passengers were able to put on the oxygen masks that popped out above them. There was a loud grinding and crashing noise as the entire tail section banged from side to side.

In the cockpit, the pilots put on oxygen masks and extended the landing gear as part of the emergency descent procedure. The captain had no control over the tail but used the ailerons on each wing to gain some stability. The tail section acted like the drag chute on a race car. For a brief instant there was hope for survival. Then the entire tail section broke away and tumbled into the darkness, taking seven passengers with it. The plane lurched so violently sideways that all four jet engines were sheared from their mountings. They soared ahead into the night like rockets and ran until the last drops of fuel were consumed. The twisting was so violent that parts of both wings were torn off, and the plane entered a steep spiraling dive toward the dark countryside below. Wreckage was scattered for more than forty miles along the flight path. Lighter pieces of plastic and fabric were carried more than one hundred miles to the east by the wind.

The phone awakened me at my home in Kansas City at 5:30 A.M. I scrambled agents to the scene, arranged for another agent to look after my thirteen-year-old son (since my wife was visiting relatives and my daughter was at college), and arrived in the office at 6:25. By 7:33 we were racing down the runway in a small single-engine plane on our way to Centerville. From the air, we could see the incredible impact the plane made as it hit the ground. Apparently the jetliner came down at about a 45-degree angle and the whole forward portion exploded from the force of the impact. Already thirty or forty cars were parked at the edge of the pasture and a curious crowd of a hundred or more stood behind rope barriers erected by the local sheriff and his deputies. We circled several times and then headed for the airstrip at Centerville. As we were coming in for a landing, our pilot remarked that he had no experience landing on grass strips. We knew he was kidding, but it did nothing to improve our mood.

When we arrived at the scene, deputies were removing mangled body parts from the broken fuselage. I could not eat anything for two days because of the utter despair I felt at such a great loss of life. My main responsibility at first was to supervise the disaster squad, which arrived from Washington later that day. The squad had obtained the passenger manifest and the fingerprints of a number of the passengers—those who had served in the military or applied for government jobs, among others. Agents also visited the homes of probable victims and collected fingerprints that could then be compared to human remains found at the crash site. In a few cases, where both arms were missing, identifications were made from dental charts.

Continental Airlines and the Civil Aeronautics Board reconstructed the airplane in a large, unoccupied building on the county fairgrounds in Centerville. The main portion of the fuselage was in relatively large pieces; behind the separation point, the pieces were progressively smaller, indicating that an explosive decompression had occurred there. The metal was deflected outward at that point, suggesting that the cause of the structural failure came from within the aircraft. Furthermore, analysis of the metal's molecular structure indicated that a powerful force had separated it rapidly. In other words, the crash was caused by a bomb in the right rear lavatory.

From this point on, the FBI investigation moved to (1) identify the guilty party and (2) collect enough evidence to prove it in court. I was responsible for the investigation at the crash scene. The Civil Aeronautics Board worked from large pieces of the outer skin of the fuselage. The FBI had to find the small pieces from the right rear lavatory and analyze the explosive residue to determine whether the bomb was constructed of dynamite, plastic explosives, or some other material. Finding the big pieces had been easy. Finding the small pieces was difficult. First, there was the problem of recognizing the small structural parts of the right rear lavatory. FBI explosives experts came to Centerville for the preliminary screening. The Boeing Company brought in a four-foot stack of construction manuals and worked hand in hand with the lab experts to describe the parts we were looking for. We had to go out and find them over a stretch of Iowa countryside ten miles wide and forty miles long. This turned out to be one of the most massive crime scene searches ever conducted by the FBI.

I knew we could not do this alone and asked the army to send two helicopters with flight crews, as well as ground search crews to work with the helicopters. We plotted out a grid pattern of the territory to be searched in order to keep track of what had been done and what remained to be done. Each helicopter would cover one square of the grid at a time. The ground crews, each consisting of two enlisted men in four-wheel-drive Jeeps, were in radio contact with the helicopters. When a piece of wreckage was spotted from the air, the pilots would direct ground crews to the site. I worked from a helicopter without doors, suspended in a chair with no arms and looking straight down. After getting over the initial discomfort, I thoroughly enjoyed the sensation. Many times when we spotted possible bits of wreckage, our superb pilot would take the helicopter down and hover just above the ground until we decided whether or not to send the ground crew in. On several occasions, he flew so low that we were underneath the foliage of the large oak trees that dotted the Iowa landscape. After several busy days, we found enough pieces to permit the lab experts to reconstruct some of the right rear lavatory. Dynamite residue was present on many of these small parts.

Agents working in Kansas City narrowed their focus to one of the passengers, thirty-four-year-old Thomas G. Doty, a Kansas City resident who had flown to Chicago and was returning home when the explosion ended his life. His body, totally unrecognizable and with most of the clothing missing, was one of seven that spilled out of the plane after the tail section was blown off. Positive identification finally was made through dental records. An autopsy concluded that Doty's injuries were consistent with those suffered by someone occupying the lavatory. FBI investigators found that Doty had purchased dynamite from the Pierce and Tarry Trading Post in Wyandotte County, Kansas, not far from his home. He had studied books on the use of explosives at the Kansas City Public Library only a few days before the crash. A witness said he had seen some brownish red round sticks in Doty's briefcase shortly before his Chicago trip, which he thought were emergency flares such as motorists sometimes carry in their cars.

Doty was known to be despondent over his finances and had declared bankruptcy. He carried $300,000 of life insurance. Of that, $250,000 was in policies covering accidental death in flight. A short time before the Chicago trip, Doty and his wife purchased a new car. Doty made a point of obtaining insurance to cover the unpaid balance on his car loan in the event of his death. Another $50,000 life insurance policy was taken out just prior to the Chicago trip.

A few days after the crash, Doty was due to face criminal charges of first-degree robbery and carrying a concealed weapon. A woman complained that a man entered her car while it was stopped at a traffic light. He struck her in the face, took her pocketbook, and ran. Two men heard the woman's screams and found Doty carrying the pocketbook. As they attempted to approach him, he pulled a pistol from inside his shirt. The two men subdued him without further incident. He told police he stopped in the area because he felt ill and found the pocketbook while he was walking around getting fresh air.

Doty was traveling to Chicago with Mrs. Geneva Fraley, a fellow employee at Luzier Incorporated, a Kansas City cosmetics firm. Doty and Mrs. Fraley were planning to open a home decorating business. Ostensibly they were in Chicago making business arrangements. Several witnesses felt there was much more to the relationship, and the couple apparently shared a hotel room in Chicago. Doty's feelings for Mrs. Fraley could not have been too deep, however, since she was on the doomed plane.

In the end, Doty left us with no one to prosecute for the terrible mass murder in the sky. All we could do was write a report documenting our conclusion that he was to blame for the destruction of Flight 11. This investigation marked my last days in Kansas City with an important success and provided some insulation from the challenges I was about to face in Washington.

SIX

FRICTION WITH
THE KENNEDYS

I N S E P T E M B E R 1962, I was brought back to Washington as second in command of the Training Division. The lateral move to
a humdrum office job dismayed me, and I considered resigning. But
I quickly discovered that Hoover had brought me back to help
rebuild the Bureau's independence following a ruthless power struggle with the Kennedy administration.

J. Edgar Hoover ran the FBI his way. In May 1924, when Attorney
General Harlan Fiske Stone had asked Hoover to take over the Justice Department's investigative arm, the Bureau of Investigation, it
was widely categorized as a national disgrace. Hoover accepted the
job on a series of conditions. "The Bureau must be divorced from
politics and not be a catchall for political hacks," he told Stone.
"Appointments must be based on merit. Promotions will be made
only on proven ability. And the Bureau will be responsible only to
the attorney general."

"I wouldn't give it to you under any other conditions," Stone
answered.

Over the years, Harlan Stone's guarantee allowed Hoover to

make the BI (the "Federal" was added in 1935) the fine instrument of law enforcement that it was when I enlisted in the ranks. There was only one attempt, as far as I know, to make it a "catchall" for political appointees, and that was in the early Roosevelt administration. But Hoover remained firm and thereby improved his standing with FDR, the Congress, and the press. The FBI may have been listed as a subsidiary bureau on the Justice Department's organization table, but in actuality it was an independent agency.

In 1961, when President John F. Kennedy appointed his younger brother to be attorney general, Hoover and the FBI faced their first serious challenge. Prior to this time, Hoover had gotten along well with most presidents and attorneys general, although there had been some friction during the Truman days. But JFK's advisers, friends, and supporters included those who resented Hoover's undeviating opposition to communism and his determination to uproot subversion. Bobby Kennedy—brash, ruthless, and politically motivated— resented the FBI's independent status. He saw the Bureau not as a law enforcement agency but as an arm of the administration.

For the first time in his career, Hoover was up against a president and an attorney general who were openly antagonistic and wanted to dislodge him. Bobby Kennedy thought of the FBI as a kind of private police department, with Hoover as its desk sergeant. He would storm into Hoover's office unannounced or summon the director to his palatial suite in the Justice Department building as if Hoover were an office boy. He struck directly at Hoover's authority by calling a special agent in charge or an agent on a case directly, violating the traditional chain of command—something no other attorney general had ever done.

The result was ill-disguised friction between Hoover and Robert Kennedy, which affected all of us in the Bureau and struck at our morale. The attorney general's most disturbing action was to circulate among high government officials a memorandum prepared by

Walter Reuther, president of the United Auto Workers, and his brother Victor, entitled "The Radical Right in America Today." It sharply attacked the FBI and Hoover, characterized as part of a "radical right" that consisted of everything from extremist kooks to the Republican Party. To the Reuthers and Kennedy, the right posed a far greater danger to the United States than the communist movement.

Bobby Kennedy was determined to take agents off important investigations to do political jobs for the Kennedy administration. Agents were assigned to pick up unfavorable comments about President Kennedy by members of the press; those who had spoken their minds were summoned by administration officials and roughly scolded. Since the Bureau had been used to do this snooping, the press was angry at us, and consequently stories that were derogatory to the FBI were leaked by the Justice Department.

On one issue, Hoover and Bobby Kennedy battled head to head. The attorney general demanded that FBI agents be detached from the Bureau and assigned to his task forces to investigate organized crime syndicates. Hoover agreed to work closely with the task force attorneys, while insisting that his agents must remain under the direction of the special agents in charge. Kennedy twisted this position when he leaked it to the press. Reporters were told that the FBI did not believe organized crime really existed, and even if it did, attempting to cope with the syndicates would reduce the FBI's impressive arrest and conviction statistics in less important cases.

To counter the Kennedy onslaught, Hoover created the Special Investigative Division at headquarters and selected Courtney A. Evans to head it. Evans had liaised with Bobby Kennedy when he was chief counsel to the Senate Labor Rackets Committee. Knowing that Evans had Kennedy's confidence, Hoover also made him responsible for liaison between the FBI and the attorney general. Soon Evans found himself trying to serve two masters. As the situation grew untenable, Evans remarked to me, "Last night, I told my family I was sure I was going to be fired, but I didn't know whether it would be by Hoover or Kennedy."

Evans served as go-between for Hoover and Kennedy on the touchy issue of telephone taps and electronic surveillance. The attorney general had been lobbying on Capitol Hill for the unrestricted use of these devices in internal revenue cases and other unspecified "serious" crimes. Contrary to the view held by many, both then and now, Hoover believed that wiretaps and bugs should be used sparingly. To protect himself and the Bureau against any repercussions from their use, Hoover made certain that the attorney general was kept fully informed and that his approval was carefully noted (just as I had made sure to show Kennedy our bugging operation in Kansas City).

The wisdom of Hoover's procedure became apparent after Bobby Kennedy left the Justice Department and became a United States senator. Times had changed, and Kennedy now was leading the fight against wiretaps and bugging. When an instance of FBI bugging during his tenure at Justice became known late in 1966, Senator Kennedy launched an attack on the Bureau, deploring what he now saw as a dirty business. In response, Hoover noted in a letter to Rep. H. R. Gross that "FBI usage of such devices . . . was obviously increased at Mr. Kennedy's insistence while he was in office." Hoover attached a memo on using microphone surveillance in New York that was written on Justice Department stationery, stamped "Approved," and signed "Robert F. Kennedy." Kennedy responded that Hoover was "misinformed" and produced a document indicating that he had not intended to approve bugging and wiretapping. Hoover released more documents to the contrary, and the matter came to an impasse. Kennedy avowed that Hoover had at no time "discussed this important matter with me." His assertion was technically true, since all discussions had been with Courtney Evans, the liaison between the FBI and the Justice Department.

Hoover considered Attorney General Kennedy "brash, impetuous, bad mannered, and undisciplined." Hoover was irritated when Kennedy demanded a hot line link between the attorney general's office and the FBI director's. The first time it was used, Hoover's secretary answered. "When I pick up this phone," Kennedy said rudely, "there's only one man I want to talk to. Get this phone on the director's desk immediately." The phone remained there until after President Kennedy's assassination, and then was returned to the secretary's desk.

There was one amusing moment in the attorney general's imbroglio with Hoover. At a time when the White House had declared war against United States Steel, there were press stories on antitrust violations by another company, Bethlehem Steel. Robert Kennedy called Hoover late in the evening and demanded that the writers of those stories be questioned "immediately." Hoover, perhaps with a touch of malice, did exactly what Kennedy demanded. Reporters were rousted out of bed in the wee hours of the morning for questioning, and they were as incensed at this as they were at the attorney general's assumption that he could compel them to reveal their sources.

This state of affairs ended when John F. Kennedy was assassinated in Dallas. RFK's influence declined abruptly and he could no longer have his way simply by murmuring, "Do you want me to talk to my brother about this?" On September 3, 1964, he resigned, and two months later he was elected senator from New York.

While JFK was alive, it was generally assumed that Hoover would be replaced by Courtney Evans soon after the 1964 election. Because of concessions he had made to RFK, however, Evans found that his power in the Bureau hierarchy dissolved after JFK was assassinated. He applied for retirement and then went into private law practice.

Hoover quickly acted to restore the FBI's prestige and independence. He replaced Evans with James H. Gale, a tough, competent veteran of battles in the field who could stand up to the Justice Department. But the reorganization also affected me. On Friday, November 13, a few minutes after he replaced Evans, Hoover summoned me to his office. I still remember the exact minute that I entered Hoover's inner sanctum—3:53 P.M.—with no idea what the meeting was about. "It's good to see you, Felt," the director said as I shook his hand. "How have you been?"

"I'm fine," I said, relieved by the cordiality of the greeting, and his use of "Felt" rather than "Mr. Felt." Hoover wasted no time. "Felt," he said, "Evans has applied for retirement and I have approved it. I have just designated Gale to replace him. I told Gale that Evans had been wishy-washy in dealing with Justice. Gale knows I expect him to stand up to them."

"You picked the right man," I answered, wondering where I fit into the picture.

Hoover continued, "I'm transferring you to the Inspection Division to replace Gale. I'm designating you chief inspector, and if you demonstrate that you can handle the assignment, you will be promoted to assistant director."

"Thank you, sir," was all I could manage. A promotion of this magnitude, making me a virtual extension of the director, was beyond my imaginings. What's more, he held out the possibility of a further promotion into his inner sanctum.

"I want you to be firm and tough—but fair. I want you to be my eyes and ears. You will report directly to Tolson."

Again I managed, "Thank you, sir."

"I want you to handle a seat of government inspection under Gale's supervision before you take over. After that, you will be on your own. However, I want to talk to you personally before the New York office is inspected." This I could understand. There had always been a subtle rivalry between the New York office, the FBI's largest, and the seat of government.

For the third time, I said, "Yes, sir." I felt foolish but didn't know how else to respond. In my past conversations with Hoover, I had tried to contribute something, to show interest and aggressiveness, but this time I was too stunned. In the space of a few minutes, I found myself positioned at the door to the FBI's top echelons.

"That's all, Felt," Hoover said. "I expect you to do a good job."

"Mr. Hoover," I said, "I'll do the very best I can. You can count on it."

"I hope so," Hoover answered, and picked up one of the memorandums on his desk.

My transfer to the Inspection Division marked a huge change in my relationship with Hoover. As an SAC, I saw him once a year for no more than thirty minutes. During my tenure in the Training Division, I saw him only a few times. Now he would call me on the intercom and I saw him with increasing frequency for personal conferences. During his last year, I saw him or talked with him on the intercom or telephone several times a day. This association was strictly business; my only social contact with him was at a banquet of the Society of Former FBI Agents, where he was the guest of honor shortly before his death.

The chief inspector occupied a unique position in the FBI hierarchy. Operating under the direct supervision of the director and with authority to inquire at any time and any place on any matter, the chief inspector was both feared and respected. Among other duties, I was responsible for the painstaking annual search at every field office for errors, lax discipline, and infractions of the many rules set down by the director. Shortly after I was transferred to the Inspection Division, another assistant director said to me, "You are in a position where you can do a lot of good or a lot of harm." I knew what he meant. During my movement up the FBI pyramid I had learned the difference between constructive and destructive criticism. I was determined to be as constructive as possible, and during my six years as FBI chief inspector I tried to achieve a balance between Hoover's rigid demands and what I felt were the best interests of the Bureau and its personnel.

No organization is free of error, and the FBI was no exception. Hoover knew this and demanded that all errors be uncovered and all responsibility fixed. When inspectors detected mistakes, they initiated corrective action and made recommendations for suitable discipline, almost always by letter of censure. Field agents complained of "nitpicking" and of censure letter "quotas" imposed on inspectors and their aides. The chief inspector bore the brunt of this criticism no matter how fairly or compassionately he tried to act.

However understandable the agents' reactions, their complaints were usually unjustified. For one thing, Hoover would not accept an inspection report that found a field office or national division to be in perfect condition. Had I submitted such a report it would have been inaccurate, and Hoover would have removed me from the Inspection Division at once. In addition, I could not accept an inspector's assurance that he had reviewed hundreds of case files and found them to be completely free of error. Given the tightness of rules and regulations, there were always mistakes of varying magnitude in the investigation of complex FBI cases.

Most inspectors unofficially corrected minor errors that might have aroused Hoover's ire and led to disciplinary action—and they saw to it that the burden of censure letters was equally shared by a number of agents. And there were enough serious matters to report to satisfy Hoover's appetite for disciplinary action. Recommendations for this kind of action, moreover, had to be carefully evaluated and worded since Hoover or Tolson would sometimes upgrade the punishment despite the inspector's recommendations. If there was bias on our side, it was in the direction of leniency. But at no time could I let the director get the impression that the Inspection Division was "soft."

I had learned how to win Hoover's approval: keep your argument brief and concise. Throughout my career, I had insisted that every document prepared for the director be short and to the point. I worked hard to polish and perfect my own memorandums, and this was appreciated by those above me. As chief inspector, with agents' careers in my hands, my memorandums proposing disciplinary action had to justify the recommendations. It was also essential to avoid words and phrases that might inflame Hoover. My years of experience in preparing material for Hoover's eyes trained me to see and hear like the director—and to think like him.

SEVEN

HOOVER'S ENFORCER

THE FIRST THING I had to do as chief inspector, I decided, was shake things up. For as long as I could remember, the New York field office, the FBI's largest, was the first to be inspected each calendar year. But my mandate was to be fair, and it was not fair to give New York the kind of predictability denied to other offices. Hoover wanted my inspectors to evaluate an office as it normally operated. So in January 1965 I surprised New York by not showing up (secretly rescheduling its inspection for the spring) and surprised several smaller offices by sending inspectors to their doorsteps instead. (Seven years later, Acting Director L. Patrick Gray took the surprise element out of these inspections by ordering that offices be given two weeks' notice. This may have created a more relaxed atmosphere, but it did not contribute to an on-your-toes efficiency.)

Before I acted on my plans, I asked to see the director for approval, hiding the purpose of my meeting to lessen chances that somebody would tip off New York. "Mr. Hoover," I said, "you told me that you wanted to confer with me before I began an inspection of the New York office. I am planning to take the entire staff up there on Sunday, April 4, and commence the inspection on Monday morning."

Hoover looked at me steadily. "That's fine, Felt. I was beginning to wonder when you were going to start."

"That's why I didn't want to wait any longer. I have completed inspections of two medium-size offices and I think I am ready to take on New York."

Hoover smiled, as if understanding why I had put off the New York inspection. "I am not sure that I ever had a chief inspector who was really ready to take on New York. There's a good crew up there, but sometimes I am convinced they don't see any need to pay attention to what we tell them."

He seemed ready to terminate the interview, but I wanted his approval for another violation of old procedures. "Mr. Hoover," I said, "I have made intensive advance preparation and, with your approval, I want to cut down the time in New York from the usual four weeks to three."

He frowned. "All right, but don't take too many short cuts, and if you need to stay longer be sure you do so."

"Yes, sir," I said as he was rising to his feet. "I'll see that you get an inspection report on the New York office as good or better than what you have received before."

He nodded and turned back to the work on his desk. I walked out of his office thinking over what he had said, and I knew exactly what he meant. We referred to it in the Bureau as the "New York attitude." That office was big, handled some of the most important cases, and employed some of the most capable and experienced agents in the service. Not surprisingly, those agents sometimes thought of themselves as superior and somehow apart from the rest of the Bureau. The smaller offices sometimes had difficulty getting the New York office to cover leads for them. Sometimes the New York office had very important work on its hands, but there was no excuse for shunting aside another office.

On Thursday, April Fools' Day, the entire staff was ordered back to Washington. The inspectors were instructed to report on Sunday afternoon prepared for a three-week inspection assignment, and word spread that they would be going to either Los Angeles or San Francisco. Their hopes were dashed when they arrived at the Justice Department building and saw the Greyhound bus parked outside, indicating that their destination was New York.

After we arrived and checked into the hotel, I called John F. Malone, assistant director and SAC of the New York office. "Where are you?" asked Malone, an old friend.

"I'm at the Dryden East Hotel. I just arrived."

Sounding pleased, he said, "What are you doing in New York? Is there anything I can do to help?"

"John, I brought the whole inspection staff with me. We are going to start your inspection tomorrow morning."

Obviously less than pleased but still friendly, Malone said, "Oh? When you didn't come in January, I figured you would wait until it was a little warmer. But now is as good a time as any. We're always ready for the inspectors."

I knew Malone was a Hoover loyalist who ran a tight office—too tight in the view of many New York agents. As I hung up the phone, I wondered if I had really surprised him. If not, Malone was a good actor.

Early the next morning, the inspectors and their aides reported to the New York office, a large building on East 69th Street that had been converted from warehouse space and looked it. However, the facilities were efficiently laid out and economical. The executive office space included a large conference room and an elegant private office. Malone was there to greet us when we arrived. When I introduced him to the staff, he made a few friendly remarks and then left us to begin our work.

One of the first things I noticed as I settled into the executive office was a small closet housing a toilet and wash basin. I learned afterward that this perquisite had been built after the director had inspected the new quarters. He was accompanied by a friend and of course Clyde Tolson. Unfortunately for the taxpayers, the friend asked for directions to the toilet and was escorted to the spartan men's room on the far side of the large building. Hoover expressed no concern about this inconvenience, but Tolson did and instructed that toilet facilities be installed adjacent to the private office. This $5,000 expenditure had to be hidden somewhere in the Bureau's bookkeeping. Hoover never visited the New York office again, and the facility became the private washroom of the SAC.

I tried to look at the inspection from the viewpoint of a harried field official, bearing in mind my responsibility to the director. The first two or three days of an inspection involved considerable wheel spinning as the aides got organized and the office adjusted. I resolved to make sure everything was productive from the very first minute. And it was. With Malone's full cooperation, the New York office moved into high gear immediately. When the agents realized they could be rid of us in three weeks, they became highly cooperative. It did not take me long to realize that the office was operating well. Results attested to that. I was able to suggest a few streamlining changes to help the office function more efficiently.

On April 23 the inspection was completed on schedule, and we even finished early enough to ride the Greyhound back to Washington on government time, unheard of in Hoover's days because he preferred that official travel be done on overtime. The streamlined inspection was effective and everyone, including the director, was pleased.

Being Hoover's eyes and ears meant receiving a variety of unscheduled assignments—special projects and surveys, as they were called. The more of these projects I handled, the more Hoover turned to the Inspection Division, and in time he was directing all unusual problems to me. Some of these were major cases worthy of the character played by Efrem Zimbalist, Jr. in *The F.B.I.*, a TV series from the late 1960s. Efrem's character was a loose representation of the chief inspector, and I served as FBI liaison and technical adviser to MGM studios during production.

Not all cases were worthy of a TV drama. Helen Gandy, Hoover's private secretary, was one of the FBI's most powerful people. In her sixties, she had been with the director before he ran the Bureau. She was bright, alert, and quick tongued. Knowing how close she was to the boss, everybody in the FBI tried to ingratiate themselves with her. But when a letter to Hoover marked "Personal" was delayed, he ordered me to make a complete inspection of his office. This put me in a no-win situation. I couldn't blame Miss Gandy, but there was nobody else to blame.

Searching for a way to please everybody, I made a careful study and analysis of operations in the director's office, including mail flow, personnel management, and communications. But everything worked smoothly, and I was hard-pressed to think of improvements. I suggested pay raises for the two clerks in the telephone room, who handled calls to and from the director's suite, kept a running log of everything that happened in Hoover's office, and maintained the director's commitment calendar. But I needed something more impressive than that. Finally the Exhibits Section, which ordinarily builds displays and evidence models, helped me out. Its experts designed a massive operating desk for the telephone clerks, allowing them to organize and share their tasks more efficiently. The contraption looked like a modern airline ticket office, and everybody—most importantly Hoover—was extremely pleased.

Sometimes Hoover threw me into high-stakes bureaucratic battles, including those between the FBI and Central Intelligence Agency (CIA). One particular case was cloaked in secrecy. On March 14, 1969, Thomas Riha, a thirty-nine-year-old Czech-born professor of Russian history at the University of Colorado, disappeared from his home. The FBI knew of Riha's whereabouts but could not tell local authorities because this might jeopardize confidential sources. However, an FBI agent secretly briefed a CIA man, who in turn told Joseph R. Smiley, the president of the university, who made a statement that Riha was "alive and well." When Hoover learned what had happened, he was angry and demanded that the CIA identify its FBI source. This the CIA man in Denver refused to do.

A second inflammatory incident grew out of the Liaison Section in the Domestic Intelligence Division, where ten FBI agents maintained contacts with other government agencies. One of these agents, Sam Papich, dealt exclusively with the CIA. Papich had an effective working relationship with the CIA and shared the concern of CIA director Richard Helms that the FBI was not moving aggressively enough against foreign agents in the United States. (This also was a concern of Papich's boss, William C. Sullivan, then assistant director in charge of the Domestic Intelligence Division.) In 1970, when Papich retired, he wrote a polite but critical note to Hoover urging more action. Hoover was furious and told me he believed the Papich letter had been drafted by the CIA.

As a result of these two cases, Hoover called me into his office and said, "I want to abolish the Liaison Section. It's costing us a quarter of a million dollars a year, and other agencies obviously benefit more from it than we do. Let the supervisors handle their own contacts with other agencies."

"Let me look into it," I answered. "I think we can work out something effective. What about the White House? Do you want to continue direct liaison there?"

Hoover thought briefly. "Cut it all out except the liaison with the White House." Clearly the director had made up his mind and nothing was going to change it, even though the established system worked well. In 1972, Acting Director Gray reestablished the Liaison Section, though on a smaller scale.

Often FBI inspectors were assigned to help resolve investigative problems in the field. As far back as the mid-1930s, Hoover made a practice of sending Bureau officials to the scene of major cases. Hugh H. Clegg was sent to the Midwest in 1934 to direct the raid on the Little Bohemia Lodge in Wisconsin, from which John Dillinger, "Baby Face" Nelson, and other gangsters escaped after a shootout in which one FBI agent was killed. Inspector Earl J. Connelly led the squad of agents who killed the notorious Ma Barker and her son in a Florida gun battle. In the same spirit, Hoover put me on a no-win assignment in Kansas City. My experience in this numbingly difficult case against the city's Mafia was valuable in my later showdown with the Nixon administration over Watergate.

My task was to accelerate our investigation into the gangland slaying of Salvatore Eugene Palma, a notorious mob hoodlum in Kansas City. I had learned a great deal about Palma when I was SAC in Kansas City. He was a good "soldier" in the local Mafia. He did everything exactly as he was told and never attempted anything on his own without first clearing it with top Mafia leaders. His first arrest came on December 22, 1949. He pleaded guilty to second-degree burglary and was sentenced to a two-year prison term, but he was immediately granted a bench parole. Since then, he had been arrested on twenty different occasions for burglary or robbery. No charges were brought in any of these cases.

Palma also pursued several legitimate business endeavors. For a while he was part owner of the Pancake Patio Restaurant, which was destroyed by fire on January 1, 1965. Investigators suspected arson, but nothing was ever proven. He was a co-owner of the National Consignment Company, which became insolvent in January 1964. He was also involved in a women's hosiery distributorship that burned to the ground in 1964. Was this guy unlucky or what?

While I was SAC in Kansas City we suspected but could never prove that Palma obtained most of his income from supermarket heists in other cities. Consequently he came under suspicion in the spring of 1965, when three masked men robbed a Fort Worth super-market, shooting one employee and escaping with $20,000 in cash. The getaway car was later found abandoned, but the local police investigation came to a dead end. Then, out of the blue, a package broke open in a Kansas City post office. A clerk noticed that it contained about $20,000 in currency and notified postal inspectors, who also found an automatic pistol inside. The package bore a fictitious return address in Fort Worth and was addressed to an unknown person at a vacant house in Kansas City. It is a federal offense to use the mail service to transport stolen property or unregistered weapons across state lines, so the Kansas City FBI office was notified.

Working closely with postal inspectors, agents staked out the vacant house at the address. The letter carrier was briefed to stop at the place and conspicuously make inquiries around the neighborhood. On the second day of the stakeout, a taxi driver claimed the package and drove away, our agents trailing along. The cab led us directly to Palma. He denied any knowledge of the package or the events in Fort Worth, but further FBI investigation developed sufficient evidence to present to a federal grand jury. On September 2, 1965, Palma was indicted for violations of the Federal Firearms Act, interstate transportation of stolen property, conspiracy, and mail fraud.

This marked the beginning of the end for Palma. He feared being tried in federal court, where Mafia influence counted for nothing. He was not a Mafia leader, but he had been around long enough to know who had done what to whom and was familiar with many details of ongoing Mafia operations. The Mafia, therefore, considered his use-fulness ended. On the day he was to appear in federal court for arraignment, he was kidnapped from federal marshals and his body was later found in a local cemetery, right next to his father's grave. He had been shot once in the back and once through the temple, in true gangland style. Mafia leaders said Palma committed suicide; they didn't address how he had managed to shoot himself in the back.

The Kansas City chief of police, Clarence Kelley, formally requested that the Bureau take charge of the investigation and send an official from Washington to direct it. Kelley, a former Bureau agent and a good friend of mine, knew the ropes. Why not have someone to share the blame with if the investigation led nowhere? Because of my background in Kansas City and my responsibility as chief inspector, that someone turned out to be me.

Gangland slayings go unsolved more often than not, and although I liked investigative challenges, I also wanted some prospect for success. I selected Harold "Red" Campbell, one of the inspectors on my staff, to go with me. He wasn't thrilled either. It was a bleak day when Red and I stepped off the plane at the old Kansas City airport in the bend of the Missouri River.

Campbell and I worked in Kansas City for more than five months, but we never built a case strong enough to present to a federal grand jury. We knew who the hit man was, but it was like investigating Watergate: nobody would talk. During the first ten days, we stirred up a beehive of activity. We sent a long and impressive teletype to Hoover every day summarizing developments. As the days passed with fewer and fewer leads, however, it became more and more difficult to prepare the daily teletype. After thirty days without much progress, we were reduced to gathering intelligence information about the principal suspect. We went from one mob hangout to the next trying to stir something up. We were lucky we didn't get whacked.

After two months we had no reasonable prospect of solving the case. I called Cartha "Deke" DeLoach, who had replaced Alan Belmont as assistant to the director in charge of all FBI investigative operations. Maybe I couldn't argue with the director, but I could argue with Deke.

"Deke," I said, "we are wasting our time here." DeLoach listened politely as I went into a long narrative describing our progress and explaining the low probability of success.

Then he said, "You and Red might as well face it, Mark. You haven't solved the case and the director will not let you come back until you do."

"Deke, you know perfectly well that this gangland killing will probably never be solved," I insisted. "These people know damn well if they talk they'll end up in the Missouri River wearing cement boots. There's nothing more Campbell and I can do here that the Kansas City office can't do just as well. Please try to make the director see that." I hated myself for whining.

"Right now is not a good time," DeLoach said. "I'll get back to you as soon as I can, but in the meantime, keep working."

I called Audrey at regular intervals, and each time she wanted to know when I was coming home. As the weeks dragged into months, she began to wonder what exactly I was doing in Kansas City. Red and I stayed to see spring come to the Great Plains, but my mood didn't lighten. I was spending time thinking of ways to get Deke instead of the killer.

Finally I got a break. One Saturday night in April, I was in my room at the Pickwick Hotel watching the *Beverly Hillbillies* when I heard a loud knock at the door. Standing to the side of the entrance, I asked who was there. A feminine voice replied, "Your escort, sir."

To my great surprise and delight, it was Audrey. She had hopped a TWA flight to Kansas City. That Saturday night was one of the best in my life.

We slept in on Sunday morning and at about eleven we took the elevator down to the coffee shop for breakfast. Red Campbell had a room on the tenth floor, just below me, so we stopped to pick him up. When the elevator doors opened on the tenth floor, there was Campbell, waiting to get on. He started in and then paused, not knowing whether to get on or get off. Clearly he thought he had stumbled onto an indiscretion.

"Red," I said, "this is my wife. Audrey, this is Red Campbell, who has been helping me."

"I'm pleased to meet you, Mrs. Felt," he said, his disbelief registering on his face. As we rode the rest of the way down, his skepticism subsided and he grew embarrassed. Audrey began to laugh, and Red and I joined in. It was against FBI rules to have your wife with you on an assignment, and Red couldn't even imagine that I would permit my wife to visit me while I was investigating a major case.

Late in May, while Audrey and I were living happily ever after in the hotel, I got a call from Chief Kelley. The man who had killed Palma was found dead in his car, floating upside down in the river. There was no evidence of foul play, and the county coroner ruled the death accidental. No matter. That put an end to my stay in Kansas City. Hoover offered no criticism of my performance on the case and said nothing about my wife, but I'm sure he knew she was with me; he didn't miss much. If so, it was the only time I ever saw him look the other way when rules were broken.

People like to needle me about my inability to solve the Palma slaying before it solved itself. Efrem Zimbalist, Jr. would have solved the case in sixty minutes, less commercials, including a gun battle or two. To this day, my theory is that the mob gave us Palma's killer just to get the senior FBI people out of town.

If I stayed in Hoover's good graces, it probably had something to do with my work on a troubleshooting operation earlier in 1965. In April, the Dominican Republic had a full-scale revolution after army insurgents sought to overthrow the ruling civilian triumvirate led by Donald Cabral and to return to power the exiled former president, the leftist Juan Bosch. President Lyndon Johnson was gravely concerned and sent in the Marines, ostensibly to protect American citizens and American property.

The president demanded thorough and up-to-the-minute information on the fighting—something the intelligence community could not supply. That's when Hoover stepped into the breach. On the third day of the revolt, the director sent the president an intelligence summary outlining what the leftist insurgents were going to do on the fourth day. Events confirmed the Bureau's intel, and Hoover continued to supply the president with advance information on the insurgents' thinking and planning. The president was delighted, and for Hoover it was a feather in the FBI's cap. The information, moreover, was coming in as a result of solid investigative procedures.

Bosch was living in Puerto Rico, directing his forces by telephone. Each evening he plotted strategy with his confederates in Santo Domingo for as long as two hours. SAC Wallace R. Estill of the San Juan office had obtained approval from Hoover and the attorney general to plant a wiretap on Bosch's telephone. Subsequently FBI agents recorded every word of the revolutionary strategy sessions. This information was summarized and sent to FBI headquarters, then passed on to the president and the intelligence community, giving Johnson accurate and preemptive knowledge of revolutionary activity.

However, the quality of the Bureau's intelligence began to deteriorate because of delays in transmitting the information from San Juan to Washington. Frustrated, Hoover called a conference attended by Clyde Tolson, Alan H. Belmont, in charge of all investigative operations, "Deke" DeLoach, in charge of White House liaison, and me. Hoover cited several examples of slow transmissions from San Juan and stated flatly, "I won't tolerate any more delays like this." Tolson speculated that the agents in the San Juan office were "probably going home by 5:30." Belmont defended the agents and added that it was a complicated problem. Just then Miss Gandy entered the room. In her hand was the latest radiogram from San Juan, a fairly short summary of a telephone conversation between

Bosch and the insurgents. It had taken place eighteen hours earlier. As Hoover read the radiogram, a flush spread up from under his collar. Knowing the information would be at least nineteen hours old before the president would read it, he turned to me.

"Felt, I want you to go down to San Juan and find out what's the matter. Take whatever steps are necessary to eliminate these inexcusable delays. This information isn't worth anything when it's old."

I speculated that the San Juan office might need another encrypting machine.

"I want to get this corrected by tomorrow," Hoover said curtly.

As I walked Belmont to his office, he briefed me on the procedures in San Juan. The tapped rebel conversations had to be translated from Spanish to English and double-checked for accuracy. Then there was another delay in Washington, where the classified messages from San Juan had to be decoded.

When I arrived in San Juan at 3:15 the next morning, I was met at the airport by SAC Wally Estill. He gave me a thorough briefing as we drove directly to the office. The bottleneck was not attributable to lack of effort. Estill was averaging eight hours a day overtime, as were the other agents. When I surveyed the situation at the office, I decided that nothing further could be done about speeding up the translation of the monitored messages. The old World War II encoding equipment, secure but cumbersome, was another source of delay. Even the addition of the second machine I brought would not help decisively.

The greatest single problem lay in the radio transmission. The San Juan office had only one transmitter, and the radio operator tapped out the message a letter at a time in Morse code. Two operators were using the transmitter around the clock, but they could not keep up with the traffic.

In the radio room I noticed a piece of equipment that resembled a small computer. "What's this?" I asked the radio operator.

"That's our new encoding machine."

"Why aren't we using it?"

He explained that they were waiting for additional equipment to hook it up to the radio transmitter.

"How does it work?" I asked.

"It's a tremendous improvement over the old equipment," the operator said. "You type the message at this end and the machine automatically scrambles it. An identical machine on the other end receives and unscrambles the message as fast as it's being received. It's just like using a teletype."

"Is there any way of using it now?"

The operator thought for a minute. "We could use it if we connected it to a leased telephone line."

"Why don't we do that now?"

"It's against regulations of the National Security Agency. We can't operate it until a special lead-lined room is constructed. There might be a breach in our security. We just can't do it."

Returning to Estill's office, I told him, "If Belmont approves, we're going to order a leased telephone line and connect the new coding machine to it."

Estill frowned. "What about NSA regulations? Where are we going to put it?"

"Wally, we're going to put it wherever you decide is the most convenient place to hook it up to a leased line. I don't care if you put it beside your desk. This is an emergency and we aren't going to worry about regulations."*

We called Belmont, who agreed and promised to arrange the hook-up at his end. I assured him that the new machine would be operational before the day was over. Late that afternoon the leased

---

* This incident gives us an early example of the Mark Felt who investigated Watergate: the disciplined risk taken with a disdain for needlessly cumbersome rules. —Editor

line had been brought in and the coding machine was working at full speed. By midnight, the large backlog of summaries had been sent to the Bureau and the messages were going out on a current basis. The coding machine sat in full view for all to see in the center of the agents' room, but I was certain that security was not compromised. The bottleneck was broken. I had accomplished my objective in one day, as Hoover had demanded.

The seeds of another rift between the FBI and CIA grew out of the Dominican crisis. The CIA was supposed to have sole responsibility for intelligence gathering outside the continental United States. President Johnson was disappointed with CIA efforts in the Dominican Republic and pleased with the FBI. Much to the chagrin of the CIA, he ordered Hoover to establish an office in Santo Domingo. It took Hoover nearly two years to convince the White House to close the office.

None of those gathering storm clouds darkened my horizon. Just before I left Puerto Rico, Hoover called and told me to take a short vacation.

"How short?" I asked.

"Don't push it, Felt," he replied. I called Audrey, who happily accepted my invitation to fly down to San Juan for the weekend.

EIGHT

THE 1960S:
ATTACK OF THE RADICALS

B Y THE MID-1960s, Hoover had conditioned a full generation of Americans to respect the FBI as the ultimate guardian of law and order. The lawyer-agents who filled its ranks hunted criminals with ruthless professionalism. The G-Man in suit and tie was lionized in TV dramas and worshiped by children who sent away for their Junior G-man badges. The Bureau was a pillar of the establishment, a status that began to hurt it in the turbulent 1960s. In the years of protest, the FBI and Hoover became prime targets of the New Left on campuses across the nation. Left-wingers equated the FBI with the KGB (the Soviet secret police), and this misidentification seeped into the press and found growing expression among the more bewitched and bothered opinion makers. With our national penchant for overreaction, the pendulum began to swing from blind approval of everything the FBI did to equally blind rejection.

The biggest blemish on the FBI's image came late on the evening of March 8, 1971, in a Pennsylvania town appropriately named Media. The FBI resident agency was broken into and more than a thousand classified government documents were stolen.

The rationale for the Media burglary came several months ear-

lier, on November 19, 1970, when Hoover testified before the House
Appropriations Subcommittee, asking for additional agents. Hoover
refused to follow the political and media trends by lending
respectability to leftist agitators, whom he saw as criminals and
friends of Moscow. Some of his testimony was given in executive
session, but one sensational portion came out in open session:

> One example has recently come to light involving an incipient plot
> on the part of an anarchist group on the east coast, the so-called
> East Coast Conspiracy to Save Lives. This is a militant group self-
> described as being composed of Catholic priests and nuns, teach-
> ers, students, and former students who have manifested opposition
> to the war in Vietnam by acts of violence against Government
> agencies and private corporations engaged in work relating to U.S.
> participation in the Vietnam conflict.
>
> The principal leaders of this group are Philip and Daniel Berri-
> gan, Catholic priests who are currently incarcerated in the Federal
> Correctional Institution at Danbury, Connecticut, for their partic-
> ipation in the destruction of Selective Service records in Baltimore
> in 1968.
>
> This group plans to blow up underground electrical conduits
> and steam pipes serving the Washington, D.C., area in order to dis-
> rupt Federal Government operations. The plotters are also con-
> cocting a scheme to kidnap a highly placed Government official.
> The name of a White House staff member has been mentioned as
> a possible victim. If successful, the plotters would demand an end
> to U.S. bombing operations in Southeast Asia and the release of all
> "political prisoners" as ransom. Intensive investigation is being con-
> ducted concerning this matter.

Hoover's statement was accurate and reflected the results of FBI
probing. However, it was gratuitous because he was appearing
before the subcommittee in support of adding agents to combat

organized crime. Pertinent or not, it made headlines. News stories disclosed that the intended kidnap victim was Henry A. Kissinger, the president's national security adviser.

Left-wing activists William M. Kunstler and Rev. William C. Cunningham branded Hoover's statement a "far-fetched spy story." They stated that if Hoover had "the evidence he claimed to have" his duty would be to see "that the Berrigans and their alleged co-conspirators are prosecuted." Other critics felt that the Hoover remarks constituted prejudicial pretrial publicity that violated the constitutional rights of the Berrigans.

Sensitive and unaccustomed to this kind of criticism, the FBI reacted with consternation. The background material about the Berrigans had originated in the Domestic Intelligence Division, but the man who headed it, William C. Sullivan, quickly disclaimed responsibility. He insisted that although he had furnished the information to Hoover, he had warned against its use. Hoover's reaction was to bring the case to a speedy conclusion.

On January 12, 1971, Attorney General John Mitchell announced that a federal grand jury in Harrisburg, Pennsylvania, had returned indictments against Philip Berrigan and five others on charges of conspiring to kidnap Henry Kissinger and blow up the heating infrastructure of federal buildings in Washington.

The trial commenced on February 21, 1972, and was marked by defense histrionics inside the courtroom and demonstrations outside the courthouse. On April 5, 1972, a tired jury found Berrigan and Sister Elizabeth McAlister guilty on four counts of smuggling contraband letters at the federal prison in Lewisburg, Pennsylvania, but was unable to reach a verdict on the charges of conspiracy to kidnap Kissinger, blow up heating tunnels, and raid draft board offices. The defendants and their counsel—Kunstler, Leonard Boudin, and Ramsey Clark—were jubilant, particularly when the Justice Department decided not to retry the case.

The Berrigan victory encouraged the extremist left, which was determined to strike the FBI in more damaging ways. I was affected only indirectly. Long before the trial started, Hoover had given me the task of supervising the security of FBI resident agencies, anticipating attacks against the FBI by Berrigan supporters.

On Wednesday, March 9, 1971, I was in New York on a routine inspection of the field office. I had just started to shave that morning when the phone rang. It was the night supervisor at the New York office.

"The Bureau wants you to call as soon as possible," he said. "And they want you to call on the secure line."

"What in the world do they want?"

"I don't know," came the expected reply. "They didn't say." They never do. I dressed, rushed to the office, and picked up the phone at 7:30. The Bureau switchboard operator put me through to Edward S. Miller, my top assistant in the Inspection Division. He told me that burglars had broken into the FBI's resident agency at Media, Pennsylvania, near Philadelphia.

"Apparently they got away with a lot of serials," Miller said, using the FBI's internal term for file documents. Using a crowbar, the raiders had broken the locks on every filing cabinet and made off with hundreds of documents, including many that related to foreign intelligence. A group calling itself the Citizens Commission to Investigate the FBI called a local paper to claim credit for the burglary.

Within thirty minutes I was on the Metroliner for Philadelphia. A midnight raid was not unexpected. Draft boards around the country had already been burglarized by war protestors. In one instance the Berrigan brothers had poured animal blood over the files. A raiding party also attempted to burglarize the FBI resident agency at Babylon, Long Island, but was unable to break through the masonry wall. The burglars left the public corridor in a shambles.

At this time Hoover tasked me with determining what precautionary steps should be taken to ensure adequate protection for sensitive FBI material. I discovered that only a few resident agencies were located in federal buildings with twenty-four-hour guards. Some of these offices had secure vaults. Most, however, were located in commercial office space with minimal protection. The answer was to furnish each office with a filing cabinet as strong as a safe and sealed with a combination lock. A good burglar-proof cabinet safe would cost just under $1,000; 475 of the 536 resident agencies would require one or more cabinet safes.

The problem was that the FBI did not have $500,000 to spend on cabinet safes. The only workable solution I saw was to recommend added protection for key resident agencies close to colleges and universities with a great deal of activist ferment. My first reaction to the Media burglary, therefore, was to check my memory: Had I picked Media as one of the resident agencies to receive the new cabinet safes? When Ed Miller assured me that I had, I breathed a sigh of relief.

At the Philadelphia field office, word came that Hoover wanted to talk to me as soon as possible. When I called, he told me that a contingent of laboratory and fingerprint experts had been sent from Washington to help with the investigation. He instructed me to inquire narrowly into the breach of security, and I assured him that he would have a memo on his desk when he arrived for work the following morning. When I arrived at the Media office, the experts were looking for evidence to help identify the burglars. What I wanted to see, though, was the safe, and there it was—the biggest type of two-door, burglar-proof, fireproof cabinet safe that money could buy—untouched and unscratched in the middle of the office.

The burglars did not even attempt to jimmy this monster. I suspect they stole away thinking that they had failed in their mission, that the really secret documents were locked away in the big safe.

The regular file cabinets, no match for a determined burglar with a crowbar, had been destroyed.

I began my inquiry by asking the senior resident agent to open the safe. Inside, where sensitive documents should have been stored, were several two-way radios, assorted Bureau firearms, handcuffs, a blackjack, and a copy of the National Crime Information Center operation manual, a public document. The resident agents at Media completely missed the point, but the Citizens Commission to Investigate the FBI did not miss a single important document.

Hoover was enraged, and so was I. The senior resident agent in charge had failed to protect Bureau documents by putting them in the safe, and I recommended stern disciplinary action; he was suspended for a month without pay and given a punitive transfer to the Atlanta field office.

On March 22, Senator George McGovern of South Dakota and Representative Parren Mitchell of Maryland, both outspoken critics of the FBI, received packages of selected material from the stolen files. Both men immediately turned the material over to the Bureau, and McGovern publicly stated that he would not associate himself with "illegal actions of this nature." The Citizens Commission to Investigate the FBI publicized only items that put the FBI in a bad light. Contrary, explanatory, or mitigating papers—memoranda rescinding a previous order or censuring a particular action, for example—were excluded. While elected officials had shied away from handling the material, the press showed no such compunction. The *Washington Post* described the classified documents taken in the Media raid, and the *New York Times* and other publications printed excerpts from the stolen files.

In March 1972, a publication calling itself WIN produced an eighty-two-page pamphlet purporting to be a full reproduction of all the documents stolen from the FBI at Media. It was entitled *The*

*Complete Collection of Political Documents Ripped Off from the FBI Office
in Media*—an answer to charges that only damaging documents had
been released to the press—but the pamphlet included only a few
selected documents.

Publication of the FBI documents resulted in a great outcry
against FBI practices depicted as reprehensible and un-American.
Over the years Hoover had been praised by Roger Baldwin, the
founder of the American Civil Liberties Union, and Morris Ernst, an
ACLU guru, for safeguarding the rights of the citizenry. This fact was
forgotten as charges that the Bureau was a secret police were dusted
off. In the documents released, the names of those under investigation were excised, whereas the names of those cooperating with the
FBI were exposed, leaving them vulnerable to vituperative attack.

A telephone operator at Swarthmore College had allowed an FBI
agent to see the long-distance telephone records of a philosophy
professor, a gesture that was held up as an invasion of privacy. It was
never mentioned that the professor was under suspicion of harbor-
ing several fugitives from justice. Another document concerned the
investigation of a traveler to East Germany who had visited a number of communist camps. When the FBI learned that the subject
was fourteen years old, it dropped the case. But one pertinent fact
was omitted. The FBI had opened the investigation at the request of
U.S. military authorities in West Germany.

The FBI was accused of racism when the Media documents
showed it attempting to recruit informants in black neighborhoods.
The FBI directive, however, plainly stated that this recruitment was
intended to give the Bureau advance warning of riots at a time
when the nation's inner cities were tinderboxes.

The Media papers also included an investigative report on
Jacqueline Reuss, the daughter of Rep. Henry S. Reuss, a Wisconsin
Democrat. This raised a furor, but the Bureau's interest was justi-
fied. Jacqueline was active in Students for a Democratic Society, an

organization that was a seedbed for campus violence in the late
1960s. Two local police departments and another government
agency were also keeping tabs on the congressman's daughter.
Some claimed that the FBI's investigation of Reuss was really a
flanking attack on the Congress—though her file contained nothing
more than a perfunctory list of her educational achievements in the
United States and France.

For the most part, the Media papers dealt with routine FBI business. One memo reported on a Rochester, New York, police department program to enlist the Boy Scouts in the war on crime. Another
described how FBI offices were linked to the National Crime Information Center to trace people as well as firearms, stolen cars, and
other items. A precise directive instructed special agents on what
authorization they needed to use wiretaps, spelling out the provisions of the Omnibus Crime Control Act of 1968. There were transcripts of telephone taps on the Black Panthers, instructions on how
to cope with rioters, and a number of investigative reports.

The Media papers were relatively innocuous, with one exception: an interoffice routing slip that referred to "COINTELPRO—
New Left," a bureaucratic phrase for FBI counterintelligence
programs aimed at uncovering potential and actual violence and
subversion by the extremist right and left. This clue was overlooked
until March 1972, when Carl Stern, a bright young reporter for
NBC, made a formal request for all FBI documents relating to
"COINTELPRO—New Left" under the provisions of the Freedom
of Information Act. When Stern's request was refused, based on
certain exemptions in the act, he filed suit in federal court, which
ruled that the documents should be made available to him. This
opened the floodgates.

The media highlighted material dealing primarily with the New
Left and extremist black groups. It ignored documentation of FBI
actions against the Ku Klux Klan and other organizations of the

extreme right. The public was given the impression that COINTEL-PRO was designed solely to combat leftist political activity rather than to combat violence on both ends of the political spectrum.

An exhaustive investigation to identify the perpetrators of the Media burglary ended in frustration. The Bureau learned who they were but could not develop the evidence to prove its case in court—in large part because peers and sympathizers of the culprits, wrapped in media martyrdom, refused to talk. But the impact of the disclosures went far beyond the leftist fringe. The selective and widespread publication of the stolen documents damaged the FBI's image, possibly forever, in the minds of many Americans.

NINE

TO WIRETAP
OR NOT TO WIRETAP

T HE FBI's public reputation went into decline just as the
Bureau was coming under unprecedented attack in Washington. In the Nixon administration, which took office in 1969, a White
House–Justice Department cabal worked to turn the Bureau into a
political tool of those in power. The New Left and the media were
attacking the FBI for abusing civil rights while Hoover was fighting
to keep the Bureau loyal to its old disciplines and insisting on procedures that should have gladdened the hearts of civil libertarians. His
principled stand led President Richard Nixon and his aides to create
the unofficial Plumbers unit to conduct national security and political intelligence missions that the FBI would not touch. This strategy
led to undercover capers by Nixon operatives E. Howard Hunt and
G. Gordon Liddy as a means of "protecting" national security at any
cost and, indirectly, led to Watergate.

Hoover had always stood for investigative techniques that
respected the Bill of Rights. He took that same stance in 1936, when
he was called in by President Franklin D. Roosevelt and ordered to
investigate communist and Nazi organizations. When Hoover

protested that he had no authority to embark on domestic intelligence gathering, the president dug up a federal statute permitting the secretary of state to sanction such activity. Secretary Cordell Hull was summoned to the Oval Office and, in the presence of Hoover, wrote out his authorization, which was locked up in the White House safe. On September 6, 1939, the statement was released by President Roosevelt:

> The Attorney General has been requested by me to instruct the Federal Bureau of Investigation of the Department of Justice to take charge of investigative work in matters relating to espionage, sabotage, and violations of the neutrality regulations.
>
> This task must be conducted in a comprehensive and effective manner on a national basis, and all information must be carefully sifted out and correlated in order to avoid confusion and irresponsibility.
>
> To this end I request all police officers, sheriffs, and all other law enforcement officers in the United States promptly to turn over to the nearest representative of the Federal Bureau of Investigation any information obtained by them relating to espionage, counterespionage, subversive activities, and violations of the neutrality laws.

These directives were repeated almost verbatim by later presidents.

The FBI crippled the German intelligence apparatus before Pearl Harbor. Japanese operations were almost nonexistent in the United States as a result of FBI effectiveness. But before the war ended, Hoover had become aware of the activities of espionage agents and those who sympathized with our Soviet ally. This "friendly" interest was directed toward U.S. nuclear capabilities. Soviet agents stole our atomic secrets and the technical details of our highly sophisticated proximity fuse, not to mention a wide range of other military information.

Passage of the Smith Act (1940), first invoked against the Socialist Workers Party (Trotskyites), and other statutes broadened the scope of FBI investigative authority. The Smith Act prohibited teaching or advocating the overthrow or destruction of the U.S. government or the government of a state, territory, or other entity by force or violence or conspiracy to do so. The act made no mention of foreign involvement.

Information passed on to President Truman by J. Edgar Hoover in 1945 laid bare a pattern of communist infiltration into the highest reaches of the U.S. government, designed to pervert and misdirect policy as well as conduct espionage. The government employees loyalty program also put tremendous new investigative burdens on the FBI.

The FBI conducted domestic intelligence throughout the 1950s with the full knowledge and encouragement of both executive and legislative branches and with the strong support of the American people. During the 1960s, however, questions began to arise about the proper role of government in this area. Numerous violent and revolutionary groups began to form, obliterating the distinction between foreign and domestic operations against the government and people of the United States.

The civil rights struggles that came after the Supreme Court's antisegregation ruling in 1954 intensified the FBI's mission. During 1957 and 1958, more than one hundred bombings and attempted bombings, motivated by racial or religious hatred, were committed in the United States. Reacting to the growing evidence of such outrages, Congress enacted the Civil Rights Act of 1960, expanding the FBI's jurisdiction over bombings and bomb threats, and interference with court orders and election matters.

The civil rights movement gained momentum and public support in the early 1960s. At the same time, it became the target of vili-fication by the Ku Klux Klan and other merchants of hate, who saw a communist behind every banner or sign that urged desegregation and equal rights.

Some communists joined civil rights organizations, and a few maneuvered themselves into positions of influence over the policies and programs of legitimate groups. Furthermore, young dema-gogues thirsting for personal power and recognition were attracted to the civil rights movement like moths to a flame.

Given these circumstances, violence and bloodshed were inevitable. The FBI was called on time and again in the 1960s to exceed its authority by providing physical protection to persons engaged in civil rights activities. It refused and was accused of hold-ing back. On the other hand, the FBI resisted pressure to ignore or neglect its duty to enforce provisions of the federal civil rights statutes, and for this it earned the enmity of the forces on the oppo-site side.

The FBI saw its proper role as the prevention of violence and the protection of life and property. It continued its investigations to identify and apprehend terrorists jeopardizing the civil rights of other Americans. But increasingly the problem became one of how to distinguish between persons and organizations intent on violence and those that merely employed inflammatory rhetoric. It was also a problem of staying abreast of the plans and activities of those who ignited violence. This required both criminal investigation and intel-ligence work.

Confronted with this situation, should the FBI employ methods sanctioned by higher authority since 1936? Or should it take a safer but less effective course and bow to growing pressure from the media, Congress, and civil libertarians to shut down its domestic intelligence operations?

For Hoover, always sensitive to the moods of Congress, a straw in the wind was the hearings held by Senator Edward V. Long of Missouri to investigate the Internal Revenue Service for electronic surveillance activities in the drive on organized crime during the early 1960s. This development led the director to call me into his office in mid-1965 to tell me that he wanted a "substantial" cutback in the number of FBI wiretaps. I was directed to review the case files and eliminate the least productive wiretaps. Hoover did not offer any guidelines, nor did I ask for any. I simply said, "Mr. Hoover, I'll attend to it." Hoover anticipated widespread internal opposition to the reduction, but it was his custom in those years to toss me the difficult administrative problems and expect me to solve them.

This particular challenge brought me into open conflict with William C. Sullivan, the assistant director in charge of the Domestic Intelligence Division, who had used his status as one of Hoover's favorites to rise through the ranks and would eventually turn on the director and try to unseat him. I had previous experience with Sullivan and knew he could be difficult to deal with when crossed, throwing tantrums, for example, and engaging in backstabbing.

I had no interest in a head-butting contest with the mercurial little man known for his Napoleonic complex. Instead, I went to his superior, Alan H. Belmont, who was at that time assistant to the director in charge of all investigative operations. Belmont, a highly regarded official with a superb background in intelligence matters, was a pragmatist.

When I entered Belmont's office, the usual blue haze of cigar smoke hung in the air. I explained Hoover's instructions to me and requested his support. Belmont replied forcefully, "Mark, we can't cut back on wiretaps without reducing our effectiveness." He argued that cutbacks had been made through the years and the number of taps was reasonable. Wiretap requests were carefully screened and recommended to Hoover only when they were completely justified, he said—and the need for the taps was reviewed at regular intervals after they were in place.

I knew that what Belmont was saying was true. Ninety-five percent of the wiretap installations involved foreign intelligence cases, and they provided valuable information to the government. But I was new in my position as assistant director in charge of the Inspection Division and had yet to learn how to influence Hoover without incurring his wrath. So I pressed on with my assignment and did not let myself be diverted by Belmont's argument.

"Al," I said, "that's not the point. The director wants a reduction and that is what we are going to give him. It would be much better if I had your cooperation."

"I'm not going to help you tear down the effectiveness of the FBI," he said brusquely.

My only course was to review all current wiretap files to rank them in some order of priority. After a week of twelve-hour days I was ready to take the first step. I selected the case of an individual suspected of cooperating with the intelligence service of a Soviet satellite country. In my opinion, this wiretap could be discontinued without critical damage to the United States, and the case could be handled by conventional means, albeit somewhat less effectively. I then dictated a memorandum summarizing the case and suggesting that the wiretap phase of the investigation be discontinued. I recommended that the matter be presented to the executive conference. These conferences were meetings of all top FBI officials at Bureau headquarters, usually minus the director, held at irregular intervals when important policy considerations arose, generally about three or four times a month.

In spite of the public's image of "Hooverized conformity," the executive conference was anything but a group of yes men. Arguments for and against a given proposal were aggressively debated before a vote was taken. Associate Director Clyde Tolson, who customarily chaired the meetings in Hoover's absence, encouraged participation by everyone and frequently called for opinions. Afterward, but preferably the same day, the proponent of the matter under consideration would prepare a succinct memorandum summarizing the proposal and the arguments pro and con. The memo was then routed to Hoover for final decision.

Usually he agreed with the majority, but sometimes he took the minority position or even an entirely new position. In any case, the executive conference provided Hoover with the dialectical input of all his top assistants, minus the wrangling. Under this system he received more candid views than he would have if he had personally chaired the meetings.

When I presented my recommendation for discontinuing the wiretap to the executive conference, there was a cold silence. Even Tolson opposed me. When the vote was taken, I was the only one voting to discontinue.

The result was sent to the director and he returned my memorandum with a brief notation: "I agree with Felt." I expected this because it was his idea in the first place, but it did not enhance the popularity of the Inspection Division.

We went through the exercise two more times. I argued alone for the suspension of a wiretap, and the director agreed with me. My approach was much too slow for what the director had in mind, and even though the score was now three to nothing, I went back to Alan Belmont. He was the key to the whole issue.

"Look, Al, let's be practical about this. I know that you are opposed to further cutbacks. I understand your position, but we can't go on with me chipping away at your wiretaps one at a time. You know that the director wants a substantial reduction and is going to agree with me. Why don't you accept the inevitable? You are in a better position than I to decide which taps can be discontinued with the least disadvantage. More importantly, if the initiative comes from you, the director won't think you're dragging your feet."

Belmont puffed slowly on his cigar. He blew out a big cloud of smoke and stared at the ceiling. Finally he gave me his full attention. He wasn't smiling. "How many do you want to cut?"

I had already decided on a figure. When my review program started, there were seventy-eight in operation. My efforts, so far, had reduced this number to seventy-five.

"Al, we are going to cut them down to thirty-eight."

Again there was much puffing and a further detailed examination of the ceiling. The blue haze in the room grew thicker, and after an interminable period Belmont lowered his gaze and said very slowly, "All right, we'll do it."

"Good," I replied, relieved that the matter could be settled without wasting more time in the executive conference. "This is the logical way to handle it."

"You are probably right," he replied, "but Sullivan is going to be furious."

"I know, I know. It won't be the first time."

The next day the Domestic Intelligence Division submitted a memo recommending the discontinuance of thirty-seven wiretaps. Each was identified by case title and file number. When it came out of Hoover's office, there was the penned notation, "O.K. H." in the familiar blue ink of authority.

Only a few months later, a disheartened Belmont submitted his application for retirement, effective December 30, 1965, thus creating a vacancy in the number three position in the FBI hierarchy. Hoover chose Cartha Dekle "Deke" DeLoach, assistant director in charge of the Crime Records Division, which handled press relations, research, and congressional liaison. Shrewdly playing his cards, DeLoach had insisted on handling all contacts with Vice President Lyndon B. Johnson during the Kennedy administration; the two hit it off because they were alike in many ways. DeLoach was a behind-the-scenes power in the American Legion and he had influential friends on Capitol Hill.

Ever the master at charting his way through the bureaucratic shoals of Washington, Hoover trimmed his sails to adjust to the new wind coming from the White House when he selected DeLoach, who was to continue his personal liaison with Johnson in the Executive Mansion. The relationship became so close that the president had a special White House phone installed in DeLoach's bedroom. There was never any doubt that he was the president's choice to succeed J. Edgar Hoover, but events conspired against him.

The rising tide of resentment against U.S. involvement in Vietnam blasted DeLoach's hopes of becoming FBI director when it forced President Johnson to retire to his Texas ranch on the Pedernales River. Not long after he lost his political mentor, DeLoach retired from the FBI and took a high position with the Pepsi Cola Company.

Hoover replaced DeLoach with his personal favorite—William C. Sullivan. Sullivan was more than a hothead. He was extremely intelligent and well read. An excellent conversationalist, he could be ingratiating when it served his purposes. He had expansive writing talent and cultivated Hoover shamelessly with flattering letters and unusual gifts from his travels. Dealing with Tolson and Hoover required finesse and patience. Sullivan would plant a seed and later convince them that it was their idea.

Hoover addressed subordinates in certain characteristic ways. If Hoover had any reason to address me as a young agent, he would have called me "Mr. Felt." When I was promoted to the position of assistant special agent in charge and thus became a Bureau official, he started addressing me as "Felt." This was true of all Bureau officials except two, Tolson and Sullivan. While the rest of us were "Nichols," "Mohr," "Rosen," "Belmont," "Felt," Hoover addressed Tolson and Sullivan as "Clyde" and "Bill." Tolson was Hoover's longtime confidant and daily luncheon companion, but Sullivan was granted the same level of familiarity. It was an indication of the high regard Hoover had for Sullivan until the very end.

Sullivan's appearance was the antithesis of what the director expected—a matter of enormous importance in Hoover's mind. Sullivan was short, barely over the minimum height of 5 feet 7. He was pale and drawn and gave the impression of poor health. He dressed atrociously and his clothes looked as though they had been slept in, as indeed they sometimes were. On one occasion he appeared for a conference with Hoover wearing muddy shoes, and he borrowed a clean pair from a subordinate. They were two sizes too large, and he had to maneuver them like snowshoes.

I can't explain why Hoover accepted these idiosyncrasies from Sullivan. Perhaps Hoover felt sorry for Sullivan. Perhaps he regarded him as a surrogate son. But the fact remains that the agent who rose to highest favor would have been voted by the rest of us as the least likely to succeed.

Sullivan harbored grudges, and he never forgave Hoover for taking away wiretaps or ending surreptitious entries. As head of the Domestic Intelligence Division, Sullivan was concerned that the FBI was not doing enough to combat and disrupt violent elements in the New Left. He sincerely believed that the restrictions placed on him by Hoover impaired the Bureau's ability to protect the citizens of the United States.

At one point he said to me, "The boss is wrong! We have to get the job done in spite of him!"

"Bill," I replied, "the Bureau can have only one boss."

"The director is wrong. You have got to help me convince him."

I drew a deep breath. "Bill, we've talked about this before. I understand your problems but we are going to get the job done in spite of the restrictions—not in spite of the boss. After you have made your position clear, either support him or get out."

I could understand some of Sullivan's frustrations. Calls on FBI manpower for field offices in the South, a result of civil rights demonstrations and counter–civil rights violence, had cut down on the number of agents available for foreign and domestic intelligence matters. I did not realize then that Sullivan was biding his time and waiting for an opportunity to have his own way.

He got it when Tom Charles Huston, a former army intelligence officer on the White House staff, received an assignment from presidential assistant John Ehrlichman to prepare a report on campus disturbances and New Left violence, a problem deeply disturbing to President Nixon.

Huston came to Sullivan on June 19, 1969, and wanted a full FBI report on New Left foreign connections. From this meeting grew a close relationship between the two men that Sullivan skillfully used for his own purposes. Sullivan repeatedly complained to Huston about Hoover's refusal to employ wiretaps and surreptitious entries, and about the "question of coordination, the lack of manpower, the inability to get the necessary resources," all presumably attributable to a director who had lost his grip and should be relegated to the dust heap.

Huston and Sullivan developed what a Senate Committee later described as a working alliance to further their ambitions. Huston saw himself as a kind of White House gauleiter over the intelligence community, riding herd on the FBI, the CIA, the Defense Intelligence Agency, and the National Security Agency, imposing his ideas of how they should move against subversives and dissidents. Sullivan believed that with Huston's backing, he could undermine Hoover's position with the president and succeed him as director. If Sullivan did not actually draft the notorious Huston plan—which called for wiretappings, burglaries, mail openings, and similar tactics against antiwar groups and others—he certainly inspired it.

The plan was conceived when Nixon, at Huston's urging, created the ad hoc Interagency Committee on Intelligence to review and suggest improvements in collecting intelligence against the New Left. Hoover was named chairman and, at Huston's prompting, Sullivan was appointed chairman of the staff subcommittee that would actually write the guidelines for policy recommendations. As a Senate investigation later concluded, Sullivan's role seemed to be to identify desirable changes in the intelligence services; Huston was to take what was desirable and make it feasible, through his position as the White House man charged with responsibility for domestic intelligence.

When the final report of the ad hoc committee was drafted, the CIA, the National Security Agency, and the Defense Intelligence Agency approved of its tough measures. Sullivan knew this would be bitter medicine for Hoover, so he added a sugar coating by recommending that Hoover be made director of all domestic intelligence-gathering operations. But Hoover balked. Wise in the ways of Washington, he told Sullivan that the ad hoc committee would go out of business once the report was submitted. If the report was approved by the president, the FBI would have "sole responsibility" for implementation in the domestic intelligence field. If the plan backfired, the FBI would be blamed. Much to Sullivan's disappointment, Hoover instructed that footnotes be added to the report embodying the FBI's specific objections.

The authors submitted the Huston plan to the president on June 26, 1970. At first it was greeted with silence. Undaunted, Huston prepared a memorandum for presidential assistant H. R. Haldeman—purportedly a "domestic intelligence review." Reflecting Sullivan's thinking, the document began with a lashing attack on Hoover, stating that the director's objections were "generally inconsistent and frivolous" and that the other agencies had recommended an end to all investigative restraints. Hoover was "bull-headed as hell," the memo said, and "getting old and worried about his legend." It was "imperative" to move ahead, and if necessary the president should have a "stroking session" with Hoover. "We can get what we want without putting Edgar's nose out of joint."

On July 14, Haldeman informed Huston that the president had approved the plan. When Hoover found out, according to Sullivan, he "went through the ceiling." He got Attorney General John Mitchell to agree with his position, and Mitchell took their objection to the president, who agreed to recall and rescind it. Sullivan got off the hook by blaming his brainchild on the heads of the other intelligence agencies—all the time privately berating me and others for not going to the mat with the director to lift the ban on wiretaps and surreptitious entries.

I had another confrontation with Sullivan when he proposed that the FBI open investigative files on every member of the radical Students for a Democratic Society. This was a ridiculous proposal. In the first place, only a few SDS members actually advocated or participated in violence, and there was no justification for investigating the others. In any event, manpower considerations would preclude opening thousands and thousands of new cases. Sullivan argued strenuously for this proposal. I recommended that the matter be discussed at the executive conference, and an angry Sullivan muttered to himself as his proposal won only two votes, a defeat approved by the director.

More controversies would erupt before Sullivan's days with the Bureau ended. He had already left his mark on the record of the stormy case involving Martin Luther King, Jr.

TEN

WATCHING
MARTIN LUTHER KING, JR.

P ROBABLY MORE misinformation—and disinformation—has surrounded the case of Dr. Martin Luther King, Jr. than any other FBI investigation. Rumor, gossip, conjecture, fact, and malice have been stirred together to put the Bureau in as bad a light as possible. Setting the record straight becomes a formidable task, but it is worth doing. The story of the King investigation demonstrates the stresses and strains connected with FBI operations and how Hoover managed these pressures.

In September 1957 the director issued a memorandum to all special agents in charge concerning the Southern Christian Leadership Conference (SCLC), which was headed by Dr. King:

> In the absence of any indication that the Communist Party has attempted, or is attempting, to infiltrate this organization, you should conduct no investigation in this matter. However...you should remain alert for public source information concerning it in connection with the racial situation.

In the years that followed, the FBI compiled information on a number of organizations—including several that espoused the cause of civil rights and/or opposed America's military involvement in Southeast Asia—which had become targets of communist infiltration efforts.

This was part of the Bureau's responsibility, as mandated by presidents and attorneys general since the 1930s. And there was no doubt in our minds, or in the minds of those who kept a close watch on communist activities, that the American Communist Party was attempting to capture positions of influence in the civil rights and antiwar movements.

On January 8, 1962, Hoover sent a report to Attorney General Robert Kennedy stating that influential members of the Communist Party were in fact attempting to infiltrate the SCLC and that a member of the Communist Party served among King's top advisers. Some months later, Hoover reported to the attorney general that one of King's staff members was "a member of the National Committee of the Communist Party." In its final report, dated April 23, 1976, the Senate Select Committee to Study Governmental Operations with Respect to Intelligence Activities set forth the above information and identified two alleged communists associated with King as "Adviser A" and "Adviser B."*

With the written approval of the attorney general, wiretaps were installed on both the office and home telephones of Adviser A [Levison]. Bobby Kennedy's concern over possible ties between King and the communists ran deeper than Hoover's. Both the attorney general and his brother, President John F. Kennedy, were closely tied in the public mind with Martin Luther King, Jr. and the civil rights movement. Bobby realized what political damage could result for

* Since this was written, the advisers have been publicly identified as Stanley Levison and Jack O'Dell. —Editor

the administration if it became known that King was working with communists. The attorney general needed to have the facts in order to bring pressure on King to sever any damaging ties. Therefore, directly and through his aides, he not only authorized but also pressed for an in-depth investigation, including telephone taps.

Both he and the White House, moreover, were anxious to know what King was up to. The Kennedy administration welcomed FBI reports about King's meetings with his advisers, details of his strategy, and the attitudes of civil rights leaders.

Or at least it did until King and Hoover began to feud. In the autumn of 1962, King picked up a false charge made by the Southern Regional Council—that the FBI was deliberately dragging its feet in civil rights cases—and compounded its falsity. "One of the great problems we face with the FBI in the South," King said in a *New York Times* interview, "is that the Agents are white Southerners who have been influenced by the mores of the community. To maintain their status, they have to be friendly with the local police and people who are promoting segregation."

This was patently untrue, as I know firsthand. The majority of agents working in southern offices were northerners. Furthermore, the Bureau's ranks were as open to qualified blacks—southern or northern—as they were to everyone else. The Bureau was actively trying to recruit agent applicants from minority groups to prevent just this sort of criticism. The number of black FBI agents remained small because blacks with the necessary qualifications chose better-paying or more prestigious jobs. Bobby Kennedy pressured Hoover to accept unqualified blacks, but the director stood firm. He was not going to lower his standards just to please the Kennedy administration.

Always sensitive to criticism of the Bureau, Hoover reacted strongly to King's charges. At his instruction, Deke DeLoach and the SAC in Atlanta called King to give him the facts. In both instances, a secretary took the message and promised that the reverend would return the call. He never did, which convinced FBI officials that King didn't want to hear the facts.

The Bureau's memorandums about Adviser A [Levison] and Adviser B [O'Dell] had left Bobby Kennedy badly shaken, and he had Assistant Attorney General Burke Marshall, who was in charge of the Civil Rights Division of the Justice Department, speak to King about the problem caused by his associations. King flatly refused to drop Adviser A [Levison], who was a close personal friend. But he did promise Marshall that he would cease contacts with Adviser B [O'Dell] because of his communist association.

King's promise to Marshall was intended to placate the young attorney general, but in June 1962, the Bureau intercepted a telephone conversation between King and Adviser A [Levison] in which they worked out a small deception. King would continue to use Adviser B [O'Dell] as an unofficial assistant, but without any formal connection with the Southern Christian Leadership Conference. "No matter what a man was," King said, "if he can stand up now and say he is not connected, then as far as I am concerned, he is eligible to work for me."

The Bureau subsequently sent a series of memorandums to Attorney General Kennedy, reporting the continued association between King and his suspect associates, including Adviser B [O'Dell]. On a memorandum from the Bureau dealing with a secret meeting of King, Adviser A [Levison], and Adviser B [O'Dell], Kennedy penned a notation to Marshall: "Burke—this is not getting any better." Once more Marshall was dispatched to Atlanta to urge King to break off the worrisome relationship. It had little effect, and in June 1963, Hoover directed a memorandum to top officials in the FBI in which he detailed a conversation with Robert Kennedy:

The Attorney General called and advised he would like to have Assistant Attorney General Burke Marshall talk to Martin Luther

King and tell Dr. King he has got to get rid of [Levison and O'Dell], that he should not have any contact with them, directly or indirectly.

I pointed out that if Dr. King continues this association, he is going to hurt his own cause as there are more and more Communists trying to take advantage of the movement and bigots down South who are against integration are beginning to charge Dr. King is tied in with the Communists.

Marshall talked to King once more and summed up the conversation in a memorandum to Hoover.

I brought the matter to the attention of Dr. King very explicitly in my office on the morning of June 22 prior to a scheduled meeting which Dr. King had with the President. This was done at the direction of the Attorney General, and the President separately. [I] strongly urged Dr. King that there should be no further connection between [O'Dell] and the Southern Christian Leadership Conference. Dr. King stated that the connection would be ended.

Apparently as a result of these conversations, the civil rights leader wrote a letter to Adviser B [O'Dell] stating that he had been cleared by the FBI but had to resign from the SCLC because "the situation in the country is such . . . that any allusion to the left brings forth an emotional response which would seem to indicate that SCLC and the Southern Freedom Movement are Communist inspired." This allowed the attorney general to respond to queries from congressional leaders about King's contacts with the formulation that there had been attempts to infiltrate the civil rights movement but King resisted them.

Attorney General Kennedy, however, was not fully satisfied that King had severed his connections with Adviser B [O'Dell]. At one point he suggested that the FBI subject King to "technical surveillance," meaning wiretaps or microphones. Hoover agreed but insisted that the request be made in writing. Kennedy pulled back from this.

There was continuing debate inside the Justice Department over the King problem. Courtney Evans, the liaison between the attorney general and the FBI, wrote that although the Civil Rights Division was not concerned, "Andrew Oehmann, the Attorney General's Executive Assistant, has counseled him [the attorney general] that in his judgment there is ample evidence there is a continuing relationship with [O'Dell] which Martin Luther King is trying to conceal."

Again Kennedy brought up the subject of electronic surveillance. Hoover warned of the political consequences if such coverage became known and questioned its feasibility, since King moved about the country. Telephone taps of King's home and office required authorization by the attorney general, and Kennedy signed the order in October 1963.

But the measures went beyond telephone taps. Beginning three months later, microphones were placed in various hotel and motel rooms occupied by King. The issue of who authorized the microphones and who knew about them still generates controversy. I cannot produce hard evidence that Attorney General Kennedy knew of these microphones, but I am convinced that he did. Both Nicholas Katzenbach, Robert Kennedy's successor as attorney general, and President Lyndon Johnson knew of them, as FBI records clearly show. Some of the last of the microphones were authorized by William C. Sullivan without prior consultation with Hoover or any other superior. On the memorandum written by Sullivan noting installation of these microphones, Associate Director Clyde Tolson noted, "Remove this surveillance at once," and Hoover wrote, "Yes." A further note by Tolson said, "No one here approved this. I have told Sullivan again not to institute a mike surveillance without the Director's approval." Hoover noted, "Right!"

The microphone surveillance and telephone taps on King and the SCLC demonstrated conclusively that the civil rights leader maintained his contacts with communists, contrary to his promises, and attempted to keep this knowledge from the attorney general. And when the puritanical director read the transcripts of the tapes disclosing what went on behind Dr. King's closed hotel room doors, he was outraged by the drunken sexual orgies, including acts of perversion involving several persons. Hoover referred to these episodes with repugnance as "those sexual things."

The tapes recorded a running account of King's extramarital sex affairs. On his journeys about the country to promote civil rights, he received numerous women in his hotel rooms, and it was all there to be heard, right down to his cries in the throes of passion. Many male visitors joined in.

I am not passing judgment on King's morals, and some may actually envy his sexual exploits. The point is that it was his personal conduct, more than the attacks on the Bureau and his association with communists, that inflamed Hoover. The director embarked on a campaign to discredit Martin Luther King, Jr., whom he regarded as a hypocrite unfit to lead the civil rights movement. Hoover was a straitlaced man and did not tolerate even the appearance of alcoholic or sexual irregularities among Bureau personnel. He was incensed that a man preaching morality to the nation should comport himself as King did.

These three factors—King's continued involvement with communists despite his promises to Attorney General Kennedy, his unfounded attacks on the Bureau, and his marathon adulteries—led to what the media seized on as a "feud" between King and the FBI. Various reporters alleged that Hoover had offered to play the King tapes for them, but when Attorney General Katzenbach, who succeeded Kennedy in 1964, asked the reporters to confront Hoover with these allegations, the reporters declined, preferring not to challenge the old lion while he was still alive.

As the conflict between Hoover and King heated up, some civil rights leaders called for an open confrontation. But as one of King's legal counselors warned with astonishing frankness, this could be the "beginning of an Alger Hiss–type dilemma." The director brought the matter to a head at a meeting with a group of women reporters. In response to a question, Hoover cited some of King's accusations, demolished them, and said for the record that the civil rights leader was "one of the most notorious liars in the country" and "one of the lowest characters."

In the uproar that followed, King suggested that Hoover was "faltering." In a telegram, he said that he was "appalled and surprised at your reported statement maligning my integrity. What motivated such an irresponsible accusation is a mystery to me." He suggested a meeting with Hoover but added that he had "sought in vain" for a record of any attempt by the Bureau to arrange a meeting—an assertion that could have been true only if his associates had deceived him.

They did meet, and there are several versions of the session. The account of Andrew Young, a King aide who went on to become ambassador to the United Nations, stresses the long lecture that Hoover delivered on the FBI's work. Deke DeLoach's notes highlight a conciliatory speech by King in which he lauded Hoover and the Bureau—"a love feast." I feel sure Hoover warned King, who never publicly attacked the Bureau again.

Irresponsible allegations later were made charging that the FBI participated in a conspiracy to assassinate the black leader. But no thinking American will place any credence in these charges. In fact, the FBI protected King from injury and possible death, even though it had no authority for protective intervention. When the FBI learned from informants of planned violence against civil rights demonstrators, it simply let the planners, as well as the local police, know that the FBI knew of their plans. That was generally enough to defuse tense situations. In 1977 a Justice Department task force appointed by Attorney General Griffin Bell said it "found no evidence of FBI complicity in the murder."

The task force criticized FBI actions to drive King out of the civil rights movement, most egregiously the composite tape sent anonymously to King in November 1964. The known and verifiable facts are that William C. Sullivan sent an FBI agent from Washington to Miami with a package to be mailed from there to King. Sullivan had prepared the package, according to his later testimony, and it contained a composite of the microphone surveillance tapes. Sullivan testified that the order to prepare the tape and send it to King came, indirectly, from Hoover and Tolson.

Included in the package with the tape was a letter that seemed to advocate King's suicide:

King, look into your heart, you are a colossal fraud and an evil vicious one at that. But you are done.

King, there is only one thing left for you to do. You know what it is. You have just 34 days to do this. There is but one way out for you. You better take it before your filthy fraudulent self is bared to the nation.

Sullivan denied knowledge of this letter, but in 1975, four years after he retired from the FBI, a copy of it was found in his private files, which had been sealed at his departure. Sullivan claimed the letter was a "plant." The only logical explanation, it seems to me, is that the project was Sullivan's brainchild and was carried out without the knowledge or authorization of the director. There is nothing to indicate that Hoover was aware of Sullivan's actions.

Brilliant and fragile: Mark's favorite
photo of Audrey, taken in the 1930s

Love in dramatic times: Mark with Audrey in
Ocean City, MD., shortly after their marriage
in 1938

Dreams of glamour: The newlyweds in their first Washington apartment

A taste for adventure: Mark, 17,
on a trip to California in 1930

Destination Washington: A quiet young man on the rise

What Depression? The law student showing off his Chevrolet coupe

A Hooverite from the start: Mark in his Seattle office in the late 1940s

"The power and strength of this man": Mark (left) with Hoover (third from left) at the "seat of government"

The right kind of publicity: Mark as a firearms instructor in Salt Lake City, late 1950s

Lone Ranger: Mark takes responsibility for the FBI's black bag jobs on national television, in 1976

Taking a stand: Mark greeting FBI supporters outside court during his 1979 trial

The importance of commitment: Mark and Audrey (seated) with Mark Jr. and his wife, Wanda, in 1984

"Your mother has committed suicide": Mark with Audrey, who shows bruises from her cosmetic eye surgery only days before her death in 1984

Rebel on the farm: Joan with her four-month-old son, Kohoutek (now Will), in the converted chicken coop where she lived, 1974

Generation gap: Joan as a young actor at Stanford in the 1960s

The pull of family: Mark with Joan (wearing a wig during chemotherapy treatment for breast cancer) at a 1986 convention of former FBI agents

The power of love: Posing for a 1994 portrait with Joan's children Will, then 20 (left), Robby, 15, and Nick, 13 (seated)

Setting standards: Grandson Mark III, a doctor, working on his residency in emergency medicine at Orlando Regional Medical Center

Eldercare: Mark with Joan and caregiver Bola outside their home in Santa Rosa, California, in 2005

"I'm not Deep Throat. I'm the guy they used to call Deep Throat": Mark Felt at age 91

ELEVEN

PURGING AN FBI RENEGADE

W ILLIAM C. SULLIVAN was a symptom of his times. Having risen as a favorite of Hoover's, he sought to boost his progress by playing on the paranoia and political obsessions of the Nixon administration. Whether Hoover and Tolson approved of Sullivan's actions or even knew about them is unknown. As head of the Domestic Intelligence Division, Sullivan had access to top officials of the Nixon administration and fed the growing White House fear of the New Left. Sullivan ingratiated himself with Henry Kissinger, Nixon's national security adviser; Alexander Haig, Kissinger's deputy; and Robert Mardian, an assistant attorney general who headed the Internal Security Division at the Justice Department and claimed to have direct contacts in the Oval Office. Sullivan stayed in constant touch with the CIA and other branches of the intelligence community.

In my opinion, Sullivan was responsible for the excesses in domestic intelligence gathering in the Nixon White House. When Sullivan appeared before the president's intelligence advisory board, his comments on FBI operations tended to emphasize his personal frustrations at restrictions imposed by Hoover and his complaints about what he saw as Hoover's conservatism.

In spite of all this, Hoover held back and there was no open conflict until October 1970, when Sullivan addressed a group of newspaper officials at a meeting in Williamsburg, Virginia. During the question-and-answer period, Sullivan was asked to comment on the current threat of the Communist Party USA and possible communist connections with the New Left. Sullivan told the newspeople that the old, Soviet-style Communist Party had been greatly contained through the years and did not pose a serious current threat.

Sullivan's answer made headlines across the nation. A high FBI official, the press reported, had minimized the communist threat. Hoover was furious. For years he had emphasized that the CPUSA was "an integral part of the international Communist conspiracy." Hoover contended that the CPUSA, however circumscribed by the FBI, was still giving secret aid and comfort to the New Left and its terrorist offshoots. Sullivan might have salvaged the situation by protesting that he had been quoted out of context, which was true, but he refused to give in. Having watched his machinations, I am convinced that he decided to make an open bid for power. Already one of his aides was saying that Sullivan would be the new director within a few months, enthroned by friends in the White House and the Justice Department.

Skirmishing between the two men began in earnest. In the investigation of Daniel Ellsberg, accused of leaking secret Pentagon papers to the press, agents submitted a memorandum requesting Hoover's authority to interview Louis Marx, a toy manufacturer and friend of the director's—and the father of Barbara Ellsberg, Daniel's wife. In one of his blue-ink notations, Hoover wrote "No. H." The memorandum was routed to Assistant Director Charles Brennan, a member of the Sullivan faction, who later claimed that he misread the notation and thought it said "OK. H." In fact, however, the interview was conducted before Hoover's permission was sought.

When Hoover discovered this, he was livid. This was deliberate insubordination, and knowing that Brennan was Sullivan's right-hand man made him doubly angry. He ordered Brennan demoted to SAC in Cleveland. Two days later, the director received a telephone call from Attorney General John Mitchell indicating White House displeasure and asking Hoover to cancel the transfer. Whether it was a request or an order, Hoover decided to go along with it. Those of us in the Bureau could see that Sullivan had used his White House contacts to force Hoover to capitulate. Newspaper pieces by colum-nists Robert Novak and Rowland Evans, among others, attacked Hoover and stated that he was too old to control the FBI.

Differences between Sullivan and Hoover became a fact of life for us in the Bureau. In the spring of 1971, President Nixon person-ally asked Hoover to expand FBI liaison coverage in foreign coun-tries. Hoover did not agree, but he pushed the change through the Bureau leadership to accommodate Nixon. Sullivan went along at first but suddenly reversed himself and came out in strong opposi-tion, perhaps to please his friends in the CIA, who resented what they considered FBI incursions into their jurisdiction. His memoran-dums grew bitter and insubordinate. And when the policy went through nonetheless, the FBI again came under attack from Evans and Novak for trying to force its way into a field that was the respon-sibility of the Central Intelligence Agency. The arguments and the language were exactly what Sullivan had used inside the Bureau.

Sullivan had to go.

Hoover made his move in true bureaucratic fashion. He realigned channels of authority so that Sullivan was shifted to a lower rung on the ladder. I learned of this when Hoover called me into his office on July 1, 1971.

Not wasting time on amenities, Hoover informed me of his plan. "Felt," he said, "I am creating a new position in the chain of com-mand. I am calling it deputy associate director, and it will be the number three position in the Bureau. You are the one I have selected for this assignment."

This surprised me and I thanked him. I did my job in a way that was meant to please the director, but it never occurred to me that high responsibility was so close.

"Felt," he continued, "I need someone who can control Sullivan. I think you know he has been getting out of hand. You have been the only one to curb him."

"Yes, sir," I replied. "He and I have been bumping heads frequently. I know what the problem is."

"Watch everything that comes out of the Domestic Intelligence Division very closely," Hoover warned. "I want to slow them down. They are going too far."

"Mr. Hoover, I'll do my best. I understand the problem and I know what to do about it."

Hoover waved his hand, and the interview was terminated. "Keep me informed," he added, "and let me know what the problems are."

I left Hoover's office and set about the task of restoring order and morale to the Domestic Intelligence Division and putting the reins on Sullivan. He did not fail to recognize the point of my promotion. My first directive was to soften the rhetoric of the intelligence letters that his division sent to the White House and intelligence agencies.

On August 28, 1971, two months after I was appointed over him, Sullivan wrote a letter to Hoover airing his resentment and frustration. In doing so, he inadvertently provided Hoover with sufficient cause for requesting his retirement. Hoover called me in to read Sullivan's letter and I was shocked by the vicious tone and rambling text. Sullivan typed the letter himself and submitted it replete with mistakes and smudges. Hoover called me again later the same day. "I showed the letter to the Attorney General. He told me I had no choice but to get rid of Sullivan and that's what I'm going to do."

On September 3, 1971, Hoover wrote a formal letter to Sullivan: "Submit your application for retirement after taking the annual leave to which you are entitled." He then appointed Alex Rosen, the assistant director in charge of the General Investigative Division, to succeed Sullivan in the top intelligence job. Sullivan did not respond but he did take his annual leave, and we waited for the next development.

As that drama unfolded, I came up with a way to replace his ally Brennan as assistant director for Domestic Intelligence. The White House wanted Brennan on the Ellsberg case, and I suggested to Hoover, why not reassign him to that case permanently? Hoover thought it over and agreed. He also went along with my recommendation to replace Brennan with Edward S. Miller, then serving as inspector and number one man in the Inspection Division. Miller had served under me in the same capacity and I could vouch for his competence.

Sullivan did not go quietly. Several days before he left on annual leave, I learned of files in his possession relating to wiretaps that the FBI had conducted for the White House. These secret files had never been indexed, and only Sullivan and a few of his confidants knew all their details.

These wiretaps later became known as the "Kissinger wiretaps," but the atmosphere of denials and finger pointing made it impossible to fix responsibility inside the White House. At the time, Henry Kissinger was director of the National Security Council and the wiretaps were placed on members of his staff suspected of leaking information and on members of the press suspected of receiving it.

When I learned about these sensitive files, I sought a conference with Hoover, and he told me to get the files from Sullivan and keep them in my office. But the files were nowhere to be found. I asked Miller, working with a trusted aide, Thomas J. Smith, to search all the file cabinets in Sullivan's office and all other logical places they could think of. They had no success. As a safety precaution, I ordered the lock combinations on these cabinets changed, which led to newspaper accounts that Sullivan found himself locked out of his office when he returned from annual leave.

Miller and Smith searched the entire Domestic Intelligence Division and finally located six file cabinets chock-full of confidential FBI research material. These cabinets had been maintained in Brennan's office and all were marked "Sullivan—Personal." But none of these were wiretap files, and the material was returned to its place in the regular files.

When Sullivan returned from his annual leave during the last week of September, he found Rosen occupying his office. Yet he made no move to retire and on September 30, Hoover wrote another letter telling Sullivan that he was being relieved of all duties and placed on annual leave status pending his application for retirement. This time Sullivan gave up, and on October 6 he submitted his application for retirement.

When I confronted Sullivan about the missing files, he said he had given them to Brennan with instructions that they be delivered to Assistant Attorney General Robert Mardian. Brennan confirmed this story but denied knowing what was in the files. None of us believed him.

While this was going on, Sullivan was cleaning out his personal effects. He pointedly left one item: his autographed picture of J. Edgar Hoover. He seemed edgy and upset that we would not let him get into the locked file cabinets. We now know why: they contained the only copy of the so-called suicide letter to Martin Luther King, Jr.

Sullivan's last day was memorable. FBI officials were glad to see him go but worried about how he would attack the Bureau. I accused him of being a "Judas" and he challenged me to a fistfight. He was like a little banty rooster and I think he really would have fought me had I accepted his challenge, although I am half again his size.

Later in the day, after I briefed Hoover about these developments, he paused a long time before he slowly shook his head and said thoughtfully, "The greatest mistake I ever made was to promote Sullivan." Then he turned and looked out the window at Pennsylvania Avenue. I left him alone with his thoughts.

I stayed on the case of the missing wiretap files. My investigative team learned that the taps were installed at Kissinger's request. He denied it was his idea, but the record shows that he called Hoover three times from Key Biscayne, Florida, on May 9, 1969, and the first tap was placed on Morton H. Halperin, one of Kissinger's principal aides on the National Security Council, who was suspected of leaking information to the *New York Times.*

Subsequently taps were placed on Helmut Sonnenfeldt, Daniel I. Davidson, Richard M. Moose, Anthony Lake, and Winston Lord, all of whom worked for Kissinger on the National Security Council. When these taps did not disclose the source of the leak, coverage was extended to John P. Sears, deputy counsel to the president; Col. Robert Pursley, aide to Melvin Laird, secretary of defense; William H. Sullivan, deputy assistant secretary of state for Asian affairs; Richard F. Pederson of the State Department; William Safire, a presidential speechwriter; and James W. McLane, executive assistant to Robert H. Finch, secretary of Health, Education, and Welfare. The taps also covered newsmen—Henry Brandon of the *London Sunday Times;* William Beecher and Hedrick L. Smith, both of the *New York Times;* and Marvin Kalb, a correspondent for CBS. Agents recalled that Sullivan had arranged for French authorities to place a wiretap on syndicated columnist Joseph Kraft, who was writing and broadcasting from Paris at the time.

The last request for a national security tap was made on December 14, 1970, and all coverage was discontinued around the end of May or the first part of June 1971. Because Sullivan personally maintained the wiretap files, they were never indexed in the general files or the electronic surveillance index. Sullivan kept them until his losing confrontation with Hoover. Seeking to ingratiate himself with

Mardian and the White House, he told Mardian about the wiretap files and suggested that Hoover would use them to blackmail President Nixon. Mardian reacted as expected and notified the White House. The files eventually ended up with White House aide John Ehrlichman.

Shortly after Sullivan retired, an Evans and Novak column dated October 11, 1971, reported the event. The column referred to restrictions that Hoover imposed on Domestic Intelligence, to the detriment of counterintelligence work. Subsequent columns were equally critical of Hoover and later of Acting Director L. Patrick Gray. FBI insiders were convinced that the information in the columns was supplied by Sullivan.

Such tactics kept his name in play. During the summer of 1972, Sullivan received a telephone call from Attorney General Richard Kleindienst, offering to make him director of the newly established Office of National Narcotics Intelligence in the Justice Department. The new office would serve as a computer clearinghouse for intelligence information gathered by government agencies. Sullivan accepted, and by August 1972, less than a year after his departure from Washington, he was back in a prestigious position. Mardian confided to Edward Miller that Sullivan had been given the high-paying job to keep him from writing a book about what he knew.

Sullivan offered advice to Gray on several occasions but received a cold shoulder. When Gray's candidacy for permanent appointment as director of the FBI appeared to be foundering, Sullivan renewed his efforts to take over the FBI Directorship. He inundated Robert Mardian with letters about the FBI, commenting on its budget, its management, and many other topics. Mardian, who had moved over to the Committee to Reelect the President, encouraged the letters, hoping to keep Sullivan quiet until after the November presidential elections. Sullivan also wrote several letters to Attorney General Kleindienst about how he would change the Bureau.

The White House wanted to keep Sullivan quiet about Nixon administration abuses; it also wanted to find out from him how previous administrations had misused the FBI. Both Nixon and John Dean, his chief counsel, saw this as a possible escape hatch from Watergate. If Nixon could prove that other presidents had abused the FBI, this might deflect criticism of him.

In February 1973, Nixon discussed this possibility with Dean. "Hoover was my crony," the president added. "He was closer to me than Johnson, actually, although Johnson used him more. . . . I think we would have been a lot better off during this whole Watergate thing if he had been alive. Because he knew how to handle the Bureau. He would have scared them to death."

Nixon and Dean explored allegations about Johnson's tactics during Nixon's first victorious presidential campaign. "We were bugged in '68 on the [campaign] plane," Nixon said. "God damnedest thing you ever saw." Actually, Deke DeLoach told John Mitchell, Nixon's plane had not been bugged, but the FBI had traced toll call records from telephones near the Agnew plane when it was parked on the ramp at Albuquerque in 1968.

In his conversation with Nixon, Dean mentioned that Sullivan was disgruntled and "has a world of information."

"You think Sullivan is basically reliable?" Nixon asked. "Why would he want to play ball?"

Dean explained that Sullivan badly wanted to get back into the FBI.

"That's easy," Nixon replied.

"He might tell everything he knows," Dean said. "He's a bomb!"

Dean called Sullivan to the White House and asked him point-blank to prepare a memorandum listing examples of political use of the FBI by previous presidents. Sullivan, still ambitious to become FBI director, saw this as a chance to further ingratiate himself with the president.

He prepared two memorandums, which Dean later turned over to the Senate Watergate Committee. In the first, he offered "to testify in behalf of the Administration." The facts, he said, "would put the current Administration in a very favorable light." The second memorandum detailed instances of questionable use of the FBI by previous presidents. Both documents were typed personally by Sullivan in his familiar rough style.

The second memorandum read in part:

> To my memory, the two Administrations which used the FBI the most for political purposes were Mr. Roosevelt's and Mr. Johnson's. Complete and willing cooperation was given to both. For example, Mr. Roosevelt requested us to look into the backgrounds of those who opposed his Lend-Lease Bill. . . . Mrs. Roosevelt would also make some unusual requests. The contrary was also true in that the Roosevelts would indicate to the FBI they were not interested in the FBI pushing certain investigations too far if the subjects were ones the Roosevelts did not want derogatory information on.

Among other cases, Sullivan said, Roosevelt was not interested in pursuing allegations that Sumner Welles, the undersecretary of state, had made homosexual advances to a porter on a railroad train.

Johnson had his own uses for the Bureau, Sullivan said. He "would ask the FBI for derogatory information . . . on Senators in his own Democratic Party who were opposing him, which he would leak to Everett M. Dirksen, the Republican Leader of the Senate, who would use it with telling effect against President Johnson's opponents."

Sullivan also disclosed Johnson's use of a special FBI squad at the 1964 Democratic Convention in Atlantic City. The squad bugged Martin Luther King, Jr.'s hotel room, tapped the storefront office used by black groups, and set up a network of informants to infiltrate various factions at the convention. These sources supplied a steady stream of information to President Johnson.

Sullivan cited the case of Walter Jenkins, the Johnson aide who was arrested on a morals charge in a YMCA men's room, as well as the alleged bugging of Agnew's campaign plane (which he knew to be untrue), the wiretapping of the South Vietnamese embassy, and the surveillance of Anna Chennault. Johnson thought she was a contact between Republicans and the South Vietnamese, and that she tried to delay peace negotiations until after the 1968 elections, thus giving a political advantage to Nixon.

Much of Sullivan's memorandum was sheer fiction, and he was unable to document any of his charges. It was therefore of no value to Nixon, and when John Dean later turned it over to the Senate Watergate Committee, it was set aside as a basis for inquiry.

Sullivan's shotgun blasts at the Bureau prompted allegations and attacks on the Bureau in the media, in various anti-FBI books, and in the reports of the Senate Intelligence Committee. Thus Sullivan had the revenge he sought, but at a heavy cost to the internal security of the United States and the future effectiveness of the FBI.

TWELVE

WHITE HOUSE HARDBALL

S ULLIVAN'S DEPARTURE eased my aggravation but not my workload. In my job as the Bureau's new number three man I had to please both Tolson and Hoover. For many Americans, the FBI is a collection of Efrem Zimbalist, Jr. types, implacably tracking down lawbreakers in TV-thriller fashion. In actuality, the FBI hunts a full range of violators from ordinary criminals to organized crime figures to white-collar thieves. It provides fingerprint identification services, a science laboratory, a training division, and a computerized network on open crimes. In the Hoover era, the Bureau worked under tight supervision, a clear chain of command, and with a highly disciplined and motivated force of agents.

Most of the paperwork passed through my office, including memorandums on major cases and policy matters. I also reviewed important letters addressed to people outside the Bureau, appointment letters to new special agents, TV scripts, and hundreds of other papers. A heavy volume of material nonetheless went to Tolson, who in turn passed it on to the director. I found out the hard way that I should not initial any material going to Tolson or Hoover unless I could anticipate their questions, and they usually made very probing inquiries.

One of my responsibilities was to fully brief Tolson on any action taken by the director between 11:30 A.M. and their shared lunchtime, which always began at noon sharp. Hoover expected Tolson to be up to the minute on any actions taken and this was part of their mealtime discussion.

The new job also required Saturday duty. Hoover and Tolson rarely came to the office on Saturday or Sunday, but the director wanted to know what was going on. Crime never takes a day off. I had to be at the office no later than 11:00 A.M. on Saturday to review the accumulated material and decide which should be sent to the director and which could wait until Monday morning. Frequently I would add explanatory comments and recommendations. When I had completed my review, which took from two to three hours, I would put the documents in "the pouch"—an old, worn briefcase— and take it to Miss Gandy, who then handed it to Tom Moton, who drove it to the director's house. Hoover skimmed through the material on Saturday and studied it carefully on Sunday. Each Monday morning, the material came back from the director's office with notations and instructions.

For Tolson, I made all recommendations for promotions and transfers of top-level personnel. I worked six years as head of the Inspection Division, and most of the special agents in charge, the assistant special agents in charge, and those eligible for promotion to such positions had worked for me at one time or another. As Tolson gained confidence in me, he accepted my recommendations and actions without question. He was frequently ill, and on those days I acted for him.

Hoover never discussed Tolson's rapidly deteriorating health with me. Though he was still mentally sharp, he did not have the physical stamina to keep up day-to-day operations. He frequently was absent, and he had difficulty reading because of strokes in the retinas of his eyes. It was obvious to me that my promotion was more than a device to put pressure on Sullivan. Someone had to begin taking over Tolson's functions.

I took a desk in a cubby hole office in the spartan, overcrowded four-room suite occupied by Tolson and his staff of five. The long, high walls of the reception room were mostly bare except for a few small pictures. The faded gray carpeting was spotted with stains accumulated over the years and so worn in places that the backing showed. The offices reflected Tolson's frugality. He refused to have a new carpet installed, even though the tattered one had become eligible for replacement many years earlier.

The associate director looked tired and weak and older than his seventy-two years. His face, always thin, had become wrinkled and drawn. Burdened with the debilitating effects of strokes and other serious medical problems, and battered by the demands of the perfectionist Hoover, Tolson was a difficult man to work for. Getting along with him required tact, finesse, and patience. Knowledge of his physical problems helped me cope with him.

I felt sorry for this old man, who was ashamed to let anyone know how seriously disabled he was. A stroke left him crippled in one leg, but he could move about in the privacy of his office. However, he could not keep up with Hoover's brisk pace at lunch. Instead of the customary one or two steps to the rear, which was his mark of deference to the director, it became twelve or fifteen steps. Hoover confided to me one day that he purposely kept up the pace to force Tolson to exert himself, in the hope this would speed his rehabilitation—or at least keep him alive.

Tolson had once been a tough and capable administrator. Like Hoover, Tolson spent most of his adult life with the FBI. He came to Washington when he was eighteen years old and worked in the War Department while he went to night school at George Washington University, receiving a B.A. degree in 1925 and a law degree in 1927.

He became a special agent of the FBI on April 28, 1928, and held various important positions at FBI headquarters before being promoted to associate director, the number two job, in 1947, a role Hoover created to give Tolson more authority.

Tolson wielded this authority with an iron hand, functioning more as a buffer than an innovator. His all-consuming passion was to protect the director from mistakes, criticism, and the pressures of strong, dynamic officials at FBI headquarters who were pushing the interests of their respective divisions. Everything that went to Hoover passed through Tolson's office first, and his tendency to react negatively considerably reduced the pressure on the director. Tolson also enjoyed his role as Hoover's confidant. Hoover needed someone with whom he could discuss high-level personnel problems and other administrative issues.

Their offices were located on the fifth floor of the Justice Building at the corner of 9th Street and Pennsylvania Avenue. Hoover had a long suite of offices extending down the 9th Street side, but his private office was back-to-back with Tolson's, separated by a small vestibule that opened onto the corridor and the elevator lobby. Tolson's back entrance was only a few steps away from the back entrance to Hoover's private office. Both always arrived and left through these rear doors.

As I assumed Tolson's responsibilities, I was on tap from early in the morning until 10:30 at night—when Hoover was no longer accessible except for a major emergency. A hot line was installed that connected my home to the FBI switchboard. The extension to that phone in my bedroom had a red light that went on when I was called and remained on if the call was unanswered. To maintain constant contact when I was away from both home and office, I kept a page boy—a small radio receiver about the size of a cigarette pack that emitted a high-pitched signal when headquarters needed me. I would then call in from the nearest telephone.

The page boy could be a nuisance. I would rush to the phone only

to be asked some routine question. To make matters worse, calls purporting to be from the White House came from individuals who
wanted to feel important. Robert Mardian, an assistant attorney general, liked to give the impression that he practically lived in the Oval
Office. On rare occasions I had direct calls from President Nixon .

On Saturday, July 24, 1971, at 9:30 A.M., Hoover called me on the
hot line. "Felt," he said, "I just received a call from Egil Krogh at the
White House. The president is gravely concerned about a story that
appeared yesterday in the *New York Times.*" William Beecher had
written a story that set forth the U.S. backup position in the strategic
arms limitation talks.

"The president is furious," Hoover said.

"Mr. Hoover," I answered, "I don't blame the president for being
mad. That's like playing stud poker with your hole card exposed."

Hoover said the president had designated Krogh, the presidential
aide who headed the Plumbers unit, to handle the leak inquiry.
Krogh requested FBI polygraph machines and technicians to help
interrogate suspected leakers, and Hoover complied. He told me to
attend a White House meeting at 2:00 P.M. that day.

First I called the Saturday supervisor at the Bureau to have the
Times story read to me. It was headlined "U.S. Urges Soviet to Join in
Missiles Moratorium." In devastating detail, the article described the
American backup position in the strategic arms limitation talks—the
minimum the United States would settle for if its initial proposals
were rejected. Since the Soviets now knew our bottom line, U.S.
negotiators could achieve nothing more than minimal expectations.

I called Assistant Director Ivan Conrad, who headed the FBI lab.
Conrad was in charge of the polygraph equipment and trained the
agents who operated it. Conrad had been very disappointed when
Hoover had barred use of the polygraph more than seven years ear-
lier, responding to the demands of highly vocal civil libertarians.
Conrad had great confidence in the machine, as did many of us in

the FBI. Though it was less than 100 percent accurate, it helped weed out the innocent and allowed us to focus on those with doubtful readings as well as those who refused to take the test.

Conrad seemed more than a little upset when I told him the polygraph was back in fashion. "Mark," he said, "we just can't do it. Our equipment is covered with dust in the warehouse at Quantico. The agent operators haven't had any practice for seven years. This is a terrible mistake."

"Ivan," I told him, "we're going to do it anyway. Start getting the instruments back to Washington and lining up the best operators. We may have to do some tests as early as tomorrow. On Monday, we will have to be ready to go all-out. The boss said the president was very upset."

By the time I arrived at the White House, several machines had been dusted off and were on their way from Quantico. In addition, Conrad had arranged to borrow some machines from the New York City police department, which sent them to Washington in FBI cars.

I was the first to arrive for the White House meeting—or so I thought. A balding little man, dressed in work clothes and dirty tennis shoes, was shuffling about the room, arranging the chairs, and I took him to be a member of the cleaning staff. He turned out to be Robert Mardian, who had been reached on the tennis court with orders to attend the meeting.

Egil "Bud" Krogh chaired the meeting. Others attending were David R. Young of the White House staff, who seemed to be assisting Krogh; Gen. Alexander Haig, at that time Kissinger's chief deputy; E. Howard Hunt, a nondescript man who said practically nothing; and two representatives from the Defense Department's Office of Legal Counsel. It was the first time I had met any of them, although I had talked to Mardian on the phone.

Krogh explained the president's concern over the growing problem of leaked national defense information. An article by Beecher that appeared on May 9, 1971, reported the secret bombing of Cambodia and triggered student protests and the Kissinger wiretaps. On June 13, the *New York Times* had begun publishing the stolen Pentagon papers, which at the very least may have enabled other countries to break the U.S. diplomatic code.

According to Krogh, the principal suspect was a strategic weapons expert at the Defense Department on leave from a large university. He was known to have had recent contacts with Beecher. We were informed that the suspect's office would be searched that afternoon by Pentagon authorities, and in due course the FBI would give him a lie detector test. Mardian then argued forcefully for the use of wiretaps. I suggested that we should first obtain a court order under the provisions of the Omnibus Crime Control and Safe Streets Act of 1968. But Mardian brushed this aside, stating that the act applied narrowly to organized crime. He was wrong, but he would not listen to the facts.

Krogh told me that he would be in touch about the use of the polygraph. I have since learned that after the meeting adjourned, Krogh immediately reported to the president and John Ehrlichman that "we've got one person that comes out of the Department of Defense, according to Al Haig, who is the prime suspect right now. He had access to the document and apparently he has views very similar to those which were reflected in the Beecher article. And it would be my feeling that we should begin with him and those immediately around him before going to a dragnet polygraph."

"Polygraph him!" the president ordered. "I want that to be done now with about four or five hundred people in State, Defense, and so forth, so that we can immediately scare the bastards."

The following Monday, I received a terse phone call from Krogh. "We have decided to let the Agency [CIA] handle the polygraph interviews," he said, and apologized for causing the Bureau any difficulty. Obviously John Ehrlichman wanted to punish the Bureau for what he saw as reluctance to get involved in work that the Plumbers later undertook. Krogh seemed embarrassed, but he could not have known that the Bureau was relieved rather than angry at being brushed aside. I immediately called the director to tell him of the White House turnabout. He merely thanked me for calling. I'm sure he was relieved too.

There is a sour postscript to this. Krogh conducted a full-scale investigation to determine the source of the leak on arms talks. The suspect was given a polygraph examination by the CIA, but it was inconclusive. As ordered by the president, the investigation was broadened to include others at the Pentagon and the State Department. The CIA conducted the investigation and all polygraph tests with no conclusive results. I made some powerful enemies at the White House and the Justice Department for my "lack of cooperation."

On August 19, 1971, at 6:45 P.M., just as I was getting ready to go home, I received another phone call from the director. "Felt," he said, "I have just received a long-distance phone call from Lawrence Higby, who is with the president at San Clemente. He wants a full field investigation of Daniel Schorr. I don't know what position Schorr is being considered for, but the White House is in a hurry. Get the investigation started at once and set a short deadline."

Who's Who listed Schorr as a reporter and broadcaster for CBS News. He had a waspish temperament and was disliked by his colleagues at CBS and elsewhere in the media. The White House did not identify what government post he was presumably slated for, but that was not unusual. In fact, the Bureau preferred it that way; if there were leaks we could not be accused of them. I immediately called Lorenz H. Martin, chief of the Special Inquiry Section responsible for investigations of this nature, and briefed him on Hoover's order.

It was a tough assignment but could be completed in three days; however, a dangerous number of loose ends would be left. Martin ordered agents in the field to drop other investigations and concentrate on Schorr.

Agents investigating presidential appointments went directly to the candidate. Schorr helpfully furnished information on his past employment, past residences, close associates, references, names of relatives, and everything else he was asked about. He also expressed his pleasure at being considered for a high government position.

Among those at the top of the list of interviewees was Richard Salant, president of CBS News and Schorr's boss. Perturbed because Schorr seemed to be looking for other employment, Salant called the New York FBI office. He said that he had just talked to Schorr by telephone and quoted him as saying that he was not considering taking any position with the government, that he did not know anything about it, and that he did not want to be investigated by the FBI. This was relayed to the White House, where security chief Alexander Butterfield's office called back with instructions to drop the investigation.

When I learned of this turnabout I was shocked. Obviously someone had made a serious mistake. Could I have misunderstood Hoover when he ordered the full field investigation? I called him right away and said, "Mr. Hoover, possibly Higby was confused and only intended to ask for a file search on Schorr."

"No," the director told me. "Higby was very definite about it. He specifically asked for a full field investigation. Let him worry about it."

In fact, as we later learned, someone at the White House, angered by Schorr's broadcasting, hoped to find something derogatory about the newsman in order to silence him. Perhaps Higby did not know the difference between a file check and a full field investigation. Ron Ziegler, the White House press secretary, denied any attempt at intimidating Schorr and said the CBS broadcaster had been considered for an appointment in the "environmental area."

No one believed him. Schorr posed as a martyr, claiming that he was harassed by the FBI and that the few hours of interviews had an "impact" on his "relations with employers, neighbors, and friends." In the end, the Schorr fiasco got the newsman a lot of publicity—and demonstrated once again the inclination of Nixon's White House to use the FBI for its own political purposes.

THIRTEEN

A PRELUDE TO WATERGATE

T HE FBI lab was J. Edgar Hoover's pride and joy. Its technicians were—and are—skilled in scientific crime detection, and its equipment is probably the best in the country, if not the world. It serves not only the Bureau but police departments throughout the United States. Its goal is complete objectivity in the analysis of criminal means and methods, from forged documents to ballistics. But even the lab was pressured by the Nixon administration to become a political arm of the White House.

The pressure intensified when John Mitchell resigned as attorney general to direct President Nixon's reelection campaign. To replace Mitchell, Nixon nominated Richard Kleindienst, deputy attorney general, and then named Pat Gray, assistant attorney general in charge of the Civil Division, to move into the Kleindienst slot. Confirmation hearings before the Senate Judiciary Committee began in February 1972, with Gray acting as unofficial counsel for the attorney general designate. The hearings included a serious allegation that the Justice Department had been improperly influenced in settling a major antitrust suit against International Telephone and Telegraph. Kleindienst denied any pressure or influence, and the hearings were closed.

A few days later, on February 19, columnist Jack Anderson exploded a bombshell. He published the text of a memorandum purportedly written on June 25, 1971, by Dita Beard, an ITT lobbyist, to one of the company's vice presidents, W. R. Merriam. The memorandum baldly implied that there had been a payoff in the antitrust settlement. If Dita Beard was to be believed (the more cynical members of the Washington press corps saw the memo as a self-aggrandizing effort), Attorney General Mitchell had told her that the suit would be settled favorably in return for a $400,000 cash contribution and services to the Republican National Convention. The convention was scheduled to be held in San Diego, where the company's Sheraton subsidiary owned a hotel. The next day, Anderson charged that Kleindienst had lied when he testified about the ITT case.

Dita Beard was one of Capitol Hill's more flamboyant characters—hard drinking, hard swearing, and not above giving her employers an exaggerated sense of her importance and effectiveness. But her memorandum raised legitimate questions about the probity of the Nixon Justice Department, the White House, and Richard Kleindienst. And it could be damaging to the president's reelection campaign.

The FBI first became involved when Robert Mardian called me. I had met him earlier at the White House meeting regarding national security leaks and already had formed a vaguely unfavorable impression of him. He called from the office of Senator James O. Eastland, chairman of the Judiciary Committee, and told me that the committee had issued a subpoena ordering Beard to appear but she had vanished. Senator Eastland had requested that the FBI locate her and serve the subpoena.

I did not like the assignment, which smelled of politics. But Hoover cleared Eastland's request, and FBI agents located Beard at the Rocky Mountain Osteopathic Hospital in Denver, where she was being treated for a heart ailment. Beard's doctor permitted the subpoena to be served but said that she was not well enough to travel to Washington. Consequently committee members traveled to Colorado and interviewed her inconclusively.

That did not end the matter, however. On March 10, I received an urgent telephone call from Pat Gray. He explained that he had to see me about a very important matter and appeared in my office a few minutes later. Almost six feet tall, with closely cropped hair and weatherbeaten face, he looked like the submarine commander he had been during World War II. He took no time getting to the point and gave me a brief rundown on the new uproar. Then he handed me a large manila envelope and said, "The original Dita Beard memorandum is inside. The Judiciary Committee got it from Jack Anderson, and we need to know whether it is authentic. I would like the FBI lab to identify the typing, check the paper for watermarks, and determine if there have been any erasures."

"We can do that," I assured him.

"We don't want the memorandum altered in any way," he ordered.

"All right," I answered, "but that may limit what tests we can do."

"I understand that, but we must not alter the document in any way," he insisted.

I agreed, got clearance from the director, and sent the document to the lab by special messenger. Less than an hour later, Gray's office called and demanded that the memorandum be returned immediately. A startled Ivan Conrad retrieved the memorandum and sent it back to Gray. Conrad called later to tell me that technicians had photographed the memorandum, which would allow them to identify the probable make and model of the typewriter used. On March 11, we informed Gray of that.

Four days later, Gray was on the phone again to tell me that he was returning the Beard memorandum together with six pages of typewritten notes made by Brit Hume, an investigative reporter for Jack Anderson who had interviewed Beard. Gray wanted the lab to examine the memorandum and the notes without altering them in any way.

"Mr. Gray," I said, "I am sure you realize that what we can do is very limited without access to the typewriters in question and without known typing specimens for comparison."

"I know, I know," Gray answered, "but that's the best I can provide. Tell them to do what they can."

Again the documents were turned over to the lab—and again Gray's office called asking for the urgent return of the memorandum. This back-and-forth troubled me but I relayed the message to Conrad, who expressed annoyance.

"Look, Mark," he said. "With such limited access to the memo and no material for comparison purposes, there is nothing we can do except to say that the Beard memo and the Hume notes were not typed on the same machine."

The next day, Gray called me yet again. He was sending me copies of Beard's initials because she had denied that the initials on the memorandum were hers. Exasperated, I told Gray, "You are asking us to compare copies with copies, but this will make any positive conclusion impossible."

"Please check them anyway," he insisted.

Conrad duly called to say that the lab could arrive at no positive conclusions, and I hoped this would end the game. But I was wrong. Twenty-four hours later, John Dean, the White House counsel, called me. He explained that private document examiners working for ITT had obtained three sets of documents typed on the same machine as the Beard memo, but at different periods between June 2, 1971, and February 18, 1972. According to Dean, ITT's experts concluded that the Beard memo had been typed in January 1972 instead of June 25, 1971, as it was dated, conclusively proving that the memo was a forgery. He wanted the ITT findings confirmed and said he would have the original memorandum delivered to me from the Senate Judiciary Committee and the typing specimens from the Washington ITT office. But he would not permit chemical analysis to test paper, ink, and so on. As before, Conrad did the best he could.

On March 17, Beard issued a statement that was released simultaneously by her attorney and Senate Republican leader Hugh Scott. It read, in part, "I did not prepare it [the memo] and could not have.... I have done nothing to be ashamed of and my family and I—and in a sense, the whole American Government—are the victims of a cruel fraud." Against this there would be Jack Anderson's testimony that Brit Hume, his assistant, had gone over the memo line by line with Beard before he published it and she confirmed its authenticity.*

At 9:00 A.M. on Saturday, March 18, I called John Dean to advise him that the FBI findings raised the strong presumption—though no positive conclusion—that the Beard memo was typed at or about the time it was dated. Dean sounded annoyed and argued that in the absence of a positive conclusion, the FBI lab report should be modified to avoid conflicting with the ITT analysis. I told Dean it was completely out of the question. When he realized that I would not "budge," as he put it, he asked that I check with Hoover.

"Tell him the request comes from the White House," he stressed. When I told Hoover of my conversation, he exploded. "Call Dean right back and tell him to go jump in the lake. I cooperate when I can, but this request is completely improper."

---

* A bizarre sidelight: The White House sent E. Howard Hunt, later of Plumbers and Watergate fame, to interview Beard in Denver. Beard's son, Robert, told newsmen, "The man refused to identify himself. He seemed to have inside information about what would happen next." The visitor was "very eerie, he did have a red wig on cockeyed like he put it on in a dark car. I couldn't have identified my brother if he was dressed like that." Hunt's visit was subsequently verified. The red wig had been borrowed from the CIA. —Editor

When I informed Dean that the director had firmly refused, he was angered by our refusal to "cooperate." But the White House did not give up. At 1:30 P.M. on the same day, Mardian called me—from the White House, he said—to notify me that he had just dictated a memorandum directing the FBI to conduct whatever investigations and examinations were necessary to determine the authenticity, or lack of it, of the Beard memorandum. He said Senator Eastland had insisted on this. Mardian's memorandum set a 10:00 A.M. Monday deadline for our report. Agents were immediately sent to the ITT office, where they took typing specimens from the typewriter used by Beard's secretary and obtained other memorandums typed on that machine on or near the date of the original document.

Pat Gray got the lab's report well before the deadline. Though the findings were not categorical, they made a strong case that the original Beard memorandum was prepared on or about June 25 and that it was authentic. The known specimens and the original memo were returned to Dean by courier at his urgent request. The following day, Gray personally returned the lab report to me, advising me that Senator Eastland wanted the substance of the memorandum incorporated in a letter to him.

At 7:30 P.M. that day, John Dean called me. "Has the final lab report gone to Senator Eastland yet?" he asked.

"No," I said. "But it is on the director's desk for his signature."

"I must talk to the director before it is delivered," Dean said with urgency.

"John, I'm sure he'll talk to you, but be sure to call as soon as possible after 9:00 A.M."

Shortly after nine o'clock the next day, Hoover had me on the intercom. "Felt, the White House wants some document examiners hired by ITT to look at the original memorandum and talk to our examiners before we send the final report to Senator Eastland. The memorandum actually belongs to ITT, so I saw no objection and I told Dean it would be all right. Tell the laboratory."

I immediately made arrangements with Ivan Conrad and let John Dean know where the examiners should report. The ITT experts did not arrive until 5:30 P.M. The group consisted of Martin Tytell, a typewriter expert from New York; his wife, Pearl, a specialist in document examination; Walter McCrone, a spectrogram expert from Chicago; and a lawyer representing ITT. They were trying to prove that the original Beard memorandum had been written in January 1972 and was therefore a forgery. But their arguments were unconvincing, and the FBI experts stuck firmly to their opinion that the memorandum was written on or about the date it bore and was probably authentic. The ITT people then asked for permission to cut certain letters from the memo, which McCrone would take to Chicago for testing in his laboratory. When Ivan Conrad refused, the ITT lawyer asked to use a private phone and called the White House. Within fifteen minutes, Conrad received a call from Hoover directing him to comply with the ITT request to mutilate the document. Later Hoover told me that he had given his permission after receiving a call from John Ehrlichman, who argued that ITT was entitled to do what it wished to the document since it was the company's property. Hoover had yielded to this White House pressure.

Still stalling, the ITT experts did not return to the FBI Lab until 1:45 the following afternoon, March 23. They cut the fifteen letters from the Beard memo and departed. At 3:45 P.M. the formal FBI lab report was delivered to Senator Eastland. At 7:00 P.M. Dean called me.

"Has the formal report been delivered to Senator Eastland?" he asked. I told him that it had been delivered that afternoon.

There was a long pause, and then Dean asked, "Did you change it or was it in its original form?"

"It was in its original form."

Another long pause. "I see," Dean said curtly and hung up without another word. He was furious that I did not bow to White House pressure to change the report.

Ten minutes later, Mardian called to say that Senator Eastland was complaining about a leak: Senator Edward M. Kennedy had called him to see the report before it reached the Senate.

At 10:45 on the following day, Dean appeared at my office. He said that Walter McCrone, working in his Chicago laboratory, had prepared a spectrographic report on the memorandum. "He is convinced the Beard memo is a forgery," Dean said. "I want him to talk with your lab people."

I wondered why McCrone had called the White House instead of the Bureau, but all I said was, "Oh? Okay, John. I don't believe our lab men have much confidence in McCrone—not after what he told them before. But I'll ask the director. I'm sure he'll approve."

"I'd appreciate that," Dean answered. "You can reach me in the attorney general's office during the next hour. After that, I'll be back in my office."

"Where's McCrone?" I asked.

"He's here in Washington. We'll make him available on short notice." The White House was still in the act.

"That's fine," I said. "I'll call within the hour. I'm sure we can arrange the meeting for today."

"We will appreciate that," Dean said huffily, and with no further comment he left my office.

When I explained the situation to the director, he remarked, "They are persistent, aren't they? Go ahead and set up a meeting between Conrad and McCrone. Let me know promptly what the results are."

"Okay," I answered. "I don't know what McCrone has to present but I doubt very much our lab is going to change its position." I knew how meticulously Conrad worked. He was not given to snap judgments.

The director laughed and said, "No. I don't think so either."

At 1:00 P.M., McCrone was at the lab. After the meeting, Conrad called to say that McCrone had nothing new to offer and was rather apologetic in his presentation. I sent a short note to the director giving him the facts and then I called Dean. He was not in his office so I left a message with his secretary describing the outcome of the meeting. Dean did not return my call.

The White House attempt to discredit the Dita Beard memo eventually helped bring about the undoing of Attorney General Kleindienst. He had testified that "I was not interfered with by anybody at the White House [to settle the ITT case]. I was not importuned. I was not pressured. I was not directed." The Beard memorandum, along with White House documents subsequently made available, contradicted him. On May 16, 1974, he pleaded guilty to a misdemeanor charge that he had not testified "accurately and fully" about the handling of the ITT antitrust settlement and admitted concealing his communication with President Nixon about not proceeding further against the company. Kleindienst was fined $100 and given a thirty-day suspended sentence.

I was sorry for Dick Kleindienst. But looking back, I am glad that the FBI resisted White House pressure to participate in a cover-up that in some ways was a prelude to Watergate.

FOURTEEN

"HOOVER IS DEAD"

T UESDAY, MAY 2, 1972, began like any other day. I was up at
5:45 A.M. and ate breakfast while scanning *Washington Post*
headlines so that I could answer Hoover's questions about the key
stories. By 6:45, I was on my way to the office, arriving there well
before the official workday began in order to review the overnight
teletypes and memorandums awaiting my action.

At 9:00 A.M., the day officially began. There were conferences,
phone calls, and discussions with other Bureau officials. For me, the
day would not end until 6:30 or 7:00 P.M., when the director left. It
was a Bureau tradition that the director was the first to leave; in any
case, we had a lot of work to keep us at our desks, often long into
the night.

Shortly before 9:00 A.M. the two administrative assistants, Tolson's and mine, and the two secretaries came in. Messengers arrived
with large bundles of Bureau communications. Dorothy Skillman,
Tolson's assistant, told me that he would not be coming in—no surprise, because his minor strokes often kept him away from his desk.
I filled in and made the necessary decisions, hoping that he would

not later disagree. At 9:45 A.M., John P. Mohr, the assistant to the director in charge of administrative operations, walked into my office. I was surprised because usually he communicated on the intercom.

"He is dead," John said, enunciating each word carefully. I thought he was talking about Tolson.

"Did he have another stroke?" I asked.

"Hoover is dead," Mohr said. He watched as my expression changed to disbelief and then shock.

Tolson's death would not have surprised me, but I could not grasp the reality of Hoover's death. Just yesterday he had been his usual energetic self. It seemed impossible. Of course a seventy-seven-year-old man can go at any time, but I never thought Hoover could leave the scene so suddenly.

"He died sometime last night or early this morning. Annie, the housekeeper, found him," John said. Dr. Choisser said it was a heart attack.

"Miss Gandy called me shortly after nine and I went up to see her," John said. "I talked with Tolson at Hoover's house and he asked me to handle funeral arrangements and notify the attorney general. Tolson is taking this pretty hard."

"What was Kleindienst's reaction? What did he say?"

"Not much at first," John replied. "I told him that Tolson instructed Miss Gandy and me to handle the funeral arrangements, and I asked him if he wanted me to notify the White House. He said no. He wanted to call the president personally, and he was sure the White House would want to announce the death."

I was relieved to have someone else handling the funeral arrangements because the days ahead were going to be difficult. I said, "That's fine, John. Tolson won't be coming in, and whatever you and Miss Gandy decide will be okay with me."

John turned to leave and said, "I'll fill you in on more details later, but I want to tell all the assistant directors before they hear the news by the grapevine."

I broke the news to my two agent assistants, my administrative assistant, and the two secretaries. They were dumbfounded, and one started to cry. Dorothy Skillman was on the telephone hearing the news from Miss Gandy. She was worried about Tolson.

I said, "This is going to be very rough on your boss."

"I know," she replied. "I don't know how long he'll last without Mr. Hoover's support."

"Don't worry about it today," I said. "We'll have plenty of other things to keep us occupied for the next few days." As I turned to leave the office, her tears started to flow.

The White House did not formally announce Hoover's death until a few minutes before noon, but word spread throughout the FBI and the Justice Department before that. Wives and friends were called and, of course, there were leaks to the press. It didn't occur to me to call my wife, who called me at midmorning. She had just received the news from our stockbroker, who had read the story on the wire service tape. News photographers had gathered in front of the Hoover home.

Looking back at those first hours, it is hard to assess my exact sensations. I felt no personal loss because my relationship with Hoover had been restricted to the office. Hoover had once fraternized with some of his top officials, but during his later years Tolson was the only Bureau confidant who had a social relationship with the director.

Hoover turned to me in 1971 because Tolson's weakened physical condition left him unable to cope with many daily responsibilities. He knew I had no designs on his job because I had never given him any reason to think so. I am positive I had his complete confidence. He paid careful attention to my advice and recommendations on investigative as well as personnel matters. He enjoyed talking with me, sometimes at considerable length. I feel that he respected me as much as I respected him.

This is not to say he was an easy man to work for. He was tough and irascible. He was extremely bright and had an amazing memory for detail. Allegations of senility are baseless. I had to deal with him constantly and observed him recalling details of memorandums he had seen days before.

I couldn't fill his shoes. All I could do was keep the FBI as nearly intact as possible. I knew Tolson would retire, leaving it up to me as third in command to keep the FBI on course. I had to set the example—make sure there were no operational breakdowns and prevent morale from sagging.

It did not cross my mind that the president would appoint an outsider to replace Hoover. Had I known, I would not have been hopeful about the future. There were many trained executives in the FBI who could have effectively handled the job of director. My own record was good and I allowed myself to think I had an excellent chance.

As the day went on, I reconstructed the director's last hours. It was May Day, and it began routinely. Tom Moton, who chauffeured Hoover's bullet-proof Cadillac limousine, drove it into the courtyard at the Justice Department building at three minutes past nine in the morning, slightly behind schedule, and took his passenger to the special parking space in the basement immediately adjacent to the lobby of the elevator bank at the corner nearest 9th and Pennsylvania Avenue. These elevators were almost directly in back of the director's office on the fifth floor, and it was only a few steps from car to elevator in the parking area and a few more from the elevator lobby on the fifth floor to the private rear entrance of Hoover's office.

Hoover usually had his limousine pick up Clyde Tolson at his apartment and they would arrive together, Tolson a few steps to the rear as was his custom. On this day, Hoover was alone as he left the car and strode briskly to the elevator bank.

When Hoover left the limousine, which was parked a few steps from the elevator lobby, Moton always went to a special phone and called the director's office to alert everyone: "He's on the way up." This resulted in a flurry of activity, and if there were any relaxed employees in the office before the call, there were none after.

Nothing unusual happened that day. I saw Hoover and talked with him several times on the intercom. He was alert, forceful, typically aggressive—normal in every respect.

He left the office shortly before six o'clock and was driven to Tolson's apartment, where he had dinner. Later Moton drove him home, where they arrived at 10:15 P.M. Annie Fields, the housekeeper, did not hear him come in, which was not unusual because she spent evenings in her basement apartment.

Annie said Hoover customarily let his two Cairn terriers run in the backyard after coming home late, and there was no evidence on the newspapers spread near where they slept to indicate they had not relieved themselves outside as usual. The two dogs were very attached to Hoover. The older, G Boy, died a few weeks after his master's death; Cindy moped, refused to eat, and died a few months later.

The next morning, Annie had breakfast ready at 7:30 A.M. in accordance with Hoover's strict routine, but Hoover did not come downstairs. As the minutes passed with no sound of activity from the bedroom, she began to worry. At exactly 7:45 A.M. Moton arrived with the limousine, several minutes early as always. A few minutes later, Jimmy Crawford arrived. Crawford had been Hoover's chauffeur for many years, retiring in December 1971 after major surgery. Hoover hired him to take care of odd jobs around the house. This morning he had come to plant rose bushes Hoover had purchased from a West Coast nursery. Crawford arrived early because he knew the boss would want to mark exactly where each bush should be planted.

The three of them discussed the situation and decided that Annie should knock on the director's door. Getting no answer, she tried the door. As Annie slowly entered the bedroom, she saw the man she had served for so many years stretched on the floor near the bed. She raced downstairs to get Crawford. He picked up Hoover's hand, which was stiff and cold. He let the hand drop to the floor and then took a blanket from the bed to cover the body, certain that Hoover was dead. Crawford phoned Tolson and then sent Moton with the limousine to pick him up. Annie called Erma Metcalf, an employee in the director's office, and she in turn called the director's private physician, Robert Choisser, who pronounced Hoover dead when he arrived a short time later.

Shortly before eleven, John Mohr called Joseph Gawler's Funeral Home at Wisconsin Avenue and Harrison Street, N.W., which was close to Hoover's residence. Gawler's dispatched an unmarked car capable of transporting a stretcher bearing a corpse. To avoid photographers, the car approached the house from the back alley. The coroner's representatives waited for the White House to formally announce the death and then moved Hoover's remains out the back-door, across the yard, and through the garage to the waiting car. Gawler's car left the house at 12:30 P.M.

John Mohr and Helen Gandy had been considering a Masonic funeral, but at 2:05 P.M. the White House called to advise that the president had decided on a state funeral with full military honors. The body would lie in state in the Capitol Rotunda on May 3, and memorial services would take place on May 4. The military took over the ceremonial arrangements.

May 3, 1972, dawned gray and dismal, and the mist set a somber mood for the services in the Capitol Rotunda. The heavy casket was to be placed on the catafalque built for President Abraham Lincoln and occupied by only twenty-one American heroes and statesmen before Hoover. The hearse arrived in front of the Capitol promptly at 11:30 A.M. The eight military pallbearers lifted the casket out of the hearse. Preceded by Rev. Edward L. R. Elson, pastor of the National Presbyterian Church and chaplain of the United States Senate, they carried their burden up the long steps. Mohr confided to me later that he and Miss Gandy had selected a lead-lined coffin that weighed well over 1,000 pounds, not giving any thought to the problem of carrying the casket up the Capitol steps. It must have been an incredible strain for the young men, two of whom suffered ruptures as they struggled up the steps.

Services in the Rotunda were impressive. The members of the FBI executive conference served as honorary pallbearers, and many others from the Bureau also attended. Chief Justice Warren E. Burger, whom Hoover had regarded highly, eulogized the director as "a man of unyielding integrity [whose] standards of personal conduct pervaded the entire organization so that its incorruptibility matched its efficiency."

Thousands came to pay their final respects during the afternoon and evening. The closed casket led a few sensation-seeking writers to assume that Hoover died from foul play. However, Hoover's casket was open during visitation hours at Gawler's, and there was no indication of foul play.

After Mohr had returned to his desk that afternoon, a visitor walked in. It was L. Patrick Gray III. The assistant attorney general announced that Attorney General Richard Kleindienst had directed him to review the "secret" files.

Mohr patiently explained that the FBI had no secret files he knew of. After a few words about the man whose body lay in its casket on the catafalque in the Rotunda, Gray left, apparently satisfied.

The next morning, Gray returned to Mohr's office in an agitated state, demanding to know where the secret files were kept. Again

Mohr firmly assured Gray there were no secret files. The conversation grew heated and the language became less formal. Mohr said later, "I guess I did cuss at him a little."

At this point, Gray stood, thrust out his chin, and said, "Look, Mr. Mohr. I am a hardheaded Irishman and nobody pushes me around."

Mohr also rose to his feet and in a loud voice said, "Look, Mr. Gray, I am a hardheaded Dutchman and nobody pushes me around, either." Gray turned on his heels and left. Less than three hours later, Kleindienst appointed Gray acting FBI director. Within thirty minutes of Gray's appointment, I received a telephone call from Tolson.

He said, "I want you to arrange for my retirement effective today."

I asked, "Do you want to dictate the letter to Mrs. Skillman over the telephone?"

"No," he said, "I want you to write it. Make it short, nothing fancy. Have Mrs. Skillman sign my name to it."

"All right," I said. "I'll get it to Gray this afternoon and see that it is processed right away."

I wrote the letter and couched it in softer terms than Tolson would have. Since I had had considerable contact with Gray during the Kleindienst confirmation hearings, I didn't hesitate to call him directly. I told him what had happened and he was not surprised.

He said, "Write him a warm letter accepting his application for retirement. Commend him for his many fine years of service. Write it for my signature. Date it today." He paused for a moment and then went on, "I want to have a talk with you after the funeral and I'll sign it then."

"Fine," I replied, "I'll be available. Do you want me to come to your office over there or are you going to come here?"

"I'll come over there. There is something I want to ask about, and I want to look at the space in the director's office."

"Glad to cooperate fully," I said. "I'll be here."

"Good," Gray replied, and hung up the phone.

I knew of Gray's encounter with John Mohr and I was sure he wanted to talk about the so-called secret files.

On the morning of May 4, Hoover's body was removed by Gawler's and the military pallbearers to the National Presbyterian Church on Nebraska Avenue for the memorial services.

The services were designed more to aggrandize the president than honor the director. Television coverage made seating arrangements a matter of urgent concern. The original plans called for President and Mrs. Nixon and Acting Director Gray with his wife, Bea, to sit in the front pew on the left-hand side. The honorary pallbearers, consisting of myself (as acting associate director), John Mohr, and Alex Rosen, the two assistants to the director, and all the assistant directors were to occupy the first two pews on the right.

Late in the afternoon of May 3, the newly appointed acting director bypassed Mohr, the "hard-headed Dutchman," and called James Adams, Mohr's assistant. Gray instructed that Kleindienst's seating assignment be changed. Originally scheduled to be sitting in the second row, left, with Vice President Spiro Agnew, Kleindienst wanted to sit in the first place in the first row, right, directly opposite the president and directly in front of the television cameras. Gray's instructions were carried out, and during the service the attorney general sat with the honorary pallbearers.

In his eulogy, President Nixon praised Hoover as "one of the giants" and said, "Let us honor him as he would surely want us to do, by honoring all the men and women who carry on in his noble profession by helping keep peace in our society."

As the funeral procession left the church grounds and turned onto Nebraska Avenue, there was an amazing sight. As far as the eye could see, solid lines of uniformed police officers stood on each side of the avenue. Many were from the Washington Metropolitan

Police Department, but others had come from surrounding areas. It was an unforgettable scene and I later learned it had been arranged by the military authorities.

Uniformed officers had been stationed at all intersections on Constitution and Pennsylvania Avenues. In Southeast Washington, the procession turned north on Potomac Avenue, which led directly to the cemetery where Hoover's parents were buried.

Later in the day, when I went back to the office, I waited, curious to see what my new boss would have to say. He called a few minutes after three o'clock and asked if it would be convenient for him to come to see me. A few minutes later, he walked in, extended his hand for a firm, cordial handshake, and sat down in the chair beside my desk.

I said, "Congratulations on your appointment as acting director. Frankly, most of us were hoping the president would select an insider, but I can assure you that all of us will do everything we can to help you." I was completely sincere, but I don't believe Gray trusted the FBI officials in Washington.

He smiled and said, "Thank you, Mark. I'll need all the help I can get. I am greatly flattered by the appointment. I have always had an enormous respect for the FBI." Gray added that "we will have a lot of things to talk about later, but today, the first thing I want to know about is the secret files."

"Mr. Gray," I said, "the Bureau doesn't have any secret files. There are thousands and thousands of files with derogatory information in them, some of which was obtained through investigation of FBI cases and some of which was volunteered. There are files with extremely confidential and sensitive information about espionage investigations. Many of our files are classified top secret or confidential under rules that govern all government agencies."

"Mark, I'm not talking about the regular files. Everybody knows that Hoover had his own secret files containing derogatory data on important people."

"The FBI has files on many important people," I said. "A few may have been investigated for violation of some federal statute, but thousands have been investigated for high office in the federal government."

Gray stopped me. "I know all that, but what about the files Hoover kept in his office?"

I knew more about Hoover's office files than anyone else in the Bureau—other than Helen Gandy—because those that did not fall into the category of his personal affairs were turned over to my custody.

During his forty-eight years as director, Hoover carried on a tremendous personal correspondence with the high and mighty in government. He exchanged letters with friends in all walks of life: Walter Winchell, the columnist; Clint Murchison, the Texas oil millionaire; David Sarnoff, founder of RCA; Richard Cardinal Cushing of Boston; Sherman Billingsley and Bernard "Toots" Shor, New York restaurateurs; Jack Warner of Hollywood; Lela Rogers, mother of Ginger; and many others. He wrote personal letters to incumbent presidents and remained friends with Herbert Hoover (no kin).

The director's personal files also included letters, some rather obsequious, from various Bureau officials who were trying to extricate themselves from the Hoover doghouse or ingratiate themselves with him. No doubt, some of them contained bits about prominent people, gossip that the official thought might interest or amuse Hoover. Miss Gandy maintained this correspondence and kept it out of the main Bureau files and indexes. As the years went by, the walls of her little office were lined with file cabinets. Forty-eight years is a long time, and the paper accumulates. In 1971, Hoover instructed Miss Gandy to begin weeding out this correspondence, but the work had barely begun when he died.

In addition, Hoover sometimes ordered that certain official FBI files be kept in Miss Gandy's office to prevent exposure to the eyes of rank-and-file personnel. For example, if the FBI had a file on an incumbent president, as it did in the case of Richard Nixon, whose first application for a government job had been with the FBI, it would be kept in the director's office. Extremely sensitive memorandums on Hoover's conversations with presidents were occasionally retained by Miss Gandy and could be seen only with Hoover's express permission. As a result, there was a substantial volume of official FBI materials in Miss Gandy's office, in addition to the personal papers, and these were designated the "official and confidential files."

I explained all of this to Gray, adding that the files Hoover kept in his own office "were so sensitive that he felt they should be kept on a need-to-know basis so as not to be available to the curious eyes of any agent or clerk who might come across them by chance."

Gray interjected, "Would he follow this practice if the information involved a high-placed person?"

"Sure, or the Bureau file might involve an extremely sensitive and delicate espionage investigation. We have a special file room where access is tightly limited and the cases there are mostly of a foreign intelligence nature. But, you see, all other files are kept in the Files Section, and because every Bureau employee is cleared for top secret access, there must be some exceptions, and these are the files that might be in the director's office."

Gray moved his head from side to side, thoughtfully. Obviously he still had doubts.

"Mr. Gray, why don't we go over and look at the files in Hoover's office?"

Gray smiled and said, "Okay, let's go."

I escorted Gray to his new office and we talked pleasantly on the way over. When we arrived, I introduced him to the receptionists and then took him directly to Miss Gandy's office, where I introduced him to Hoover's personal secretary of fifty-three years and to Mrs. Metcalf, who shared the space. Gray was charming and gracious to the two women.

I explained that Gray wanted to see the so-called Hoover files and view his new space. Miss Gandy smiled and said, "Well, there they are," pointing to the ten five-drawer file cabinets that filled two walls of the small office. "Most of this material is Mr. Hoover's personal correspondence—some of it going back to when he first became director." She was about to start sorting out all this material. Tolson had instructed Miss Gandy to box all the personal correspondence and have it delivered to Hoover's home. Since he planned to retire, Tolson instructed that the official and confidential files be sent to me for safekeeping and final disposition.

Gray looked casually at an open file drawer but made no further reference to these files. There was no indication that he was not completely satisfied with what Miss Gandy and I had explained.

I went on to give Gray a complete tour of the director's space, starting with the private inner office. "Mr. Gray," I said, "this furniture was obtained by Mr. Hoover when he first became director. It is almost fifty years old. You may want to replace it."

"No," he replied. "I'd like to keep it just as it is."

We next walked through the large conference room. Gray instructed that the desk at one end of the room, where Hoover had posed for pictures with visitors and employees on their anniversaries of service, be removed.

Walking through the space, we again came by Miss Gandy's office and Gray moved through the doorway to ask, "Miss Gandy, how much time will you need to clear out all of Mr. Hoover's things so that I can move in? I don't want to rush you."

"I think one week would be sufficient," she replied. "I don't want to keep you out of your new office any longer than I can help."

Gray paused a moment and then said, "Are you sure one week is enough? I'll plan on moving in on Friday the twelfth or Monday the fifteenth."

She replied, "That will be fine and I'll keep Mr. Felt posted on my progress."

Miss Gandy took one week to complete the packing process. She shipped thirty-four boxes of personal files to the Hoover house and sent twelve boxes of official and confidential files to me; I placed them in combination-lock cabinets. Miss Gandy has testified before the House Committee on Government Operations that, at Tolson's direction, she destroyed all of Hoover's personal papers except those relating to his estate. She turned them over to Tolson, who was Hoover's executor.

I made a casual review of the material Miss Gandy sent me, which was less than startling. There were folders on President Lyndon B. Johnson and President John F. Kennedy, and both related solely to administrative procedures governing liaison between the White House and the FBI. In my opinion, all of it could have been immediately returned to the general files, but I was resolved to hold the material intact and inviolate until Gray could review it for himself, since he had made such an issue of the "secret files" only a few days before. I wanted him to know exactly what was in them.

After three months of waiting for Gray to look at these files, I called in Cornelius Sullivan, an inspector in the Domestic Intelligence Division, and instructed him to prepare a complete index and catalogue. The job took him a week and when he finished, he shared my impression that the files were old and had little current significance.

I sent a copy of the inventory to Gray, but I don't know whether or not he read it; I never received a response. Looking back on it, I can't be sure that Gray ever accepted the fact that J. Edgar Hoover did not have extensive personal files crammed with all kinds of material that could be used to blackmail presidents, attorneys general, and other government officials. At least he stopped talking to me about it, and I assumed he believed me.

After briefly inspecting his new office and its files, Gray asked me to convene a brief meeting of the executive conference. I looked at my watch; it was 3:30. "How about four o'clock?" I asked.

"Four will be fine."

At three minutes to four, I was waiting outside the door to the reception room. Soon Gray came into view, striding forcefully down the long corridor. I escorted him through the reception room, down the corridor, past the raised and curious female heads, and into the conference room where FBI officials were seated at the long table.

As we entered, the officials rose to their feet and I led Gray to the head of the table. I said simply, "Gentlemen, this is Mr. L. Patrick Gray III, the newly appointed acting director of the FBI." There was a round of applause before the officials took their seats, waiting to hear what their new boss had to say.

Gray is an excellent speaker. He anticipated hostility and chose his words to be reassuring. He praised the FBI as the "finest law enforcement agency in the world" and he complimented the dedication of the FBI officials who made it that way. He expressed sympathy and understanding about the loss of a great leader and said he would not be surprised if we felt some misgivings about an outsider coming in. He explained that he would make changes and had to administer the FBI according to his own views. But he was careful to say, "I want to maintain the FBI as an institution."

As the group broke up, everything I heard was favorable to our new boss. My feelings were mixed. I felt resentful that an outsider was taking over, yet at the same time I was impressed with Gray's strength and sincerity. I determined to do everything I could to help him become a successful director. My purpose was to preserve the FBI as I had known it for so many years, and I felt this could best be done by helping the new chief.

Yet I never lost the tremendous admiration I had for Hoover. He fought ruthlessly for his causes and was as tough as the bulldog he resembled. I am proud of the FBI, and it was Hoover who built it into the finest law enforcement agency in the world. It may never be the same.

FIFTEEN

THE DIRECTOR'S LEGACY

J. EDGAR HOOVER was a complex man. The media, whether building him up in the 1930s as the great gangbuster or tearing him down as a storm trooper in the late 1960s and early 1970s, were never able to see more than one side of him. Yet he was more consistent than the caricatures indicated. His commitment to civil rights, for example, spanned his career. After Pearl Harbor, President Roosevelt ordered the relocation of loyal Japanese Americans to concentration camps. The one man of high rank in the federal government who sought to prevent this unjust treatment was J. Edgar Hoover. Thirty years later, Hoover jeopardized his relations with the Nixon White House by categorically barring FBI "black bag jobs" and drastically reducing the number of wiretaps and electronic surveillances, even in national security cases.

Hoover was the complete director, self-assured and totally in command. He had no political ambitions and repeatedly fought off attempts to expand the FBI's jurisdiction beyond its capabilities. He knew the political game and played it to the hilt with presidents, attorneys general, and the Congress, but his goal never went beyond greater independence for the FBI—and for himself as its creator and director. He basked in the power and the adulation that his position brought and in the perquisites that went with it. He was proud and pleased to be the only official besides the president to have an armored limousine. This extra protection was provided after Hoover personally led raids against gangsters in the 1930s and received numerous death threats.

In later years, as political attacks on him multiplied and became increasingly shrill and unfair, Hoover experienced loneliness and a fear that his life's work was being destroyed. His sense of public relations sometimes deserted him, and he lashed out as he never would have in the past. Yet in his day-to-day work he remained as methodical as ever. He never relaxed his demands on himself or on the Bureau.

I can testify to the J. Edgar Hoover I knew. When crossed or angered, he could be scorching and even vindictive, but on most occasions his compassion made it necessary for him to screen himself from subordinates in his FBI world. He was a soft touch to the right personal approach and insisted that most of his official contacts be in writing since it was much easier for him to be firm that way. This is undoubtedly one of the reasons he separated his personal life from his office life.

Hoover was protective of Bureau employees. For example, when former governor Grant Sawyer of Nevada criticized an FBI action, Hoover reacted sharply to set the record straight. Sawyer then stated that he had not intended to attack the FBI or Hoover personally. He said that his remarks had been intended only for the local FBI office. Hoover quickly responded, "Let me reiterate my oft stated position that as long as I am director of this Bureau, any attack on an FBI employee who is conscientiously carrying out his official duties will be considered an attack on me personally."

Hoover led a life closely circumscribed by the set patterns he had developed over the years. He seldom left his desk, and on his few vacation trips he kept in constant touch by telephone, including weekends. I know from personal observation at close quarters that he was fully aware of all the workings of the complex FBI machine that he directed—a mastery that his successors have not emulated. This is not to say that Hoover had no sense of humor or that he did not fully appreciate the pleasures of fine dining and visits to the race track.

Hoover loved his house, his yard and garden, and his dogs. The house was maintained meticulously. His collections and memorabilia were always carefully dusted and positioned. Sloan's Auction House on 13th Street N.W. frequently alerted him to sale items he might find interesting—and usually he did. Hoover's home did not look ornate—it looked lived-in, like the lounge chair on the deck off his bedroom where he sunbathed when Sunday weather permitted.

He took great interest in his yard and garden and selected the numerous shrubs. He even had a small garden plot and took great pride in the tomatoes that his gardener helped him to grow.

Hoover loved his two terriers and indulged them to the extent that their careless toilet habits occasionally required new linoleum on the kitchen floor and eventually artificial turf in the backyard. Hoover paid for it (not taxpayers, as critics claimed) and also put up with a lot of kidding about it from his friends.

J. Edgar Hoover was one of the most self-disciplined men I have ever known and he expected the same from those who worked for him. His insistence that others measure up to the standards that he set for himself gave him a reputation as an inflexible martinet. But he could and did make fun of himself. He liked to describe visiting Alcatraz prison and buying a canary from the Bird Man, one of the prisoners, as a present for his mother. It turned out to be a sparrow dyed yellow—and Hoover always laughed the hardest when retelling the story.

Among his personal associates, Hoover was known as a prankster, even in formal settings. During one official reception—for a visitor from the Royal Canadian Mounted Police—Hoover and Tolson followed their usual routine. They arrived a bit late and were served drinks—Jack Daniels and water for Hoover and Johnnie Walker Red Label scotch and soda for Tolson. Hoover made a short welcoming speech and then marched out with Tolson following behind. That was a signal for guests to hit the hors d'oeuvres. Among the first to reach the table was a top Bureau official who had some difficulty meeting Hoover's weight standards. As the FBI man made himself a large sandwich, Hoover and Tolson rushed back in and made straight for the official, who stood frozen with the sandwich halfway to his mouth, "Ah-ha!" Hoover announced. "I knew when I left the room you would be the first to reach the food." With that, he turned and strode out again, Tolson at his heels. After a few seconds of shocked silence, everyone roared with laughter.

Personally and officially, he was a frugal man, and this allowed him to build up an estate that was appraised at more than $500,000 including his house and personal property. His investments were conservative and designed mainly to produce dividends. He could have earned more had he left the government. Corporate heads courted him but he turned down fabulous executive positions. Howard Hughes told Hoover he could name his own salary.

He also had political opportunities. In a 1955 letter, Joseph P. Kennedy, father of John, wrote to Hoover that he had heard broadcaster Walter Winchell tout the director for president. "If that should come to pass," Joe Kennedy wrote, "it would be the most wonderful thing for the United States, and whether you were on a Republican or Democratic ticket, I would guarantee you the largest contribution that you would ever get from anybody and the hardest work by either a Democrat or Republican." Hoover rejected such suggestions.

Hoover respected the taxpayers who provided FBI funds. The Bureau's budget was one of the most tightly controlled in the government, and Hoover was perhaps the only administrator in Washington history to return unexpended funds to the Treasury at the end of the fiscal year. "I must explain every item in our budget and how the money is used," he once said. "I never want any secret fund, a lump-sum appropriation for which I don't have to account. I want to account for every cent because an unexplained fund is dangerous."

Hoover's critics forget that he had been called in to clean out a corrupt and politics-ridden Bureau of Investigation because of his reputation for efficiency and administrative ability, as well as his puritanical moral streak. He would tolerate no financial or sexual looseness among his subordinates; he once fired a male clerical employee who allowed his girlfriend to spend the night with him. His difficulty in adjusting to the Kennedy administration stemmed partly from his contempt for JFK's philandering. Personality differences put him at odds with Attorney General Robert F. Kennedy, and Hoover's contempt for the alleged affair with Marilyn Monroe added to the antagonism. The famous confrontation with Dr. Martin Luther King, Jr. resulted from Hoover's disgust after he learned of the civil rights leader's marathon sexual and drinking exploits.

Hoover made up his mind quickly and decisively. Major changes, policy decisions, and high-level transfers were ordered with sometimes terrifying speed. Many of Hoover's directives, as well as some of his outbursts, were written in bright blue ink in his angular hand at the bottom of memorandums and correspondence. The language of these commentaries could be blistering. These outspoken expressions of Hoover's views were never meant to be seen outside of the FBI, but they later came to light under the sweep of the Freedom of Information Act, which destroyed the confidentiality of the Bureau's business and operations. For outsiders who invited his wrath, Hoover would use such words as "jackal," "scurrilous," or "mental halitosis." Insiders could be put in their place by having their ideas branded as "ridiculous" or "atrocious." On one Hiss case memorandum, at a time when Rep. Richard M. Nixon seemed to be going in both directions, Hoover wrote, "I wish this young man would make up his mind."

When FBI veterans tried to minimize Hoover's use of marginal notes by shrinking the margins of their memorandums, Hoover would resort to his memo pad to be sure his views were fully and succinctly set forth.

Hoover had a memory like an elephant. He never forgot or forgave what he regarded as a "cheap shot" directed at himself or the Bureau. He once explained this to me: "It depends on whether something comes from the heart or the head." He could rail against a mistake, but once convinced it was an honest error of judgment or even a stupid action, he could forgive. He would never forgive what he regarded as a malicious attack.

Hoover had his idiosyncrasies and those around him could only learn to live with them. For example, he would not tolerate tardiness. Outsiders could expect appointments at a specific date and time and would be received punctually. But agents desiring to see him were placed on the open-ended "appointment list." Hoover would see them at his convenience, and it was up to them to be available near a phone in Bureau headquarters. To ensure they did not miss their appointments, the agents came in to the office no later than the director, ate lunch when he did, and waited until he had left in the evening before ending their vigil. This stand-by alert could last for several days. One field official was unavailable when Hoover called for him. The director was unmoved by the young man's explanation and apology and ordered him passed over for promotion. He later relented and restored the young man to the promotion ladder.

Hoover was bright, alert, and vigorous throughout his life. One reason is that he took good care of himself. He had an annual physical, and every morning Valerie Stewart, the chief nurse of the FBI health service, gave him a vitamin injection. He kept abreast of medical developments, and I recall several occasions when he mentioned articles he had read on such matters. He insisted that I eat one banana each day for potassium, which, he assured me, was "good for your heart."

Hoover was brisk and to the point in his conversations with FBI officials. But once I gained his confidence, he would sometimes digress from the business at hand to chat about other matters. He was particularly worried about the health of his closest friend and associate, Clyde Tolson, and he often discussed this with me. Once he told me that he suggested setting up a punching bag in a corner of Tolson's office so that Tolson could hit it when he felt tense and needed to relieve his frustrations. "I can leave my problems behind when I leave the office at night. Tolson can't and he needs to get rid of his tensions."

He was always charming and gracious with women and children. Wives left his office glowing when they were received with agent husbands who had been congratulated by the director for an anniversary or for a job well done. My wife, Audrey, accompanied me to Hoover's office for a picture-taking ceremony on my twenty-fifth and thirtieth anniversaries of Bureau service. Both times he was highly complimentary about me when I was out of hearing. In October 1971, when Audrey and I attended a private reception before the Silver Anniversary Dinner Dance of the Society of Former FBI Agents, Hoover kissed her on the cheek and said, "Your husband has been of tremendous help to me."

Martha Mitchell, wife of the then attorney general, was also captivated by Hoover's charm. (She called him "Jedgar.") At her invitation, Hoover made a rare public appearance at the American Newspaperwomen's Club in May 1971. In her introduction, Mitchell paid tribute to Hoover's many years of service by quipping, "When you have seen one FBI director, you have seen them all."

Hoover, whose caricature had just appeared on the cover of *Life* magazine as a Roman emperor, apologized for showing up in a conventional suit. He added, "I regret to say that my toga did not get back from the cleaners on time."

I have often heard Hoover talk at informal gatherings of Bureau officials and foreign liaison representatives and was always impressed by his impromptu wit and fluency. I later learned that like other famous men—including comedians such as Bob Hope—he carefully prepared these off-the-cuff remarks and memorized them for "spontaneous" delivery.

Hoover was rumored to be a homosexual. These innuendoes were based on his confirmed bachelorhood and his close association with Clyde Tolson. A New York newspaper, which for years had aimed steady fire at Hoover, assigned reporters to "prove" the charge. Finally it dropped the story without confirming it and said it had been threatened by the Bureau. I never heard of any such threats and I never saw any indication of homosexual tendencies in Hoover. To my knowledge, neither did any of my colleagues in the FBI. Hoover was married to his job. The FBI and his home were his all-consuming interests. He could have retired on full pay, but he chose to remain. He did have a close association with Tolson. They conferred frequently during the day and they invariably ate lunch together, most often at the Mayflower Hotel. On Wednesday they had dinner at Tolson's apartment, on Friday at Hoover's house. Their only vice was going to the races on Saturdays when the horses were running and where Hoover consistently lost his two-dollar bets.

That association was not without its rifts. As he did with all other high-level subordinates, Hoover occasionally became displeased with Tolson. Other officials in the Hoover "dog house" were bypassed in the daily business of the Bureau until he cooled off. With Tolson the strain was greater because he interacted with Hoover constantly.

I know from my talks with Hoover that he was genuinely fond of Tolson, as an older brother might be. He looked after him and worried about his precarious state of health.

An aggressive and energetic man, Hoover could keep several feuds going at once—and he enjoyed it. He was certainly stubborn. In matters of internal Bureau discipline, his blue-inked notations in personnel files often refreshed his recollection of unpleasant things past. But in most instances he forgave and forgot. Hoover was always fair and evenhanded with me, and I have good memories of the years I spent working for him, no matter how exhausting they were. But there were times when he overreacted toward people, sometimes over trivial matters. He would insist on disciplinary action even when the Administrative Division cautioned that it might be reversed on appeal to the Civil Service Commission or the courts, depending on the status of the employee.

For example, a young clerk once refused to cut his hair to Bureau standards. After repeated instructions to the clerk brought no results, Hoover ordered the clerk's dismissal. The clerk took the matter to a court, which ordered him reinstated with back pay—and long hair. Hoover took this in stride. Fortunately Hoover was no longer there when the clerk refused to wear a necktie in an area visited by the public.

Attempts to go over Hoover's head for any personnel action short of dismissal were foolhardy. In Hoover's eyes, this marked a malcontent to be watched and distrusted forever. On the other hand, accepting disciplinary action in good spirit could actually boost an employee's standing with him.

Hoover was an absolute tyrant on three points. An error of any sort, even a typographical mistake, in an outgoing communication was a sin punishable by censure. A second inviolate rule was that all communications from outside the Bureau had to be acknowledged within twenty-four hours. This seems like an unduly harsh rule, but Hoover explained, "It is like a clock. It can run on time or it can run slow but the number of hours in the day will always be the same." He was right. Once the twenty-four-hour rule was in effect it was just as easy to handle the mail on time as to handle it late—perhaps easier. The third point was that Hoover insisted on courtesy and promptness in answering telephone calls from the outside. The calls had to be answered before the fourth ring. Never was an operator to inquire, "Who is calling?"

Hoover was the target of allegations that he used Bureau materials and Bureau personnel for work at his home. This began when an employee of the FBI lab reported that the FBI favored the U.S. Recording Company of Washington, D.C., by purchasing equipment from that company at higher prices than the Bureau would have paid directly to the manufacturer. When the matter first came up, internal FBI inquiries determined that such use of a "cut out" was not only proper but commonplace when the purpose was to conceal for security reasons the type of electronic equipment being purchased by government intelligence agencies.

The matter would have rested there except that Rep. Bella Abzug was not satisfied with responses from former FBI officials who testified before her congressional subcommittee on government operations. According to my sources, Abzug carried her complaint to Attorney General Edward H. Levi and informed him that if he did not reopen the investigation into alleged FBI corruption, she would do so before her subcommittee. Levi hastily reimbursed the Bureau for the cost of installing locks on doors at his residence and then reopened the corruption probe.

No improprieties were found in connection with FBI purchases from the U.S. Recording Company or any other company. The department neglected to point out that most of the purchases had been approved in writing by prior attorneys general pursuant to government regulations.

The investigation turned up some questionable perquisites on the part of a few FBI officials, including the former director. One FBI official was asked to resign and was charged with a misdemeanor for using Bureau scrap material to build a bird house for his yard. Another was asked to resign after he was discovered using government funds for FBI public relations activities when such funds were not authorized. Leaks to the press hinted that these expenditures were for lavish meals in exclusive Washington restaurants for the benefit of FBI officials. When the facts were in, the dinners turned out to be rather circumspect entertainment for foreign intelligence agency heads, paid for out of funds that had not been earmarked by Congress for such purposes. There was no corruption or diversion of funds for personal use, as was intimated.

The real target of the probe started by Levi and continued by Attorney General Griffin Bell was J. Edgar Hoover. There were allegations that Bureau personnel and materials were frequently used for work done at the Hoover residence. Because Hoover was head of America's counterespionage apparatus, it would have been unwise to allow non-Bureau workmen into his home. In addition, Hoover had numerous threats against his life, necessitating unusual precautions. And finally, in every instance, Hoover meticulously paid for the cost of materials.

In the end Hoover was neither paragon nor ogre. He was a sincere man who demanded loyalty but gave it in equal measure. He was given to neither false modesty nor overbearing conceit. When the press was full of stories that he was being pushed out of office, he could read with wry satisfaction the punch line to a widely circulated story:

Nixon: I wanted to see you to discuss the matter of retirement.

Hoover: Why, that's ridiculous. You're still a young man.

Charismatic, feisty, charming, petty, giant, grandiose, brilliant, egotistical, industrious, formidable, compassionate, domineering—all these adjectives were applied to Hoover and, to a degree, they all fit him. He was widely admired and widely criticized—and he accepted this. He was a human being.

Hoover loved and believed in America. His mortal remains lie under a modest headstone in the Congressional Cemetery in southeast Washington. A more fitting recognition is his name emblazoned over the entrance of the magnificent new FBI headquarters building. His real contribution to the country, the real monument to his genius and dedication, is the Federal Bureau of Investigation itself, which, beleaguered though it has been, will survive and be strong because the nation desperately needs it.

SIXTEEN

NIXON'S FBI MAN

D URING J. Edgar Hoover's last days, pressure grew to force him out. Encouraged by Bill Sullivan, detractors seized on any episode, any controversial issue that might put the director in a bad light. White House advisers suggested privately that President Nixon was dissatisfied with a Bureau that refused to accept political dictation. These slurs came from presidential aides H. R. Haldeman, John Ehrlichman, and John Dean primarily. They were angry at Hoover's refusal to be a "team player" in connection with the Dita Beard case and Huston plan. They hinted that Hoover was "too old," he no longer "controlled" the FBI, and morale was low.

The president had ambivalent feelings about Hoover. He would have liked to have the director in his pocket, but he was aware that Hoover had strong support in Congress. Nixon was ready to bide his time, waiting for disability or death to solve his problem. Yet he made no moves to find or prepare a successor. We at the Bureau felt strongly that he would appoint someone from the ranks, and the thought more than crossed my mind that I might receive the appointment. I was next in line, my FBI record was very good, and I felt I was both liked and respected by the rank and file. Another log-ical candidate was John P. Mohr, assistant to the director in charge of administrative operations. Mohr had a distinguished service record in addition to influential contacts outside the Bureau—something I lacked.

But Richard Nixon wanted someone from the outside who would be his man, someone with no ties and no first loyalties to the FBI. His choice would have been Jerry Wilson, but the former chief of the Washington Metropolitan Police Department had been badly tarnished by his handling of the May Day demonstrations in 1971, when several thousand antiwar protesters were rounded up and herded into an improvised jail. White House aides preferred Joseph Woods, former sheriff of Cook County, Illinois, but he was the brother of Rose Mary Woods, Nixon's personal secretary. Appoint-ing him would smack of nepotism.

Attorney General Kleindienst came up with a compromise. Exactly twenty-six hours and ten minutes after the president announced Hoover's death, Nixon named the World War II subma-rine commander, lawyer, minor Connecticut politico, and assistant attorney general L. Patrick Gray III to be acting director of the FBI. It was a political appointment. Gray had been a Nixon loyalist since the two met in 1947. He had left his last military job, assistant to the Joint Chiefs of Staff, in 1960 to work on Nixon's first presidential campaign, and he left his Connecticut law practice to join the 1968 campaign. Only a few weeks before he was chosen for the FBI, Gray had been named deputy attorney general designate by Nixon in a move to consolidate his hold on the Justice Department. Now Gray would play the same role at the Bureau. He had no idea how to run the FBI, but from the standpoint of White House insiders, Gray was the ideal candidate to end a perceived lack of responsiveness in the FBI leadership.

Gray had no intimation that he was Nixon's choice until May 3, when he received a call from Attorney General Kleindienst and was told to be at his office at 2:15 P.M. because "we're going to the White House." He received the news of his promotion from Justice Department legal counsel Ralph Erickson, but didn't believe it until he heard from Nixon. "The president talked to me about the importance of the job and the fact that it had to be nonpolitical," Gray said. "The president also told me that 'ours has not been a political relationship—ours is a professional relationship based on mutual respect.'"

White House spokesmen took the same line in public, creating the impression that the Gray appointment was nonpartisan and nonpolitical, no more than an interim measure until the November election. As a White House aide put it, the president did not want the appointment to become "involved in partisan politics" as the campaign heated up. When questioned about the choice, Ron Ziegler, the president's press secretary, said, "I think you will find that Patrick Gray is not a political man."

During the first week of his tenure as FBI director, Gray continued to occupy his old space in the Justice Department, waiting for Helen Gandy to pack up Hoover's personal effects and memorabilia. He asked me to stay on to run the day-to-day operations. To provide transitional continuity, I agreed to this.

It was immediately clear that Gray brought a new leadership style. He did not smoke or drink and worked out vigorously every day. He always made a point of walking up the five flights from the basement garage to his office on the fifth floor. After twice accompanying him up the stairs, I made it a point to use a different entrance. Gray was a deeply religious man and attended seven o'clock Mass every morning.

The acting director made no secret of his intention to "woo the field," as he put it. Before his short tenure was over, he had visited every field office except Honolulu. His set speech at every stop was calculated to ingratiate himself with field personnel. Again and again, he promised to relax Hoover's rigid standards. As my friends in the field reported to me, the effect was to drive a wedge between the field personnel and headquarters.

Many of his immediate changes were meant to please the field agents. Though Hoover never put it into writing, he expected agents to dress and groom themselves like the young businessmen in their area. Hoover frowned on long hair, mustaches, and beards. The only exception, and Hoover was never told about this, was made for agents who needed beards and mustaches to move among dissenters and radicals.

Gray also discontinued several explicit rules. Hoover had required a record of each agent's time in office (TIO), meaning the hours spent actually investigating cases. Eliminating this rule made life easier for the agents. Gray also relaxed the weight standards. Agents were now permitted to let their weight go up to the "maximum" level set by insurance companies—in some cases a difference of fifteen to twenty pounds from the "desirable" level Hoover insisted on. Since he believed in physical fitness programs, Gray allowed field agents to work out, as long as they compensated for each hour in the gym with one hour of overtime. Hoover had limited this privilege to headquarters staff. Gray's most popular change was allowing resident agents to take their Bureau cars home at night. He reasoned that agents should have a car available if they were called out after hours—and it did save downtown storage charges.

Gray's field campaign required a lot of travel. During one of our first talks, he discussed the possibility of using military air command planes to visit various field offices. Trained in Hoover's tight-fisted budget management, I argued against the use of MAC because of the tremendous cost. But Gray insisted that the president did not want the acting director of the FBI being hijacked to Cuba and interrogated with sodium pentothal. I prepared a memorandum emphasizing the costs, convinced that the astronomical figures would change Gray's mind. But he simply bypassed me and asked the Administrative Division to make the necessary arrangements. Gray began using MAC on a weekly basis, frequently starting out the week from New London, Connecticut, the nearest airport to his home in Stonington. Total costs for his use of the military air command came to almost $200,000.

During his year in office Gray delivered forty-one speeches to various groups. These speeches have been criticized for their political overtones. Although Gray denies any such bias, his speeches were written by Charles Lichtenstein, a political speechwriter for a number of Republican leaders who was then employed at the Federal Power Commission. Gray chose not to use George William Gunn, a law enforcement-oriented Bureau writer.

Gray's priorities kept him away from headquarters. J. Edgar Hoover had insisted on seeing all significant memorandums and other communications, and the volume of material directed into his office was enormous. Gray could not handle this volume because of his inexperience. Also, he made it very clear to me that he wished to delegate authority. Accordingly, I sent him about 10 percent of the material that came to me. But even this was too much. After a few days in office he complained about the volume of issues hitting his desk. He emphatically told me, "I'm expecting you to run the day-to-day operations of the FBI, and until I become more familiar with procedures I will not be able to handle much paperwork." I was tempted to reply that he could help out by spending more time in Washington, but I thought better of it.

After this, I restricted the material I sent Gray to major policy decisions or memorandums such as wiretap applications that required his personal signature. Some memorandums never came back to me, and as the deadline for action approached, I frequently had to make a decision without his input. After Gray left in April 1973, I found a number of memorandums we had been looking for.

Gray thought he was working hard—and by general government standards he probably was. When he focused his attention on something, he literally smothered it. He always took work with him when he went home to Connecticut on weekends. What came back was covered with annotations in his precise handwriting—always in red ink.

To help with his workload, Gray brought four of his Justice Department staff assistants, who became known among career FBI people as the "Mod Squad." The top member of this personal staff, thirty-year-old David D. Kinley, had one main qualification, as far as I could tell: a family connection with *Parade,* the syndicated Sunday supplement. Perhaps it was a coincidence, but *Parade* published some very laudatory stories about Gray. Kinley was bright and alert and I could work with him. But there was never any doubt that his primary assignment was to advance Gray's interests, even at the expense of the Bureau. Marjorie Neenan was also loyal to Gray, but she was always gracious and easy to work with. Daniel M. Armstrong III quickly became known as the all-American boy. His experience with the U.S. attorney's office in Brooklyn had convinced him that he was an expert on law enforcement and the FBI, which was a delusion. Barbara L. Herwig was pleasant though condescending; she was a passionate advocate of women's liberation.

Gray's personal staff members, with the exception of Neenan, shared his suspicion and distrust of FBI career people. It was hard to cope with their skepticism but a pleasure to astound them with the Bureau's proficiency. None of Gray's staff had agent status or expressed any interest in attaining it. Gray was issued agent's credentials and given FBI badge number two. Badge number one was Hoover's and was retired from use.

These imported staff members interpreted the new boss better than we FBI professionals did. Gray was a compulsive note taker, and we found out that once he had made a notation concerning policy, it was almost impossible to change his mind. Frequently I could not decipher these notations. "Someone is standing on the vents," he wrote on one memorandum. Not even his personal staff could translate that for me. When I asked him what he meant, he smiled. "That's a submarine expression. When a sub is making a crash dive, all the air vents have to be quickly closed. To say that someone is standing on the vents simply means that someone is dragging his feet or obstructing progress." He would say he was holding "captain's mast" when he orally disciplined subordinates. When he said, "There's something hidden in the Claymore mines," he was referring to a serious problem that was not readily apparent.

When Gray and his staff moved into the director's office on May 12, he told a press conference that he was going to "open the window" on FBI operations. This was a complete reversal for him. During the Kleindienst confirmation hearings, Gray privately railed against the "vultures" of the press and said "the public doesn't give a damn" about many of the stories reporters were hyping. But he learned how dangerous it is to take on the Fourth Estate, and, as a friend remarked, "the hearings were the biggest thing in Pat's life up to that time. He learned the significance of the media, and now he is playing them like a violin."

The FBI was not ready for all the sunshine Gray was letting in. His first meeting of the executive conference had more to do with publicity than official business. Media representatives from all parts of the country had been invited to witness the event. After spending some fifty minutes with the press, Gray called the meeting to order. Those present spent three minutes discussing whether the FBI should hire female agents and then tabled the question when Gray agreed to study additional data on the subject.

After the other officials had left, Gray said to me, "I want to hold a brainstorming session with all the top officials. I think I can arrange to have it at Camp David if we can agree on a time when the president and his staff are not using it." I suggested using the FBI Academy at Quantico. The press, I pointed out, might attach some political significance to the use of Camp David. "I'll think about it," Gray said. I soon learned that when he said he would think about something it meant he had already made up his mind and did not want to discuss it further.

"In the meantime," he continued, "I want you to arrange for each headquarters division to prepare a position paper outlining its operations, its problems, and its plans for the future. I also want some special white papers prepared to assess the proper role for the FBI in the narcotics problem, in the establishment of an outside oversight group, and the need for a new division on planning and evaluation."

Hurriedly, Gray went on, "You are the number two in command and will be my chief of operations—but I want to be consulted on major policy matters."

"Fine," I said, "but I think we should have frequent informal conferences, you and I."

"Yes," Gray agreed. "I will be available anytime for consultation."

I returned to my office feeling encouraged and convinced of Gray's sincerity, but not for long. As Gray was moving into the director's office surrounded by reporters and photographers, the rest of us were reading the newspapers in shocked disbelief. Staring at us from the front page was Gray's announcement that the Bureau would remove all restrictions against hiring female agents. Gray was quoted as saying that "this action has been unanimously approved by the executive conference." In fact, no vote had been taken, and if it had been placed before us, there would have been fifteen votes opposed, with Gray and possibly one other official voting to hire female agents.

The issue had come up two years earlier, when a young woman in Denver, Sandra Rothenberger Nemser, applied for a position as an FBI agent. When her application was refused, she filed suit against the attorney general, the director, and the Bureau, alleging that the refusal violated the Constitution and equal employment statutes. The Nemser suit was followed by an action filed by Cynthia Gitt Edgar, a staffer for Bella Abzug, the controversial congresswoman from New York. The American Civil Liberties Union supported the two suits.

The FBI at that time almost unanimously opposed permitting women to become special agents. The FBI was a quasi-military organization with combat-type operations taking place almost every day, as agents apprehended fugitives, staged raids, and put themselves in other dangerous situations. A show of strength was often essential to ensure that an arrest was made without incident. Indeed because the FBI had so carefully stuck to this strategy, great numbers of arrests involved minimal risk. In those days, we were convinced that allowing women to participate in arrests would increase the risk for everyone.

Dwight Dalbey, assistant director in the Office of Legal Counsel, prepared the Bureau's position paper. All FBI officials opposed hiring female agents, with one exception—John Mohr. He was sure we could not defend our case successfully given the tenor of the times. "If we can't win," he said, "let's give in gracefully."

It was up to the Civil Division of the Justice Department, which Gray then headed, to defend the Bureau in the court actions, and he was anything but sympathetic to the Bureau's position. He argued that the lawsuit should not be contested and that the FBI should begin accepting female applicants for the position of agent. He refused to even listen to our arguments until Dalbey threatened to hire an outside lawyer.

Then Hoover died in the midst of the controversy, and Gray

became acting director. At that first regular executive conference meeting under the new boss, we discussed the question cursorily. Dalbey told Gray that "an extensive survey has been made in the field and you should know of the results. SACs, supervisors, and agents are unanimously opposed, and they strongly document their positions. You have not seen any of this new information and it is too long to read here. I suggest you read it first and then we can vote on the question."

Gray hesitated for a moment and then nodded agreement. But he had already made up his mind and told the media that the decision to hire female agents had been unanimously approved.

To add insult to injury, the very same day, David Kinley, Gray's administrative assistant, brought me the official communication to the field offices announcing the decision. Obviously Kinley had been working on it for some time.

After reading it, I said, "Dave, you haven't changed the minimum height requirement."

"That's right," he replied. "The boss wants exactly the same standards for females as for males."

"But Dave, a minimum height requirement of five feet seven inches limits the field to tall women. You're discriminating against average women." After a thirty-minute argument he had not changed his ground, and I called Gray. Before I could speak my piece, he cut me off.

"The women must measure up exactly as the men. There will be no exceptions," he said.

"This is discriminatory," I insisted. "You are only opening the door part way. We should be consistent."

"Mark, I don't want any more argument about it," he said. "My mind is made up. Don't push me too far."

In the end, my suspicions about the political motives of the two women who had filed suit were confirmed: neither Nemser nor

Edgar completed an application for FBI employment. In those early years of the new policy, few women applied. Since then, my arguments against hiring women agents have lost validity. Women are becoming as strong as men because of more vigorous childhood games, active sports participation, and, for some, employment at manual labor.

I still believe Gray made a serious tactical error when he misrepresented the facts to the press. He lost the confidence of the executive conference and inspired serious doubts about his honesty and good intentions. The professional staff was furious. Gray's deception was probably the deciding factor in what followed. Ten of the sixteen top FBI officials who had attended the executive conference meeting retired shortly thereafter. Various reasons were given, but I know that all ten were disenchanted with Gray because of his misrepresentation to the press. But none of that made the new acting director shy about using the media.

My first assignment for Gray was to have various divisions prepare position papers and white papers for his study. As I began to dictate instructions, I realized that I had not absorbed enough of his thinking in our hurried conference. But he was on his way home to Connecticut and unavailable for more consultation. Fortunately Carol Tschudy, my administrative assistant, understood my problem. She called my attention to a *New York Times* story that set forth in great detail a description of what Gray expected in these papers. He called them his "avenues of inquiry" and they covered everything from FBI administrative operations to organized crime to intelligence investigations to drug abuse. In time, I became used to seeing what I considered internal FBI business in the newspapers.

To Gray's disappointment, our brainstorming session could not be held at Camp David, which had been scheduled for a White House function. So Gray, his personal staff, and the executive conference journeyed to Quantico. Each operating division submitted its papers and they were discussed in depth. Gray's questions were aggressive but not always pertinent. After the first day's session, we ate dinner together in a private dining room and I was surprised to see an open bar. Liquor had never before been permitted at the FBI Academy.

As the discussions continued the next day, it became clear to us that the primary goal of the sessions was to brief Gray and his staff on FBI policies, procedures, and operations. Although he told us that his staff people were not to "wear his stripes," we soon learned how influential his staffers were. The executive conference was startled when there was no vote after we discussed the carefully prepared papers; there had always been a vote under Hoover. But now Gray himself made all policy decisions in consultation with his personal staff.

Had I been wiser, I would have retired with other members of the executive conference. I was making pennies an hour, since the retirement take-home income to which I would have been entitled almost equaled what I was earning. My salary had been frozen for several years because of the forced compression in the supergrade levels resulting from congressional reluctance to raise the ceiling on government salaries. Hundreds of my subordinates were drawing as much salary as I. Had I left in 1972, cost-of-living allowances for retired employees would have increased my retirement pay, so that my income would be greater today.

I certainly did not stay on hoping to become director if Gray failed. I realized that his failure might take the FBI down with him— as it nearly did. It was clear that the Nixon administration would not appoint anyone from the ranks. But in my fifty-ninth year, I had completed thirty-seven years of government service, thirty of them with the Bureau. As the top-ranking career official, I felt I was the logical one to provide continuity during the change of leadership. By remaining, I would have a chance to keep the FBI that Hoover had created as intact as possible. Someone knowledgeable had to train and guide the new director, and I saw this as my obligation.

When I decided to stay on, I had no inkling of the problems that lay in store for me; nevertheless, I am glad I did. I think I helped keep the FBI together. And I was never bored.

SEVENTEEN

THREE-DAY GRAY

P AT GRAY came to the FBI during troubled times. Three days after Gray moved into his new office, Arthur H. Bremer attempted to assassinate Governor George C. Wallace of Alabama, who was campaigning for the presidential nomination. It was a Monday and Gray was on his way back from Stonington, so I took the first excited call from Attorney General Kleindienst, who ordered a full FBI investigation. Although I was not sure what the FBI's jurisdiction was, I told Kleindienst that we would move immediately. Thomas H. Farrow, the Baltimore SAC, was already on his way to the scene of the shooting in Laurel, Maryland, with a group of agents. He was contacted by radio and given the attorney general's instructions that the FBI should take over the investigation. Kleindienst and I agreed that the FBI could act under the civil rights statutes, and I called him at hourly intervals throughout the afternoon to update him on developments.

At seven o'clock, I left the office knowing that everything possible was being done. Wallace was in the hospital and Bremer was in custody. When I arrived home there was a message waiting for me to call President Nixon. The operator asked me to hold and then Charles Colson, a presidential aide, came on the line. "Just a minute, Mr. Felt," he said. "The president is coming on the line." Fifteen seconds later I was talking to Nixon for the first time.

"Hello," he said. "This is President Nixon. Please bring me up to date on the Wallace case."

"Mr. President, Governor Wallace is still undergoing surgery and his condition is listed as very critical. He is in the operating room at Holy Cross Hospital in Silver Spring. Three other persons, including a secret service agent, were wounded in the shooting, but they are expected to recover. The would-be assassin, Bremer, is in federal custody and has been taken to the Prince Georges County Hospital at Cheverly, Maryland."

Nixon interrupted. "What did they take Bremer to the hospital for?"

"He was roughed up a bit by the people who captured and subdued him. Also, he was examined by a psychiatrist who says his initial impression is that Bremer is a mental case."

"How bad was Bremer hurt?" the president pressed.

"Not seriously," I answered. "He has a few bruises and contusions. That's all."

"Well, it's too bad they didn't really rough up the son of a bitch!" Nixon said.

Not wanting to comment on the president's outburst, I continued. "The FBI has assumed full jurisdiction in the case, and the way it looks now, Bremer will probably be charged with violation of the civil rights statutes."

"Is that the best you can do? There ought to be a stronger charge."

"I agree and we are discussing it now with attorneys in the Justice Department."

"Okay," he said. "I want you to give me reports on the case every thirty minutes."

I spent the next two hours alternately talking to the Bureau supervisors who were in constant touch with the Baltimore office and with the president. The president's demand that I call every thirty minutes meant that I no sooner got off the phone to the Bureau than it was time to call the president again. On my second call to the White House, Nixon said, "I want the FBI to take over responsibility for a twenty-four-hour guard and protection duty of Bremer. I don't want another Oswald case on my hands." I assured the president that this would be done and passed the word on to SAC Farrow in Baltimore, who realized what problems this would make for him.

On my third call to the White House, Nixon did not come to the phone and I talked to Colson. I told him that the Secret Service, which had entered the investigation because it was not clear which agency had jurisdiction, had found some papers in Bremer's apartment in Milwaukee that included writings, presumably Bremer's, indicating a radical bias. Colson relayed this to the president, who ordered that these papers be impounded by the FBI at once. We did not discuss the formality of a search warrant.

At 9:00 P.M., I told the president that Wallace was still in surgery and was paralyzed from the waist down. I added that Bremer's papers were being flown to Washington by the FBI. I explained that Bremer had refused to be interviewed until he could consult with an attorney. At 9:30 P.M., I talked to Colson. I had learned Governor Wallace would survive but would probably be paralyzed permanently.

At 9:50 P.M., Pat Gray called to say he had just returned to his apartment in Washington and found out about the attempted assassination when he called headquarters to check in. He said he would take over keeping the White House informed. The following day, Gray told me that he had called the White House at 10:00 and 10:30, and had spoken to Colson. Since there was little news, Colson said that no further reports were necessary unless there were unexpected developments. Gray had also talked with Attorney General

Kleindienst that evening. Both Kleindienst and Colson seemed annoyed because Gray was not on the scene when a major case broke.

One of Gray's major weaknesses in running the FBI was his lack of availability over long periods of time. More often than not, he was out of town. And even when he was in Washington, he was often out of reach in the basement gymnasium, where he would not permit any interruptions, or was locked up in long conferences with his staff. He rarely met with the executive conference. In the Justice Department, he had been known as "Three-Day Gray" because of his extended weekends in Connecticut. He was sensitive about this nickname, perhaps because it was so well deserved. Once when I was in his office conferring about a case, Gray said, "There is another important matter. Yesterday I had a conversation with a federal judge and he told me that one of my assistant directors is bad-mouthing me."

I almost choked when he complained, "This assistant director is calling me Four-Day Gray."

Suppressing an impulse to laugh, I said, "Why don't you ask the judge to name names? Make him tell you who said this and where he got his information." Gray reddened; he must have realized that I knew his real nickname. "That's all for now," he said. Later the press began calling him "Two-Day Gray," and his calendar substantiated the correction. (In fairness to Gray, he took briefcases full of work to his home in Connecticut. He wanted to become an excellent FBI director, and he loved the assignment.)

Career Justice Department officials, frustrated and angered by years of trying to impose their wishes on Hoover, had a field day after his death. They directed a string of requests to Gray or members of his personal staff that were implemented without question.

One of Gray's first acts had nothing to do with policy or procedures: he had a kitchen installed in an unused pantry closet in his office. It was furnished with a new refrigerator and an apartment-size electric range. China, silverware, and cooking utensils were purchased, and a cook was hired at a salary of $10,000 a year. To stock the kitchen, every member of the executive conference was assessed $25 as a first installment for food.

Gray also stocked a bar in the director's office, something unheard of under Hoover. Dining was in the large conference room Hoover had used for ceremonial purposes. Gray ordered a larger conference table at a cost of $5,000, but when it arrived he would not accept it because it had a Formica top. He wanted the larger table so that he could invite more people to lunch. With fifteen members in the executive conference and four staffers, it was necessary to rotate luncheon invitations in order to accommodate visiting dignitaries. Gray invited congressmen and senators to these luncheons, and assistant directors were able to attend once a month. I fared a little better, attending about twice a month. One assistant director attended only one luncheon before a second $25 assessment was made, and he later estimated that the average cost to him was $16.67 per luncheon—a hefty sum at the time.

The immediate and most noticeable effect of the kitchen and the gourmet meals—and they were that—was the cooking smells; they filled the public corridor. When Gray resigned and William Ruckelshaus took over, he retained the kitchen, as did Clarence Kelley, who made the cook his assistant.

The year 1972 was full of crises. First came the Hoover succession, followed two weeks later by the Wallace shooting, followed a month later by the Watergate break-in, all during a presidential election year. At the time, we seemed to be at odds with the White House continually. On September 8, 1972, Geoffrey Shepard, a staff assistant to John Ehrlichman in the White House, sent a memorandum to the Justice Department requesting information on criminal justice problems in fourteen designated states. It was made clear that this material would be used in President Nixon's reelection campaign. The deadline set for the FBI to submit the material was already past when we received it. Kinley, Gray's personal staffer, passed on the request to the proper division. A teletype was sent to twenty-one field offices, quoting the exact language of the request and naming the White House as its source. Neither Gray nor I saw anything objectionable about furnishing criminal justice information to the president until the text of the teletype was leaked to *Time* magazine, which blasted the acting director for politicizing the FBI. Gray hit the panic button and ordered a complete investigation of every clerk and every agent who handled the teletype to identify who had turned it over to *Time*. He was mostly concerned about what the White House, almost paranoid over the press, would say to him.

Later that month, Gray called me about another urgent demand from the White House. "Mark," he said, "I've just received a call from Lawrence Higby [Haldeman's aide]. I'm getting ready to leave for a speech in Detroit. Higby wants an FBI investigation of a burglary out in Long Beach that involves medical information about the president. Will you call him and see what it's all about?"

When I called Higby, he was excited about an incident that had occurred the day before. The office of the president's physician and medical consultant had been burglarized. "Thieves broke into the doctor's office late Wednesday night or early Thursday morning," he said. "They were trying to photograph the president's medical records, which were left scattered about the floor. The president wants the FBI to look into it."

"I'll check into it immediately and call you within the hour," I told Higby.

"Thanks," he said. "We want the FBI to go all-out on it. Someone is trying to embarrass the president."

The Los Angeles office informed me that the matter was being routinely investigated by the Long Beach police, who were convinced that it was the work of juveniles. The doctor's office had been burglarized several weeks before, and a small amount of money had been taken. On both occasions, entry had been gained through a sliding door with a faulty catch, and similar break-ins in the area also were being investigated. The president's file had been dropped on the floor, but there was no indication that it had been rifled or photographed.

When I relayed this to Higby, I added that there was no jurisdictional basis for the FBI to enter the case. Forcefully and aggressively, he demanded that the FBI "issue a press release about the case." I said, "Mr. Higby, there is no reason for the FBI to become involved in the case; besides, the FBI has no authority to issue a press release except when arrests are made by the FBI." Higby argued that there must be a press release. The only promise he got from me was that I would keep him informed. But Higby did not wait for me to call him. He called me—at least fifteen times during the next ten days. My response was always "no." I wondered why the White House was so interested in that press release. The answer came after I learned that the Plumbers had broken into the office of a psychiatrist treating Daniel Ellsberg, who had leaked the Pentagon papers. I suspected that someone at the White House, knowing that the illegal operation to photograph Ellsberg's psychiatric records was bound to be discovered, wanted to be able to show that President Nixon also had been a victim of such tactics.

Gray was doing nothing to shield the FBI from these political intrusions. By the fall of 1972, disenchantment with the acting director pervaded FBI headquarters, and the feeling was spreading to the field. Although agents had welcomed Gray, he was making the same set speech in every field office and was just telling agents what they wanted to hear. They resented Gray's airing of sensitive personnel matters in the press as part of his "open window" policy. Distrust of

Gray's personal staffers intensified as they pursued their primary aim of advancing Gray's interests, no matter what the cost to the Bureau.

On November 20, 1972, Gray was hospitalized at Lawrence Memorial Hospital in New London for abdominal surgery and did not return to Washington until January 2. He had instructed me to sign all reports and correspondence during his absence. Because he routinely spent so much time away from Washington, his extended absence had no significant impact on the already hectic pace of my activities.

When Gray returned from sick leave, we met for a private conversation. He informed me that the White House was upset again, this time about leaks in the investigation of the baffling break-in at the Democratic National Committee headquarters in Washington's Watergate complex. The suspected leaker, Gray confided, was Mark Felt.

EIGHTEEN

WATERGATE

IT'S IMPOSSIBLE to exaggerate how high the stakes were in Watergate. We faced no simple burglary, but an assault on government institutions, an attack on the FBI's integrity, and unrelenting pressure to unravel one of the greatest political scandals in our nation's history. From the start, it was clear that senior administration officials were up to their necks in this mess and would stop at nothing to sabotage our investigation. White House staffers, high and low, were either evasive or obstructive. They drew the Justice Department and the CIA into their cover-up. They used the acting director of the FBI, a political appointee, to inform them of the information we dug up and attempt to limit our inquiries.

Given Pat Gray's frequent absences from Washington, I assumed full responsibility for the day-to-day Watergate investigation, and any credit or criticism should be directed at me and me alone. I quickly found out firsthand how little pressure the FBI could apply to a sitting president. Dealing with the White House in this case reminded me of pursuing the Mafia in Kansas City, when the gangsters simply refused to talk. An agent in the Washington field office, similarly frustrated, said the investigation was like "trying to get information from the Black Panther Party." As Henry E. Peterson of the Criminal Division once said of the White House staff, "Nobody sounded innocent," and many were not. Everyone sounded like they had something to hide, and almost everyone did. This applied to not only the White House but the Committee to Reelect the President.

As the Nixon tapes prove, the president's men fought our investigation with everything they had. Chief of staff Bob Haldeman laid it on the line when he complained that the FBI was "out of control"—pushing too vigorously to determine the facts of the case. I really can't describe adequately how bad it was. As investigators trying to bring the truth to light, we could not rely on Justice Department prosecutors or even federal grand juries to bring indictments. What we needed was a "Lone Ranger," who could bypass the administration's handpicked FBI director and Justice Department leadership and derail the White House cover-up.

The FBI learned of the Watergate break-in during the early hours of Saturday, June 17, 1972. The first report came from the Washington police. Five men had been apprehended in the Watergate office building. This information was relayed to Robert G. Kunkel, SAC of the Washington field office, at his home, and he instructed an agent to get to the scene as quickly as possible. Within minutes, a second call from the police was relayed to Kunkel. An "explosive device" had been found in the offices of the Democratic National Committee in the Watergate. Kunkel immediately dispatched FBI bomb specialists to the building. He had barely put down the receiver when he received a third call—this one from police chief Jerry V. Wilson, who told him that one of the burglars had been identified as James W. McCord, Jr., a former employee of the Central Intelligence Agency.

Kunkel dressed and hurried to the field office. Agents had already examined the "explosive device" and reported that it was a microphone and radio transmitter hidden in a smoke detector case on the wall of a conference room. Kunkel then ordered an all-out investigation for possible violation of the interception of communications statute—a primary investigative jurisdiction of the FBI.

The dummy smoke detector looked like an explosive device. It contained several batteries wired together and a battery-operated wristwatch, the basic components of a bomb. The microphone and radio transmitter were obviously meant for bugging purposes, but the wristwatch was puzzling. Kunkel deduced that it was there to give a continuous signal, permitting whoever was monitoring the device to get an accurate fix on the radio frequency.

Because of the unusual circumstances, the night supervisor in the General Investigative Division notified me at home at 7:00 A.M. When he briefed me on the steps Kunkel was taking, I approved and asked that Kunkel be instructed to press the investigation energetically as a major case. At 8:30, I was in my office calling the night supervisor for an additional briefing. "This is getting rather complicated," he said. "I'd better come over to your office."

A few minutes later he was telling me what we knew so far. At approximately 2:30 that morning, a security guard at the Watergate complex noticed a partially open basement stairwell door that had tape placed across the spring bolt to prevent it from locking. He removed the tape, but when he saw the same door taped again about forty minutes later, he telephoned the police at once. Officers were on the scene within minutes. They surprised and arrested five individuals at Democratic headquarters. They were identified as James Walter McCord, Jr., Bernard L. Barker, Frank Anthony Fiorini, Virgilio R. Gonzales, and Eugenio Martinez y Creaga. They had in their possession burglary tools and eavesdropping and photographic equipment.

"What in the world were they doing?" I asked.

"Several ceiling panels had been removed as well as an air vent

cover," the supervisor said. "They had been taking apart the telephone equipment. All of them were wearing surgical-type plastic
gloves. It looks like they were getting ready to install more eavesdropping equipment or repair or put new batteries in equipment
already there."

"Where are they now?" I asked. "What did the police do with
them?"

"They're all in jail. Bond has been set at $50,000 for all but
McCord, and his bond is $30,000. They're charged with burglary."

"Have they said what they were doing?"

"They haven't said one word. They didn't even call an attorney,
but one showed up anyway. It's very mysterious."

I thought for a minute. "Tell Kunkel we've got to go all out on
this. We'll cooperate with the Washington police, but we will take
charge. This thing has all kinds of political ramifications and the
press is going to have a field day."

I thought of other aspects of the case that would have to be covered. Gray was out of town, as usual, and he would have to be
briefed as soon as I had a more complete picture.

"There's one other thing," the night supervisor said. "The
arrested men had $2,400 in their possession, including thirteen new
hundred-dollar bills."

It would be some time before we understood the significance of
those hundred-dollar bills (which eventually linked the burglars and
the Committee to Reelect the President). What sense did it make for
burglars to carry around such a sum of money? In fact, none of it
made any sense. Obviously the police had broken up some kind of
political espionage operation. But the utter stupidity of it baffled
me. What could anyone find at the Democratic National Committee that would be worth the risks?

At 10:00 A.M. I called Kunkel for a further briefing. "Mark," he
said, "there's a lot more to this than meets the eye." Shortly after the

five men were arrested and taken to the Second District station, a Washington attorney named Michael Douglas Caddy appeared at the station and said he was representing them. Because they had not made any phone calls, Caddy was asked how he knew of the arrests. He wouldn't tell the police a thing and left saying he would contact the U.S. attorney.

"Bob," I asked, "how many agents do you have working on the case?"

"Eighteen," he said after a little mental arithmetic.

"Are you sure that's enough?"

"That's enough for now, but this thing is going to expand all over the place in a day or two."

I agreed with him and asked him to keep me briefed and let me know if he ran into problems. I also told him that I would have to call Gray in Los Angeles. Hoover had been sharp, brief, and to the point, but I knew that Gray, aggressive and inexperienced, would ask many questions.

"We have a three-hour time advantage," I told Kunkel, "so I'll wait until one o'clock to call Gray. That's ten o'clock Los Angeles time. I want to brief him as completely as possible."

"We should have a lot more information by that time," he said. "We're getting search warrants to go into the rooms the subjects occupied at the Watergate Hotel."

The room search turned up an additional $3,500 in crisp new hundred-dollar bills of the same series as those found at the time of arrest. The searchers also found an envelope containing a personal check made out by E. Howard Hunt, Jr., who was quickly identified as a former CIA employee who worked at the Agency from November 1949 until April 1970. From FBI files we learned that a full-field investigation had been conducted on Hunt in July 1971, when he had been considered for a staff position at the White House. A query was made, and White House security chief Alexander P. Butterfield

told FBI agents that Hunt had been used on "highly sensitive matters" but was no longer employed there.

When I called Gray, he had already left his hotel and was en
route to Santa Ana, California, to deliver a speech at Pepperdine
University. Consequently my message had to be relayed through the
senior resident agent in Santa Ana. Gray called back after his speech
and we discussed the case at length. He seemed as surprised as I
was, and we wondered who would try such a stupid escapade. He
instructed that agents press the investigation vigorously; in addition,
he wanted a daily briefing.

I kept Gray posted at Palm Springs on Sunday, at San Francisco
on Monday, and at Sacramento on Tuesday. He returned to his office
at 7:35 A.M. on Wednesday, June 21. Waiting on his desk was a
detailed summary of the investigation to date, which I was sure he
would want to send to the attorney general. For reasons that he did
not explain, he ruled against passing it on. Much later I learned that
throughout the investigation, he was sharing all the Bureau's knowledge with the White House staff.

As the Watergate investigation started, bits and pieces of information began leaking to the press. The White House raised the roof
with Gray, accusing the FBI of leaking and ordering him to put a
stop to it. Among these leaks was a story that Gray planned to call
off the FBI investigation and would not permit agents to subpoena
the record of telephone toll calls placed by presidential aide Charles
Colson. We later learned that this leak came from the White House,
and thus it is reasonable to believe that John Ehrlichman, Bob
Haldeman, or John Dean felt the FBI had been neutralized.*

---

* Correspondent Sandy Smith of *Time* magazine, who was well connected to the FBI's upper
echelons, was the recipient of this leak. Although here Felt blames the White House, a
clever memo by a Felt aide also suggested that Democratic National Committee Chairman
Lawrence O'Brien may have been guilty of the disclosure. But the leak probably came from
Felt himself, warning Gray that if he allowed a Watergate whitewash, his career would be in
public tatters. —Editor

On Saturday, June 24, Gray called in SAC Kunkel and twenty-six agents from the Washington field office who were working on the case. He accused them of "suffering from flap jaw," and, as he later put it, "I literally put my track shoes in their backs," giving them "a strong verbal direction that we were going to press the investigation to the hilt." The agents took this accusation as a serious reflection on their integrity, but when Kunkel attempted to speak out in defense of his men, he was brusquely silenced by the acting director.

The leaks continued, however, and within a few days of the burglary Bob Woodward and Carl Bernstein were giving *Washington Post* readers details of the investigation, sometimes within hours after the Bureau had learned those details.

The White House was furious. Ehrlichman called Gray on the carpet and told him that the leaks must stop. Gray reacted by sending an inspection team to the Washington field office to question all the agents working on the case. When that did not stop the leaks, he ordered Charles W. Bates, assistant director and head of the Criminal Investigative Division, to grill the men under oath.

These actions further antagonized the agents but did nothing to stop the leaks. Numerous times when Gray was out of the city, John Dean, the White House legal counsel, called me and demanded that I take other steps to silence the leakers. I refused and pointed out to him that some of the leaks could not possibly have come from the Bureau, since they included information to which we were not privy. This did not mollify Dean. It was this series of calls that led the White House to believe that I was Deep Throat, the mysterious source Woodward and Bernstein relied on for their sensational stories about Watergate. Six months after the break-in, Gray approached me personally. "You know, Mark," he said, "Dick Kleindienst told me that I might have to get rid of you. He says White House staff members are convinced that you are the FBI source of leaks to Woodward and Bernstein."

This disclosure came as an unpleasant surprise. My contacts with Kleindienst had been frequent and friendly; I had never picked up the slightest indication that I was suspect. I could feel the anger rising in me, but I appreciated Gray's indication of support. Gray went on, "I told Kleindienst that you've worked with me in a very competent manner and I'm convinced that you are completely loyal. I told him I was not going to move you out. Kleindienst told me, 'Pat, I love you for that.'"

Startled as I was by this development, I did not want to be the one who prevented Gray from getting the permanent appointment as director. "I certainly don't want it on my conscience that I stood in the way of your nomination," I said. "I have been thinking of retirement, but I don't want it to appear that I am leaving under pressure. I am willing to accept a transfer to the West Coast as special agent in charge."

"No," said Gray, "I wouldn't do that to you. How long have you served in the FBI?"

"Thirty-one years."

Half to himself, Gray said, "I wouldn't do this to someone who has served his country and the FBI so ably and loyally."

I am grateful to Pat Gray for that.

Much later, I learned that the White House had frequently complained to Kleindienst that I was Deep Throat. No one from the Nixon White House has ever told me why I was the principal suspect, but their reasoning is obvious to me now. I was supposed to be jealous of Gray for being appointed acting director. They judged that my high position in the FBI gave me access to all the Watergate information and that I was releasing it to Woodward and Bernstein in an effort to discredit Gray so that he would be removed and I would have another chance at the job. Additionally, I had been less than cooperative in responding to what I regarded as improper requests from the White House. I suppose the White House staff had me tagged as an insubordinate.

It is true that I would have welcomed an appointment as FBI director when Hoover died. It is not true that I was jealous of Gray. Once the die was cast, I resolved, for the good of the FBI, to help Gray as much as I could.

I did talk to Bob Woodward on one occasion during the Watergate investigation. He requested an interview, which I gave him in September. To make sure I would not be misquoted, I asked my assistant, Inspector Wason G. Campbell, to be present. Woodward, however, was not looking for information. He understood my position as head of the FBI Watergate investigation: I could not release new information that might undermine our efforts to prosecute those involved in these crimes. Woodward simply wanted to check out the information he and Bernstein already had collected. He asked me to tell him what was accurate and what was not. During that first interview, I declined to cooperate with him in this manner, and that was that.

I did not tell Woodward that at the time, we were increasingly concerned about the progress of our investigation. After two months of interviews across the country, we were building a good case against the Watergate burglars. But the Justice Department was declining to authorize us to pursue a broader series of election-law violations we had uncovered, including the so-called dirty tricks that Nixon campaign operative Donald Segretti played on the Democrats. We tried to make our frustration clear discreetly in our internal memos. In one, for example, we called attention to press reports alleging that the General Accounting Office suspected violations of new campaign finance laws by Nixon's reelection committee. We pointed out that "to date we have received no requests from the [Justice] Department to conduct the investigation of matters reported by GAO," and emphasized that "Election Laws violations . . . are investigated only at the specific request of the Department." In another passage, we all but implored the Watergate prosecutor, Assistant U.S. Attorney Earl Silbert, to put us on the bigger case. "It is expected that additional leads will be requested by AUSA Silbert," we wrote, "as a result of his detailed review of Federal grand jury testimony, his preparation of indictments and further appearance of witnesses before the Federal grand jury."

But our expectations were dashed. We consistently failed in our attempts to expand the investigation beyond the Watergate break-in to a broader series of election law violations. As our frustrations grew, I began to consider the advantage we would have if a responsible member of the press could apply public pressure on the White House to come clean. If nothing else, it would speed things up. We could see from the start that the White House was trying to cover up its involvement in Watergate. If we in the FBI followed our usual investigative procedures, the administration might get away with widespread criminality. We would be blamed for that, and for not doing our duty to uphold the Constitution. This would cause citizens to doubt our honesty and would ruin the FBI's reputation as an impartial law enforcement agency. The only way to investigate these crimes would be to go outside the standards that the FBI followed so scrupulously—standards that I had enforced in the Inspection Division. But we would be blamed for that too, also hurting our reputation. In short, there was no ideal way out of this dilemma.

Debating with myself, I framed the issue this way: Did my obligation as an FBI official to work within channels supersede my duty as an American citizen to expose the truth? It always had in the past, but maybe not in this case. I met with Woodward over the next few months, again only confirming or not confirming information he already had collected from other sources. I came to respect him as an honest journalist, and I appreciated the secure public outlet he gave me.

It seems likely to me that the press was receiving inside information from more than one source. But despite reporters' best efforts, the cover-up continued. The White House was having considerable success suppressing information or putting the right spin on new disclosures. The Justice Department investigation was also undermined and contaminated by White House influence.

We already had found a White House link to the Watergate break-in through E. Howard Hunt's involvement. He was placed at the scene and eventually admitted that he was the one who called Douglas Caddy, the lawyer who appeared at the police station unbidden to bail out the burglars. This explained how Caddy knew of the arrest. We also discovered that White House records listed presidential counsel Colson as Hunt's supervisor from June 1971 until March 1972—at least four months after Hunt began to recruit secret operatives who were later implicated in the Watergate break-in. Colson's private secretary initialed Hunt's pay vouchers, and his private phone line to the White House was billed to the home address of Catherine Chenow, secretary to the Plumbers, the White House unit organized to plug leaks. A White House internal memo dated March 30, 1972, described Hunt as "very effective for us," and requested that he be shifted to the Committee to Reelect the President.

Other pieces of the puzzle began to fit together when we discovered that G. Gordon Liddy had accompanied Hunt on several trips to recruit employees for "security work" with the Republican Party. Telephone numbers in the possession of some of the arrested men belonged to Liddy at the Committee to Reelect the President. A cashier's check covering a number of campaign contributions had been given to Liddy at the committee and deposited to the account of Bernard Barker at the Republic National Bank in Miami.

Alfred Baldwin III, a former FBI agent, admitted that he had been working for James McCord and that he was assigned to monitor the microphones planted in Democratic headquarters from Room 419 in the Howard Johnson Motel, directly across the street from the Watergate. Baldwin told us that while he was occupying this room, Liddy had counted out some $18,000 in crisp new hundred-dollar bills in the presence of Hunt and had given the money to McCord.* Liddy was also known to have shredded large numbers of documents at the offices of the Committee to Reelect the President. (On July 28, Liddy was fired from the committee, ostensibly for refusing to talk to the FBI.) Baldwin also made it clear that the Democratic National Committee headquarters had been bugged for some time. Baldwin had made transcripts of the overheard conversations, which were given to McCord, who seemed to be in charge of the monitoring operation.

The FBI struck pay dirt when it found Michael Richardson, a Miami photographer. Richardson told agents that a week before the break-in, a man he tentatively identified from photographs as Bernard Barker had come to his store in a Cuban neighborhood. The man had two rolls of exposed 35 millimeter film that he wanted developed immediately and printed in eight-by-ten enlargements. There were thirty-eight negatives in all. Richardson said that they were photographs of documents, most of which had an emblem and "Chairman, Democratic National Committee" printed on them. The documents were photographed against a background of shag carpeting. Hands in clear gloves held down the corners of each document.

At every turn, FBI agents encountered delaying and obstructing tactics at the White House and the Committee to Reelect the President. For example, Dean sat in on all FBI interviews with White House staffers, which had a chilling effect. Agents encountered resistance from Dean in their efforts to obtain the records of Colson's toll calls. And they got no cooperation from Dean in their search for Catherine Chenow, the Plumbers' secretary. Kunkel did

---

* Baldwin talked to the FBI soon after the burglary arrests in June, but Woodward and Bernstein did not report his involvement until September 1972, demonstrating that Deep Throat generally refrained from leaking information not yet known to the reporters. —Editor

not believe Dean's contention that she was vacationing in Europe and Dean did not know how to get in touch with her. (In his book on Watergate, Dean admitted that he knew where Chenow was in England and sent his assistant to bring her back so that she could be coached before the FBI interviewed her.)

In addition, Dean had kept the items from Hunt's White House safe in his possession for five days before turning some of them (not all) over to the FBI. I had my own run-in with Dean over the safe. Deep Throat had leaked to the *Washington Post* that one of the items in the safe was a handgun.* This embarrassed Dean and the presidential staff because it raised questions about the effectiveness of a White House security system that would allow Hunt to smuggle a weapon past the guards. When Dean called me to ask that the FBI issue a press release denying that a gun was involved, I said, "John, that's a ridiculous request. We are not going to do it. The answer is no." Dean hung up without comment, and later that day the information officer at the Justice Department issued an obfuscating statement, presumably at Dean's request.

In late June, Washington SAC Kunkel sent Gray an airtel—a message prepared in the form of a teletype but sent by mail—bluntly highlighting the difficulties involved in dealing with the White House and asking that the Bureau take a tougher stand. I am convinced this airtel was the reason Gray later demoted Kunkel, transferring him to St. Louis.

As the cover-up coordinator, Dean had to track the progress of the FBI investigation. As we learned much later, Dean arranged to meet with Gray in the acting director's efficiency apartment in Washington. Not feeling secure even there, they conducted their

* Woodward and Bernstein never revealed that their premier source had leaked this detail. In this passage, Felt appears to be either making a guess or showing off his knowledge in a hint to discerning readers that he is Deep Throat. —Editor

business in a nearby park. As a result of this secret meeting, which Gray did not report to the FBI professional staff or to his personal assistants, Gray ordered a summary of all developments to that time. This summary, dated July 21, was directed to the attorney general and quickly forwarded to Dean.

Dean then asked Gray for the "raw files" on the case, together with copies of teletypes setting forth leads and interview results. In this way, he hoped to keep abreast of the Bureau's progress. Gray obliged by asking Kunkel for copies of these documents, explaining that he wanted to familiarize himself with day-to-day developments. Dean himself came to Gray's office to collect the first package of this sensitive material. He continued to request more material and Gray obliged him by turning over a second package of reports and teletypes on October 2, 1972. FBI agents conducted twenty-six interviews with White House staff and sixty with individuals at the Committee to Reelect the President; Dean received copies of interview reports from most. Had I known about any of this at the time, I would have done whatever was necessary to stop the transfer of sensitive material to the White House.

Agents were forced to interview employees of the Committee to Reelect the President in the presence of a committee attorney. Permission for the attorney's presence was granted by assistant U.S. attorney Earl J. Silbert, who was handling the Watergate case. The committee argued that its attorney must be present because the Democratic National Committee was suing the reelection committee for damages. But several committee employees contacted us and asked to be reinterviewed without the knowledge of committee officials. The presence of a committee lawyer during the original interview, they said, had prevented them from being completely candid. They also said that all committee employees subpoenaed to testify by the Watergate grand jury were later debriefed by committee attorneys about what they had testified.

One employee who came forward told us that Hugh Sloan, Jr., who supervised committee finances, had kept a briefcase full of money in his safe. From February to April 1972, our informant told us, Sloan had disbursed large sums to various committee officials for unknown purposes—$50,000 to Jeb Stuart Magruder, $100,000 to Herbert L. Porter, and $89,000 to Gordon Liddy. Another employee on reinterview told us that committee officials were throwing red herrings across the FBI's trail to keep us from getting at the truth. Reports on these second interviews, however, were among those that Gray provided to John Dean. Dean alerted committee officials, who challenged these employees. This certainly discouraged others from coming to the Bureau with important information.

The first concrete indication I had of Gray's role in hampering our investigation came when we began to trace the money that had been in the possession of the Watergate burglars. Agents discovered that Bernard Barker had deposited four checks totaling $89,000 in his Miami account. The checks were drawn on the Banco Internacional of Mexico City by Manuel Ogarrio, an attorney. Obviously the next step was to interview Ogarrio, but Gray flatly ordered me to call it off because it "might upset" a CIA operation in Mexico.

I did not know at the time that less than a week after the break-in, President Nixon had called H. R. Haldeman to the Oval Office for a report on the case. The two discussed the possibility of directing Gen. Vernon A. Walters, the new deputy director of the CIA, to tell Gray to "stay the hell out of this," as Haldeman put it. "We don't want you to go any farther with it."

A little later Haldeman tried to elaborate. "And the proposal would be that Ehrlichman and I call them [the CIA] in and say, ah..."

Nixon picked it up with, "All right, fine. How do you call him in...I mean just....Well, we protected [CIA Director Richard] Helms from one hell of a lot of things." (Those "things" were never specified.)

Less than two hours later, Haldeman, Helms, and Walters were meeting with Ehrlichman in his office at the White House. When Walters returned to the CIA, he wrote a memorandum recording what he was told.

> The bugging affair at the Democratic National Committee head-quarters at the Watergate Apartments had made a lot of noise and the Democrats are trying to maximize it.... The investigation was leading to a lot of important people and this could get worse.... Haldeman asked what the connection with the Agency was, and Director Helms replied that there was none. Haldeman said the whole affair was getting embarrassing and it was the President's wish that Walters call on Acting Director Gray and suggest to him that since the five suspects had been arrested, this should be suffi-cient, and that it was not advantageous to have the inquiry pushed, especially in Mexico.

Walters wrote that Haldeman told him to go to Gray and tell him "that I had talked to the White House and suggest that the investiga-tion not be pushed further." Haldeman assured Walters that Gray would be receptive because "he was looking for guidance in the mat-ter." These instructions were given to Walters, according to his memo, despite Helms's repeated assertions that the FBI investigation would not expose any covert CIA programs. The record shows that Walters did see Gray the same day to pass along Haldeman's instruc-tions. According to Walters, Gray replied that "his problem was how to low-key the matter now that it was launched.... Gray then said this was a most awkward matter to come up during an election year and he would see what he could do."

Three days later, on June 26, Walters was again summoned to the White House, where John Dean told him, "The investigation of the Watergate bugging case is extremely awkward and there are a lot of leads to important people." On June 28, Dean said to Walters, "The problem is how to stop the FBI investigation beyond the five suspects." On that same day, Helms phoned Gray, requesting that the FBI not interview Karl Wagner and John Caswell, two CIA case officers, because they were engaged in highly sensitive assignments. Gray passed this down to me as an order. I was able to stop the Wagner interview, but Caswell had already been questioned. Both were thought to have information concerning E. Howard Hunt.

The CIA was less than cooperative in other ways. Inquiries from FBI agents ran into a stone wall at the Agency or, worse still, encountered outright deception. For example, we asked the CIA about a man named Pennington, who had once been James McCord's supervisor. The CIA gave us a summary on a former employee named Cecil H. Pennington who had no connection with McCord. It was more than a year later before we learned that the man we wanted was Lee Pennington, who had been closely associated with McCord, personally and professionally.* William E. Colby, Helms's replacement as CIA director, brushed this fact aside airily by saying that "we were trying to keep publicity away from the CIA."

By July 5, the delays and obstructions hindering the FBI investigation had gotten to the point where Kunkel, Bates, and I requested an appointment with Gray to discuss the problems. Kunkel restated the points he had made in his airtel and we all argued strenuously against the restrictions that had been imposed on us, particularly the stop on an inquiry into the Mexico City operation.

"Look," I told Gray, "the reputation of the FBI is at stake. This is even more important for you as acting director than it is for us. In the future, you are going to have to convince U.S. senators that we

---

* The CIA later reported that Pennington went to McCord's home shortly after the Watergate burglary and destroyed documents that might show a link between McCord and the CIA. Pennington died, apparently of a heart attack, in October 1974. —Editor

did a good job on this case. We can't delay the Ogarrio interview
any longer. I hate to make this sound like an ultimatum, but unless
we get a request in writing from Director Helms to forgo the Ogarrio interview, we're going ahead anyway."

Gray hesitated and then looked at Bates and Kunkel. The expressions on their faces told him that he was facing near mutiny. He
drew a long breath and said, "I'll call Helms today."

"That's not all," I went on. "We must do something about the
complete lack of cooperation from John Dean and the Committee
to Reelect the President. It's obvious they're holding back—delaying
and leading us astray in every way they can. We expect this sort of
thing when we are investigating organized crime, but we can't sit
still and accept it from the White House and the committee."

"Mr. Gray," Kunkel broke in, "the obstructions we are encoun-
tering do a grave disservice to the president. I think you should call
and tell him what the problems are."

"Bob is absolutely right," I said. "The whole thing is going to
explode in the president's face." Gray demurred. He thought it would
be better to call Clark MacGregor, the new head of the Committee to
Reelect the President, who was with Nixon in San Clemente. When
we left Gray, however, I told Kunkel, "Get a teletype ready for Mexico
City telling them to go ahead with the interview. If we haven't heard
anything by the close of business today, send it."

Gray bowed to our ultimatum. He immediately called General
Walters, who noted in a memorandum, "He [Gray] said that the
pressures on him to continue the investigation were great. Unless he
had documents from me to the effect that their investigation was
endangering the national security, he would have to go ahead with
the investigation of the money transaction." Describing a meeting
with Gray on July 6, Walters wrote, "I had a long association with the
President and was as desirous as anyone of protecting him. I did not
believe that a letter from the Agency asking the FBI to lay off this
investigation on spurious grounds . . . would serve the President."

Gray called me on the intercom that same day to say that there would be no letter from the CIA and we should proceed with the Ogarrio interview. I did not tell him that instructions to that effect had been sent out the previous evening. Gray also called Clark MacGregor to inform him of the conference with his mutinous aides. As a result of that conversation, President Nixon called Gray. I have no source for what was said except Gray's testimony during his confirmation hearings. According to that account, Gray said, "Mr. President, [Vernon] Walters and I feel that people on your staff are trying to mortally wound you by using the CIA and the FBI and by confusing the question of CIA interest in, or not in, people the FBI wishes to interview. I have just talked to Clark MacGregor and asked him to speak to you about this."

The president supposedly answered, "Pat, you just continue to conduct your aggressive and thorough investigation."

The FBI worked closely with the U.S. attorney's office and with Justice Department lawyers who were handling the case before it went to the special prosecutor. They were given the results of FBI investigations on a daily basis. When it became apparent that many of the suspects and witnesses were reluctant to even discuss the case with us, let alone tell the truth, the names were turned over to Earl Silbert, who had them called before the federal grand jury, where they could be placed under oath and the inducement to tell the truth was more compelling. The evidence we collected led to the successful prosecution of the five original suspects, plus Hunt and Liddy.

At this point Gray again called Bates, Kunkel, and me into his office, ostensibly to update Gray on events. But when we took our places in his private office, the first thing Gray did was hold up a notepad on which he had drawn seven squares arranged in a circle, with a line connecting each square. There were no names on the notepad but we knew that Gray was referring to the five original Watergate burglars—McCord, Barker, Fiorini, Gonzales, and Martinez—plus E. Howard Hunt and Gordon Liddy. "Can the investigation be confined to these seven subjects?" he asked.

"We do not have all the evidence yet," I told Gray, "but I am convinced we will be going much higher than these seven. These men are the pawns. We want the ones who moved the pawns." Both Bates and Kunkel agreed with me. The investigation still had a long way to go. Gray never raised the point again. He had run up a trial balloon and it had been shot down.

No one could have stopped the driving force of the investigation without an explosion in the Bureau—not even J. Edgar Hoover. For me, as well as for all the agents involved, it had become a question of our integrity. We had been attacked unfairly for dragging our feet, and as professional law enforcement officers we were determined to go on. That we were doing a good job, moreover, cannot be denied. When Assistant Attorney General Peterson testified before the Senate Select Watergate Committee, he was able to say, "The investigation was 90 percent completed at the time the special prosecutor was appointed." In fact, the special prosecutor delayed the day of indictment for the higher-ups because he and his staff had to familiarize themselves with the intricacies of the case before proceeding.

Attacks against the FBI did not stop. One charge hurled at us echoed our internal debates. Critics said we investigated only one illegal operation—the Watergate break-in—and failed to investigate the broader campaign of so-called dirty tricks of Donald Segretti and others who were working undercover for the Committee to Reelect the President. The simple fact is that the Justice Department told us not to investigate these aspects of the case. Ordinarily the special agent in charge is authorized to use his own initiative in the investigation of criminal cases. But Justice Department authorization is required in cases dealing with the election law, civil rights statutes, and others. In the Watergate case, we furnished substantial information about the dirty tricks to the Justice Department, and in each instance we were told that no further investigation was necessary. After the special prosecutor took over, the FBI was requested to probe into this area—and it did so very effectively.

Watergate was a trying time for the FBI and a nightmarish period for me. In spite of the roadblocks, the FBI did an excellent job, as the record attests. During the first eighty-four days of the investigation, more than 1,500 people were interviewed, 1,900 leads handled, and 120 subpoenas served. In all, 130 investigative reports totaling more than 3,500 pages were submitted by 330 agents in 51 field offices who worked more than 14,000 man hours. The prosecution was based on information developed by the Bureau, and the FBI apologizes to no one for this achievement. If at times I worked outside of normal procedures and behind the back of the acting director, I did so in the hope that someday the FBI community would understand why I took these steps. I hoped these FBI loyalists would recognize the extraordinary situation in which we found ourselves and understand what I had to do to protect the country—and the Bureau.

In all fairness, I must give some of the credit for the success of the FBI investigation to the press. The FBI did a fine job under the circumstances, but there is no doubt that much of the White House involvement in the break-in and the subsequent cover-up would never have been brought to light without the help of the press. People will debate for a long time whether I did the right thing by helping Woodward. The bottom line is that we did get the whole truth out, and isn't that what the FBI is supposed to do?

ADDENDUM BY JOHN O'CONNOR

When Mark Felt last wrote for publication in the mid-1980s, he still was hiding his identity as Deep Throat. Since then, his memories of the period have almost entirely faded. As a consequence, he has never revealed three important aspects of his story: why he initiated

his high-stakes garage meetings with Woodward, how he planned
and managed those meetings, and how he escaped detection at the
FBI. With the help of his formerly secret files and interviews with
his family and colleagues, I have reconstructed below, to the extent
possible, his operational strategies. —John O'Connor

A generation later, Mark Felt's operation to expose the Nixon
administration's crimes stands out as bold, if not foolhardy. Consider the political establishment he took on—a coalition involved in
a widespread conspiracy to obstruct justice. By the time of the
Watergate break-in on June 17, 1972, Nixon's senior staff was already
busy covering up operations ranging from the Kissinger wiretaps,
the break-in at the office of Daniel Ellsberg's psychiatrist, the shadowy work of the White House "Plumbers," and an extremist plan of
political disruptions codenamed "gemstone." The capture of the
Watergate burglars heightened anxieties all around. Staffers at the
White House and the Committee to Reelect the President knew
that the arrests threatened the much broader array of campaign
dirty tricks they had approved and financed. Leaders at the Central
Intelligence Agency, aware that CIA veterans Hunt and McCord,
along with some of the CIA's old Cuban operatives, had been
caught, were concerned that the growing scandal would draw attention to their own covert operations. And the Justice Department, an
institution largely ignored by historians in this case, placed an
impenetrable roadblock in the FBI's way as it pursued these powerful forces, a silent obstruction that came perilously close to success.

As a professional investigator whose job was to catch criminals,
no matter how high ranking, Mark Felt had to contend with these
powerful forces—and with his own acting director, L. Patrick Gray,
who was sharing every twist of the FBI investigation with the White
House counsel, John Dean. On the very morning of the arrests, Felt
knew he had stumbled onto something big—a political operation, a

CIA operation, or both. He realized as well that the White House would put heavy pressure on the FBI to limit the investigation, and that nothing less than the independence of the Bureau was at stake. Felt's shrewd strategy was to turn the light on the mess his agents were uncovering, to keep public attention focused on Watergate. Only two days after the burglary, he helped Woodward on the *Washington Post*'s first big story, confirming that Hunt was connected to the White House and a prime suspect in the break-in. The ploy worked. The article made a big splash, and Felt managed to cover his tracks: Attorney General Richard Kleindienst blamed the story on Washington's Metropolitan Police Department. More *Washington Post* revelations followed quickly after that.

Numerous stories by Woodward and Bernstein seemed to emerge directly from FBI investigative reports, but none of them led directly to Felt. The reporters had interviewed many witnesses and had gleaned information from a half dozen FBI agents as well as many other sources. By night, Deep Throat confirmed what the reporters had discovered and sent them on new paths of investigation. By day, Felt played the role of Gray's loyal number two, overseeing the grilling of field agents under oath about possible FBI leaks. In one icy memo, he wrote that "I personally contacted [Washington] SAC Kunkel to point out that it appeared the *Washington Post* or at least a reporter had access to [a confidential investigative file]. I told him he should forcibly remind all agents of the need to be most circumspect in talking about this case with anyone outside the Bureau."

By mid-August, however, Woodward and Bernstein were running out of steam, and the public seemed to be tiring of the story; Democratic presidential candidate George McGovern pounded the White House, blaming Watergate on the incumbent, but voters shrugged off his speeches as so much partisan ranting. The massive FBI investigation also was slowing. Then on September 15, the Justice Department announced the indictment of seven suspects—the five burglars and their supervisors, Hunt and Liddy—and announced that no further indictments would be coming. "We have absolutely no evidence to indicate that any others should be charged," a department spokesman said. Bernstein's Justice Department source confirmed that the investigation was in "a state of repose."

Mark Felt recognized that he was contending with a quiet but highly effective curtailment of what had been a promising investigation—a silent obstruction. At this point, an FBI leader going by the book would have strictly limited the Bureau's work. Though the FBI usually had plenary jurisdiction to investigate any federal crime, it needed permission from the Justice Department to delve into violations of election laws, among others. Because a range of Republican campaign violations, including Donald Segretti's dirty tricks, fell under this provision, Justice would have to approve expanding the Watergate investigation to cover such shenanigans. But in this case, Justice defined the case narrowly, focusing only on the burglary. That limited what the FBI could do and prevented the Watergate grand jury from considering the larger conspiracy that would have led investigators right into the White House.

Even assuming that Segretti's operations should have been divorced from those of the Watergate burglars, his dirty tricks warranted a second investigation. But Justice was under no obligation to open one. The department, led by Attorney General Kleindienst and the chief of his criminal division, Henry Peterson—both Nixon loyalists—enjoyed broad prosecutorial discretion. Its leaders could open an investigation or not, as they chose. And they chose to regard Segretti's dirty tricks as routine politics (although he eventually served a brief sentence for distributing defamatory campaign literature). The chief prosecutor, Assistant U.S. Attorney Earl Silbert, was characterized in an FBI memo as "satisfied that the activities of these men [like Segretti] were political and they were not involved in nor were they part of the Watergate conspiracy." This refusal to prosecute required no public announcement and the public did not know about the allegations anyway. So Watergate was ending silently.

The Justice Department approach frustrated and angered Felt. While he saw the Watergate break-in as part of a broad spectrum of violations, Justice ordered him, in effect, to stick to the break-in. His first response was to leak the restraints that were impeding his investigation. Nearly a week before the Justice Department announced its limited indictments, Woodward and Bernstein, primed by Deep Throat, reported that the Watergate investigation had been completed and that agents had not been allowed to investigate violations of the law on political contributions. But the story raised little public outcry.

Felt knew he had to keep the Segretti case alive. Donald Segretti was a small fish, but the allegations against him—such as disrupting Democratic rallies and campaign logistics—showed the bigger point Deep Throat was trying to make: the Watergate burglary was not an isolated act, but part of a larger conspiracy. The dirty tricks were financed by the same slush fund used for the break-in and potentially implicated major administration actors: Dwight Chapin, who originally supervised Segretti; Haldeman, who was Chapin's boss and conceived of the Segretti program; E. Howard Hunt and G. Gordon Liddy, who eventually took over responsibility for Segretti's operation; John Dean, Charles Colson, John Ehrlichman, Jeb Magruder, and John Mitchell, who supervised or dealt with Hunt and Liddy; Herbert Kalmbach, Nixon's personal lawyer, who paid Segretti; and, by implication, the president himself.

In short, Felt could link Segretti both to the Watergate intruders and to the White House. If he could nail Segretti, he could negate the administration's claim that the intruders were small-timers work-

ing on their own. He also could destroy the prosecution's theory—
that the break-in was motivated by E. Howard Hunt's extortion
scheme against a Democratic official with rival business interests.

Sensing this broader conspiracy early on, Felt pushed the envelope on his investigation of the break-in, hoping that Justice would
then pursue the leads. As he told Woodward, "You don't do those
1,500 interviews and not have something on your hands other than a
single break-in." Felt managed to shine some light on the Segretti
allegations by investigating his possible connections to Hunt and the
Watergate burglars instead of his dirty tricks per se. But the Justice
Department declined to pick up on the FBI leads, concluding that
Segretti's operations added up to no more than "harassment" or
"political activities." Charles Bolz, a Felt aide, reported in mid-Octo-
ber that Assistant Attorney General Peterson "advised he was fully
aware of the extent of the FBI's investigation of Segretti and he is
also aware of the allegations as to Segretti's political harassment
activities and attempts to recruit personnel to assist in such, as set
forth in recent news articles. Mr. Peterson stated he does not believe
Segretti's activities are in violation of any federal statutes and,
accordingly, he can see no basis for requesting any additional investigation of Segretti by the FBI at this time."

By then, Mark had leaked the September story reporting that the
FBI investigation had been curtailed and had generated several internal FBI memos suggesting the silent obstruction by the Justice
Department. When these revelations failed to spark a broader investigation, Mark concluded that he had to publicize details relating to the
broader allegations, allowing the public, the Congress, the courts,
and the media to see and evaluate. And that could only be done by in-
depth journalism revealing the full scope of the broader conspiracy. If
the story were told well, any blame would accrue to the Justice
Department for not allowing a more thorough investigation.

Mark knew he was about to put himself on the line. By going

"out of the box"—cooperating closely with Woodward—he risked revealing himself as the reporter's source: he was, after all, the most senior official involved in the investigation who had not signed on to the cover-up. As he writes in this chapter, he was in the sights of both Nixon and Kleindienst. He was concerned as well about how the CIA would react to an expanded investigation. Deep Throat could have been excused for lying low at this point; instead, he raised the stakes, taking as many personal precautions as he could.

First, the old counterintelligence agent utilized clandestine protocols. He chose a quiet Virginia parking garage just across the Potomac from Washington for his nighttime meetings with Woodward and instructed the reporter to take a circuitous route to the rendezvous, minimizing the possibility of a chance observation. To signal a garage meeting, Woodward was told to move a planter holding a red construction flag to the rear of his apartment balcony. When Felt wanted a garage rendezvous, Woodward would find a round clock face, with the meeting time indicated, on page 20 of his New York Times.

Felt could easily manage this system of secret signals as he commuted from his home in Virginia. He was an early riser and drove himself to work, usually arriving around 6:00 A.M. and leaving late at night. He could cross either of two bridges and go a few minutes out of his way to pass by Woodward's apartment on his way to or from work or on a break. Felt also could stop by Woodward's apartment early in the morning, where copies of the Times were stacked in the lobby, marked with the apartment numbers of their subscribers. Drawing the rudimentary clock face would have taken a few seconds at most.

At their first long meeting in the garage during the predawn hours of October 9, Felt played the role of "teacher," as Woodward characterized him, sketching the outlines of a Watergate scandal that went far beyond the burglary.

Although Woodward was the younger man, he sought a traditional approach to the story: eliciting as many sensational headlines as he could publish. In the book he wrote with Bernstein, *All the President's Men*, he related how he confronted Deep Throat, asking for more juicy details and demanding that his source quit playing "a chickenshit game." But Deep Throat insisted they had to do it "my way." Woodward's colleagues at the *Post* also were puzzled over Deep Throat's preference for the "drip, drip, drip" of steady guidance. Woodward owed his ultimate journalistic triumph largely to Deep Throat's patient, in-depth style. Mark Felt knew, and Bob Woodward learned, that to make a real impact, the Watergate story had to be written in compelling detail over time. Readers needed a story, not a headline.

Sitting on the garage floor until 6:00 A.M., Felt helped Woodward understand the overall story of the conspiracy from isolated pieces of information that the reporter in large part already had. The lesson had begun earlier, when Deep Throat advised Woodward, "You can go much stronger." The FBI man was advising his student how to forcefully present his opening statement before the court of public opinion.

Up until this point, Deep Throat had kept his young reporter friend at a remove, providing Woodward with just enough information and perspective to keep Watergate in the public eye. But now Felt was growing desperate to keep the investigation alive. He brought Woodward much closer, sharing his deepest analysis as a seasoned investigator. For the first time, Felt shared his road map to the broad conspiracy—melding the headline-seeking aggression of journalism with the skilled investigative weapons of the modern G-man.

Deep Throat gave Woodward what lawyers call "inference," a reasoning process that is invaluable in making a good overall presentation in a complex connect-the-dots case. Reporters are trained to ask "the five Ws and the H"—who, what, where, when, why, and how—and to provide reliable sources for the answers. But Felt showed his student how to take the facts of the case and infer the overall story, as Woodward and Bernstein did in their October 10 article reporting a "massive campaign of political spying and sabotage." And Felt also offered something even more important. As a high-level supervisory official in the FBI, he provided the *Post* with an unimpeachable authority for its Watergate series and the confidence to pursue it. The October 10 story, as Bernstein later wrote, "may have been our most important: it finally made sense out of 'Watergate'; instead of the inexplicable 'third-rate burglary' described by White House press secretary Ron Ziegler, the break-in had been only part of a massive campaign of political espionage and sabotage directed from the White House."

The story electrified the country. Two weeks after it appeared, CBS anchorman Walter Cronkite, the most respected newsman in America, aired two in-depth television segments outlining the conspiracy. Immediately after the article appeared, Rep. Wright Patman called for congressional hearings into the scandal. On October 12, Sen. Ted Kennedy opened an investigation in his Administrative Practice and Procedure Subcommittee, based primarily on the October 10 article, a holding action that eventually morphed into the sensational Ervin Committee investigation.

Immediately after the October 10 story, John Dean, realizing the implications for the White House, cut short his honeymoon and hurried back to Washington. Because the story and follow-ups connected the break-in to broader allegations and the White House, a skeptical U.S. district judge, John Sirica, hectored the prosecution on unanswered questions throughout the Watergate trial. Patrick Gray was grilled by the Senate about these allegations during his confirmation hearings. Perhaps most important, the public was now fully engaged in Watergate.

As the Woodward–Bernstein stories became more sensational, they focused increasing suspicion on Felt. Though the reporters did not reveal their source, as agreed, they cited "information in FBI and

Department of Justice files," as they wrote in their October 10 story. And Felt remained conspicuous as the highest-ranking FBI official who was not assisting the cover-up. To ward off suspicion, Deep Throat played a masterful bureaucratic game designed to switch the focus elsewhere. As the White House put pressure on Acting Director Gray to plug the leaks, Gray called on his trusted number two, Mark Felt, to supervise the various leak investigations. And of course these investigations found no shortage of suspects. In the probe of the October 10 story, for example, Felt's investigators mentioned "Carl Bernstein's attempts to interview Washington field office case agent [special agent] Angelo Lano on 10/3/72, and Bernstein's repeated attempts to interview Assistant U.S. Attorneys Earl Silbert and Donald Campbell, who are responsible for the prosecution of this matter." Any of these individuals could have been the unnamed FBI and Justice Department sources cited by Woodward and Bernstein. On one report prepared by his team, Felt dramatically circled a paragraph stating that Campbell had been approached by Woodward before a leak but denied giving any comment. Felt wrote boldly capital letters, "LAST PAGE OF ATTACHED MEMO—HERE IS ENTIRE ANSWER." That was not the only time Felt tried to deflect attention from the FBI to other potential leakers. One opportunity came after Woodward and Bernstein wrote that a White House aide had composed the "Canuck letter," a slur against French Canadians falsely attributed to Democratic presidential candidate Edmund Muskie. Felt demanded that his investigators analyze whether the FBI had anything in its files about the Canuck letter. The answer was no, as he knew it would be.

Felt employed all the talents of an escape artist. After Woodward wrote that the FBI investigation of Watergate was ending prematurely—a story Deep Throat had planted—Felt wrote a scathing memo directed at Washington SAC Kunkel, ordering "comment as to whether there is any doubt in [Kunkel's] mind as to the scope of the investigation to be conducted." The hectoring tone positioned

Felt as an enforcer of the official line that the investigation was proceeding vigorously.*

By February 1973, senior FBI Watergate investigators, including
Bates, Bolz, and Washington SAC Kunkel, had been transferred—
either because they pressed the case too strongly or were suspected
of leaking. But Felt managed to keep his balance. In four months
there had been no taped conversations in the White House naming
Felt as the *Post*'s suspected source. Gray was about to testify at Senate hearings to confirm his appointment as permanent FBI director,
but he faced the hostility of a Democratic majority outraged by
Watergate, and he recognized that he might not get the job. Privately, Felt knew Gray would recommend him as his successor if
Gray's nomination failed. Felt appeared to have won a great bureaucratic victory as the Watergate investigation gathered unstoppable
momentum and he stood in line to be number one at the FBI.

Only one relatively minor obstacle stood in his way. Felt assumed
his old Bureau rival William Sullivan, who had been fired by Hoover
nearly two years earlier, was busy making friends in the Nixon
administration and had earned inclusion on the list of potential FBI
directors. Felt worried that the politically malleable Sullivan would
lead the FBI into the kind of corruption mess that Deep Throat had
worked so hard to avoid. To circumvent that, Felt leaked details of
the Kissinger wiretaps on newsmen and policymakers to *Time* magazine, all but guaranteeing that Gray would be asked about the taps
at his hearings. Gray had nothing to do with the operation, but Sullivan played a central role and was bound to see his chances for taking
the FBI's top spot crushed in the glare of publicity.

But this time Deep Throat miscalculated. Felt was among eight

---

* Felt got a break when Woodward and Bernstein blew a big story. They reported, mistak-
enly, that Nixon's campaign treasurer, Hugh Sloan, had told a grand jury that White House
chief of staff Bob Haldeman was linked to a slush fund. Felt ordered his underlings to
investigate who had access to Sloan's confidential statement to prosecutors, which did contain the allegations. The agents confirmed that the FBI had never received the statement—
but Campbell had. Once again Deep Throat escaped detection. —Editor

or nine officials who knew about the Kissinger wiretaps, and the only one who had played no role in the operation. Inevitably Felt rose to the top of the list of suspected leakers—of the wiretap story and the Watergate story as well. By February 28, Nixon and Haldeman were talking of Felt as the Watergate leaker in no uncertain terms. Their suspicion doomed any small chance he had of rising to FBI director. As it turned out, Sullivan had not been as close to the White House as Felt had sensed, and the leak actually drove Sullivan into a closer relationship with Nixon's men.

The pressures of Felt's double life were beginning to show. In a May 16 garage meeting with Woodward, he issued his warning that "everybody's life is in danger," as Woodward relayed it to Bernstein, explaining the source of that danger as "C-I-A." Felt has never fully explained his fears of the CIA during Watergate beyond a comment to Woodward that "the cover-up had little to do with Watergate, but was mainly to protect the covert operations" of the U.S. intelligence community.

The issue goes back to a more fundamental question Mark raises in his book but never answers: Why would anybody want to break into the headquarters of the Democratic National Committee (DNC), an organization that played a relatively minor role in the primary campaign? At the time, most investigators assumed that the break-in had something to do with Republicans spying on the Democrats' *campaign*. But that assumption never made much sense. Political spies would have struck after the upcoming Democratic convention in Miami, when the DNC would start actively assisting the nominee. In any event, the intruders would have bugged the DNC nerve center, including the offices of Chairman Lawrence O'Brien, not the relatively remote part of the headquarters where they actually were caught.

The intruders may have been looking for scandalous secrets. The first Watergate break-in, when the intruders successfully placed their bugs, came on May 28, 1972, a month after the arrest of a young Washington lawyer, Phillip Macklin Bailley. He represented numerous prostitutes and had connections to prominent Democrats. In June, after Bailley was indicted for violations of the Mann Act, which prohibits transporting women across state lines for prostitution (for which he was later convicted), an article appeared in the *Washington Star* suggesting his connections to a D.C. call girl ring. A few days later, the burglars were caught while infiltrating the Watergate again, this time with additional or replacement bugs and a desk key. The timing may suggest a connection between the two cases: the Watergate intruders may have been bugging a remote office used by DNC visitors to order the services of high-priced female escorts.

According to court documents, prosecutor Silbert intended to elicit salacious trial testimony showing that the burglary was motivated by Hunt's desire, perhaps unknown to other burglars, to elicit personal "dirt" for his financial gain. Alfred Baldwin, who monitored wiretapped conversations from the first break-in and bugging, was to testify that he listened to "explicitly intimate" conversations between men and presumed call girls from a phone in offices controlled by Hunt's business rival at the Democratic National Committee. (One effect of the prosecutorial theory would have been to limit the scandal to the original seven defendants and steer it away from the White House.) As Silbert was about to take this testimony, the Democratic National Committee persuaded an appeals court to block it.

As Felt suggested in his warning to Woodward, the CIA also may have been involved in Watergate, beyond the Agency's connections to Hunt and the intruders. Some analysts have speculated that the CIA was eavesdropping on the same call girl ring; the Agency may have been looking for material to help prepare profiles of politicians who used the service.

As Felt was showing his nervousness, according to FBI and news reports, Michael Stevens, a Chicago-based supplier of sophisticated eavesdropping equipment, was seeking FBI protection. Stevens had sold bugging devices to Watergate burglar McCord before the first break-in, after McCord had shown CIA credentials and said he was involved in an Agency operation. In December 1972, seven months after the burglars were caught, E. Howard Hunt's wife, Dorothy, was en route to Chicago with $10,000 in cash when she died in a plane crash. She had been coming to pay him hush money, Stevens claimed, and he suspected that the tragedy was not accidental. After receiving an anonymous threat himself, he went to the FBI, where Felt doubtless would have learned of his story.

Felt also may have known of a shadowy, CIA-connected detective, Lou Russell, who was working for McCord for cash payments and likely was in the vicinity of the Watergate during the break-in. On May 18, 1973, two days after Felt issued his warning to Woodward, Russell suffered a nonfatal heart attack. That was the day McCord (who also expressed fear for his life) was to begin his Senate testimony. A few days earlier, Russell had received a Senate subpoena for records and testimony. He subsequently claimed that poison had been substituted for his regular medicine, causing his heart attack. He died that summer, followed closely by his friend John Leon, a Washington attorney who had planned to hold a press conference with Republican National Committee chairman George H. W. Bush on his claims of past wiretap operations by Democrats.

Early that May, Woodward published a story about the Kissinger wiretaps, an operation Deep Throat had told him about three months earlier. That caused more consternation at the White House. On May 11, Nixon and his new chief of staff, Alexander Haig, discussed the strong opinions of both "Eliot" (the newly designated attorney general, Eliot Richardson) and "Sullivan" that Felt was the leaker. In June, a month after his nerve-rattling session with Woodward, Felt retired after thirty-one years of FBI service, having achieved his goal of a clean and reputable FBI investigation into Watergate. Deep Throat had performed spectacularly. The scandal unleashed forces that swept away Gray, Nixon's men, and finally the president himself. But little did Felt know that he had started a storm that later would come crashing down on another prominent victim—himself.

NINETEEN

TWISTING SLOWLY IN THE WIND

P RESIDENT NIXON made Pat Gray acting director of the FBI following Hoover's death because he wanted a politician in the job who would convert the Bureau into an adjunct of the White House machine. Before becoming president, Nixon applauded Hoover's political independence; once in the Oval Office he saw the possibilities of making the FBI a White House police force. What Nixon did not foresee was that the Bureau's professional staff would fight this development tooth and nail. Gray never understood that he minimized his impact on the FBI by spending so much time away from Bureau activities while he traveled the land making speeches. No sooner did he return from one speechmaking tour than he would be off again, beating the drums for the Nixon administration more than the FBI. His actions hurt his standing at the Bureau while failing to win the trust of the White House, which was not impressed by his job performance.

His travels and his long convalescence after abdominal surgery, together with his lack of experience with FBI operations, combined to make him an ineffective leader. As the days after Nixon's second inauguration passed, Gray became less and less confident that he would receive a permanent appointment as FBI director. One by one, others named to federal jobs on a temporary basis were given permanent status by the president, but there was no word about Gray. Suspecting that he was being shunted aside, he confided to me that he was seriously considering dropping his government career and returning to his law practice in New London.

On February 15, 1973, the White House seemed ready to drop the other shoe. Gray received a phone call summoning him to the White House the following morning. When he returned, he described to me his lukewarm reception by a blank-faced John Ehrlichman and his brief meeting with the president. During his fifteen minutes with Ehrlichman, he was grilled on his ability to handle the post of FBI director and questioned about his health. Nixon was no more sympathetic. "Pat," he said, "you're not ruthless enough in getting polygraphs to stop those leaks. Get tougher."

Gray promised that he would, but he left the White House not knowing whether he would get the appointment. On Friday, February 17, however, press secretary Ron Ziegler announced that Gray had been named the permanent head of the FBI. Noting that Gray would be the first FBI director to require Senate confirmation, Ziegler added that he was "confident" there would be no difficulties. This was gainsaid by the Senate Democratic whip, Robert C. Byrd, who let it be known that he would oppose Senate confirmation because Gray was "a bone of contention and a source of division" within the Bureau.

This should have been a warning to Gray. But instead of turning for assistance to Justice Department veterans who were wise to the ways of Capitol Hill, he relied on his personal staff for the preparation he badly needed. It was not a good time for any FBI director to face the Senate. Political bombs were bursting in Washington. *Time* had just disclosed that the FBI had been wiretapping White House personnel and certain members of the press at the request of presidential aides. During the same period, an ugly showdown in South Dakota between Indian radicals and the federal government further damaged Gray's reputation among his FBI colleagues.

The South Dakota standoff was dominating the headlines. In February 1973, about two hundred members and supporters of the American Indian Movement occupied the small reservation town of Wounded Knee, taking eleven whites hostage and demanding that Congress investigate violations of the Indian treaties as well as conditions on Sioux reservations. The White House decided against interfering or making any show of force. Attorney General Kleindienst decreed a "containment" policy. He ordered the FBI to help form roadblocks around the town, a futile attempt to stop traffic across a fifteen-mile perimeter and a misuse of agents who were assigned to the scene as investigators, not guards.

Had J. Edgar Hoover been alive, there would have been no problem. He would have refused to let agents be used in this manner. But I did not have Hoover's muscle or authority, nor did Gray. To make matters worse, Kleindienst changed FBI rules of engagement. Normally agents do not use firearms except in vital self-defense or to protect an innocent third party; under those very restrictive conditions they shoot to kill. Kleindienst instructed us to use firearms when fired on first—and then shoot to wound, not kill.

This new rule loosened restrictions on opening fire. During the seventy-one days of the Wounded Knee siege, gunfights broke out nearly every night. Thousands of rounds were exchanged, though no one had the slightest idea at whom they were shooting. It was a miracle that the casualty list wasn't longer in one of the most badly bungled government operations I have ever witnessed. Two radical Indians were killed and seven wounded. A U.S. marshal was shot through the spine and paralyzed from the waist down. One FBI agent was badly wounded in the arm. In the end, the Indians tired of

the occupation and agreed to evacuate the town, many of them slip-
ping past roadblocks.

Gray's popularity with the FBI rank and file had declined in the
wake of the Watergate investigation, but it plummeted during the
siege of Wounded Knee, when agents blamed him for failing to protect the Bureau's interests and agents' wives blamed him for unnecessarily exposing their husbands to the hazardous and bitterly cold
conditions of the South Dakota winter.

Nonetheless, Gray was supremely confident that he could handle
the Senate Judiciary Committee. He was presented to the committee
by Connecticut's two senators, Democrat Abraham Ribicoff and
Republican Lowell Weicker. Gray read a statement outlining in glowing terms his "accomplishments" during his ten months as acting
director. Then he took a step that almost guaranteed his downfall.
He offered to make the entire Watergate file available to any senator
who wished to see it. The files, he added, would be available to senators alone and not to staff. Attorney General Kleindienst was aghast
and the White House, which knew what the files contained, was furious. Even the senators were startled. "Do you mean the entire file—
lock, stock, and barrel?" an incredulous Senator Byrd asked.

"Yes, sir," Gray answered. "We are proud of that investigation."

His opening statement completed, Gray was pressed by Sen.
Sam J. Ervin, Jr. to explain a speech he had delivered the previous
August before the City Club of Cleveland. Ervin and others felt the
speech had been political. Gray insisted that the invitation had come
directly from the City Club, but he was later forced to admit that the
White House set it up. Senator Ervin then asked about the "congressional cards" that the FBI kept on senators and congressmen. These
were little data sheets on every senator and congressman that the
FBI's Crime Records Division had maintained since the early 1950s.
Each card contained biographical data and any information that
would help the Bureau maintain congressional liaison. The nota-

tions included a brief record of all dealings with the particular congressman or senator, including problems to avoid in the future. The FBI had never investigated members of Congress, congressional candidates, or governors unless a violation of federal law was alleged or the individual was being considered for a top-level government appointment. Nonetheless, Gray told Ervin that he had discontinued the practice of keeping the data cards.

Then the senator asked about an incident in September 1972, when the FBI had been used to collate criminal justice information for the political use of the White House. Gray answered that he had been out of town at the time but had admonished those responsible for acceding to the White House request. This answer came as a surprise to us at the Bureau, for it was the first time FBI agents learned that they had been "admonished."

Ervin next referred to newspaper reports that Donald Segretti, the inept dirty tricks specialist, had been shown transcripts of two FBI interrogations he had undergone. Gray opened a Pandora's box with his reply. He described how he ordered the preparation of a detailed summary of the investigation, at John Dean's request. Since it was his duty to keep the attorney general fully informed, he had the summary sent to the Justice Department, knowing it would be sent to the White House. So far so good. But like many inexperienced witnesses, Gray could not let it go at that. He had to elaborate.

"Later," he told the committee, "Mr. Dean asked to review the interview reports of the Federal Bureau of Investigation, and I submitted these to him." This was like saying he let the fox into the henhouse. Gray said that Dean denied showing the reports to Segretti, but the damage had been done: Gray had allowed FBI reports to be shown to a man under FBI investigation.

From there on it was all downhill for Pat Gray. In subsequent testimony, he hedged and attempted to evade the pointed questions of Democratic members. Sen. John V. Tunney asked, "How many people in the country have files?" It was perfectly clear that Tunney was talking about investigative files, but Gray went into a long discussion of fingerprint records and so on for the next twenty-five pages of the record.

It was Sen. Edward M. Kennedy of Massachusetts who really drew blood. "This week's *Time* magazine contains information on alleged wiretaps on newsmen—according to the article—requested by the White House, authorized by the Justice Department, installed by the FBI. How do you respond to these charges?"

Gray squirmed. "I would have to say, first, that with regard to the general matter of wiretaps..."

Kennedy interrupted. "No, just on these charges. How do you respond specifically?"

"How do I respond to these charges? When I saw this particular article and checked the records and indices of the Federal Bureau of Investigation, and I am also told that the Department of Justice checked the records of the Internal Revenue Division... there is no record of any such business here of bugging news reporters and White House people."

Gray had expected this question and he had thought out an answer that was technically true but completely misleading. There was no official record of the so-called Kissinger wiretaps in the FBI because Assistant Director Sullivan had personally sequestered the records in his own files, along with the logs and letters of authorization from Attorney General John Mitchell. Sullivan had then secretly turned them over to Assistant Attorney General Mardian, who later delivered them to the White House. Therefore, there was nothing in FBI files to indicate the existence of the Kissinger wiretaps. But Gray had unofficial knowledge of their existence, though he had absolutely nothing to do with them. Had he admitted this, he would have been home free. But as President Nixon's man in the Bureau, and out of political loyalty, he resorted to a circumlocution that led him deeper and deeper into trouble as Senator Kennedy pressed relentlessly for unequivocal answers.

Gray was not prepared for this kind of cross-examination, in effect a psychological assault, and matters became worse when Kennedy directed his fire at the FBI's handling of the Watergate investigation. Perhaps, had he been at his desk more often, Pat Gray might have been able to avoid the pitfalls and defend the Bureau adequately. With only a smattering of knowledge, however, he blundered—and it did not take Kennedy very long to expand the scope of his questioning. In written answers to some of Kennedy's questions, Gray testified that Dwight Chapin, the White House appointments secretary, had referred Segretti to Herbert W. Kalmbach, Nixon's personal attorney, and that Kalmbach said he had hired Segretti and paid him between $30,000 and $40,000 out of campaign funds between September 1, 1971, and March 15, 1972. According to Gray, Kalmbach "said he had no knowledge of what Segretti was doing to justify these expenses or to earn his salary."

In the give-and-take of questioning, Gray might have been able to gloss over many of the details, but his written statement had invidious overtones that infuriated an already angry White House. Every hour he spent on the stand marked a further erosion of White House support.

His offer to open the FBI's Watergate files to senators, moreover, put him in a damned-if-you-do, damned-if-you-don't situation. That goodwill gesture brought Gray under attack by the White House for offering the files in the first place, under pressure from the members of the committee to allow staff members to see them, and under criticism from the American Civil Liberties Union for being ready to violate the privacy of individuals under investigation.

There was no respite for the acting director when the senators

shifted to other subjects, some already covered but now rehashed
with some vehemence. Why had Gray acceded to John Dean's
demand to be present when the FBI was conducting its interviews?
Why had Gray not acted when he learned that Dean had taken possession of the contents of E. Howard Hunt's safe at the White
House? Why was Dean allowed to retain some of the contents of
that safe? How was it that he had no knowledge of the Kissinger
wiretaps?

And then Gray made his most serious mistake. While another
witness was testifying, Gray called John Ehrlichman about a terrible
secret in his closet known only to himself, Ehrlichman, and John
Dean. The White House aides had secretly given Gray two folders
from Hunt's safe with instructions that they must "never see the
light of day." (Dean himself shredded two Hermes notebooks from
the safe, one containing a list of names and the other notes made
by Hunt.)

Gray was naively unaware that the call was being recorded, but
who could have guessed that it would subsequently be made public
during the Watergate hearings? The call was a major indiscretion,
first because it delivered Gray into Ehrlichman's hands and second
because it hinted at matters that would eventually kill Gray's chances
of confirmation. Gray's first comment was, "The thing I want to talk
to you about is, I am being pushed awfully hard in certain areas and
I'm not giving an inch. And you know those areas and I think you
have got to tell John Wesley [Dean] to stand very tight in the saddle
and to be very careful about what he says and to be absolutely certain that he knows in his own mind that he delivered everything he
had to the FBI and doesn't make any distinction between..." Gray
paused, "but that he delivered everything to the FBI."

Ehrlichman replied in a cavalier tone, "Right."

Gray went on, "And that he delivered it to those agents—"

"All right."

Gray was obsequious. "You know I've got a couple of areas up there that I'm hitting hard and I'm just taking the attack."

[Ehrlichman] "Okay."

[Gray] "I wanted you to know that."

[Ehrlichman, ironically] "Good. Keep up the good work, my boy. Let me know if I can help."

[Gray] "All right. He [Dean] can help by doing that."

[Ehrlichman] "Good, I'll do it."

The "it" was to ask Dean to lie for Gray if anything came up about the documents from the Hunt safe that Gray had destroyed. Immediately after talking to Gray, Ehrlichman called Dean and said cheerily, "Hi. Just had a call from your favorite witness."

[Dean] "Which is?"

[Ehrlichman] "Patrick J. Gray."

[Dean] "Oh, really?"

[Ehrlichman] "And he said to make sure that old John W. Dean stays very, very firm and steady in his story that he delivered every document to the FBI and that he does not start making distinctions between agents and directors."

[Dean] "He's a little worried, isn't he?"

[Ehrlichman] "Well, he just does not want there to be any questions. He says he's hanging very firm and there's a lot of probing around."

[Dean, in a disgusted tone] "Yeah, he's really hanging tough. You ought to read the transcript. He makes me gag."

[Ehrlichman] "Really?"

[Dean] "Oh, it's awful, John."

[Ehrlichman] "Why did he call me? To cover his tracks?"

[Dean] "Yeah, sure. I laid this on him yesterday."

[Ehrlichman] "Oh, I see. Okay, John."

[Dean] "Laid it on him, too. You know, to confuse the issue, so I don't have any idea what he said up there today...."

[Ehrlichman, laughing] "Let him hang there. Well, I think we ought to let him hang there. Let him twist, slowly, slowly in the wind."

[Dean] "That's right, and I was with the boss this morning and that is exactly where he was coming out. He said, 'I'm not sure Gray is smart enough to run the Bureau the way he is handling himself.'"

A series of other witnesses either testified against Gray or vented their spleen at the FBI. But while their testimony was droning on in a Senate hearing room, the White House and the Justice Department were moving to put Gray in a completely untenable position. When the committee convened again to continue Gray's testimony, he was forced to inform the chairman and the ranking minority member that something new had come up. On orders from Attorney General Kleindienst, Gray withdrew his offer to allow the senators to review the FBI's Watergate files. Only the chairman, the ranking minority member, and their counsel were to have access. This alone might not have caused a great furor. Senators were too busy to sift through FBI files. But Kleindienst had also instructed Gray that he was to limit his answers to procedural matters and decline to answer anything related to substance—to keep his mouth shut about Watergate.

The White House, in effect, made Gray appear to be a part of the general cover-up. In comments to the media, Senator Tunney suggested that the Nixon administration "has decided to throw Mr. Gray to the wolves." Sen. Birch Bayh, the Indiana Democrat, put it even more bluntly. "With friends like Mr. Gray has down at the White House," he said, "he doesn't need any enemies." To compound Gray's troubles, President Nixon refused to allow John Dean to testify, on the grounds of executive privilege.

On Thursday, March 22, the last day of the hearings, Senator

Byrd administered the coup de grâce. Facing a tired and discouraged Pat Gray, the senator probed into how the FBI had handled the contents of E. Howard Hunt's safe. Referring back to June 28, 1972, Byrd said, "Mr. Dean called you at 10:45 A.M. regarding leaks concerning material delivered to the FBI. What particular leak and what specific material did he have in mind?"

"He was calling me then about those rumors that were continuing, as he put it, to the effect that the FBI was dragging its feet in the investigation and that a gun had been found in Mr. Hunt's effects. That was the subject of the call . . . as best as I can recollect it, sir."

"On that same afternoon, at 4:35, you called him. You state that you have no recollection of the substance of that call. Could it have been with respect to Mr. Hunt's properties?" Byrd asked.

Gray was exhausted. "No, I do not think it was . . . but I just don't know."

Then Byrd sprang the trap. "Going back to Mr. Dean. When he indicated that he would have to check and see if Mr. Hunt had an office in the Old Executive Office Building, he lied to agents, didn't he?"

A hush settled over the hearing room. Dean had lied in an attempt to steer suspicion away from the White House connection with the Watergate burglary. Hesitating for a moment, Gray spoke very slowly. "I would say, looking back on it now"—he paused and took a deep breath—"and exhaustively analyzing the minute details of this investigation, I would have to conclude that probably is correct. Yes, sir."

Gray knew, the committee knew, and the audience knew that the director designate had just cut himself off from White House support. And in admitting that he knew Dean lied but did nothing about it, he had destroyed his credibility and his integrity.

From that point on, Gray refused to talk to reporters. On April 5, he asked President Nixon to withdraw his nomination, since there was no chance he would be confirmed by either the Judiciary Committee or the Senate.

President Nixon's comment in acceding to Gray's request was typical. "In fairness to Mr. Gray," he said, and the phrase elicited ironic smiles in Washington, "and out of my overriding concern for the effective conduct of the vitally important business of the FBI, I have regretfully agreed to withdraw Mr. Gray's nomination."

Having allowed Pat Gray to twist in the wind, the president finally cut him down.

TWENTY

THREE-HOUR FELT

A S HE ENTERED his office on the morning of April 25, 1973, Sen. Lowell P. Weicker, the Connecticut Republican, was stopped by his secretary. Acting Director Gray of the FBI, sitting out his days until President Nixon appointed a successor, had called urgently three times, Weicker was told. Somewhat surprised—the senator and Gray came from the same state but they were hardly close friends—he returned the call immediately.

When Gray came on the line, he said, "Senator, it is very urgent and very important that I see you right away. Can you come down to my office?"

Twenty minutes later, Weicker was in the acting director's office. For a while, Gray talked despondently about his problems with the White House and the difficulties of the confirmation hearings. Then he exploded a bomb. On June 28, 1972, just eleven days after the Watergate break-in, Gray said, he had been summoned to the White House for a conference with John Ehrlichman. When he arrived, he was surprised to find John Dean there. Ehrlichman came directly to the point.

"Pat," he said, "John has some files he wants to turn over to you."

Dean then handed Gray two folders. He explained that they had come out of E. Howard Hunt's office safe in the Executive Office Building—the office Dean had denied knowing about. Dean said the rest of the material from the safe was being turned over to FBI agents who had requested it. Dean added that the folders had nothing to do with Watergate and contained "highly sensitive, classified national security material with political overtones."

"They shouldn't see the light of day and they must never become part of the FBI's own files because they are political dynamite," Dean told Gray. Then he left the office.

Ehrlichman had been more explicit. Gray told Weicker that Ehrlichman had ordered him to "deep-six" the documents. (Ehrlichman later denied making the statement.) Gray told Weicker that he kept the documents in his office for two weeks and then took them to his home in Connecticut. In December he burned them in his fireplace. He denied reading the documents—something Weicker found hard to believe.

The facts came out later, on August 3, 1973, when Gray testified before the Senate Watergate Committee. In his testimony he admitted looking at the documents before burning them; they appeared to be top secret State Department papers. "I read the first cable," he told the Watergate Committee. "I do not recall the exact language but the text of the cable implicated officials of the Kennedy administration in the assassination of President Ngo Dinh Diem of South Vietnam. I had no reason then to doubt the authenticity of the cable and was shaken by what I read.

"I thumbed through the other cables in this file. They appeared to be duplicates of the first cable. I merely thumbed through the second of the two files and noted that it contained onionskin copies of correspondence. I did not absorb the subject matter of the correspondence and do not today, of my own knowledge, know what it was."* Neither the committee nor the public could believe that Gray burned the contents of the folders without reading them.

But on that April day in 1973, Senator Weicker, without knowing what the two folders contained, realized the seriousness of Gray's confession. Already angered by White House tactics in the Watergate case, he knew that he now possessed a lethal weapon. "Don't do anything about it right now," he told Gray. "Let me think it over and decide what you should do." Naive as usual, Gray agreed.

Weicker did not take long to decide. The following day, without consulting Gray, he gave the story to a reporter friend on the *New York Daily News* and it broke dramatically in that paper. The wire services immediately picked up the account of Gray's malfeasance and the media across the country gave it heavy coverage. Weicker made no secret of the fact that he was the source of the story but insisted that he had released it to "protect" Gray.

The furor at FBI headquarters and in every FBI field office made it impossible for Gray to remain in office. On April 27, two days after his "confidential" discussion with Weicker, the acting director resigned and the news was flashed to President Nixon as he was returning from Key Biscayne on Air Force One. Hours later, Nixon publicly accepted the resignation. The terse announcement did not mention a successor.

I talked with Gray shortly after Nixon's comments and we discussed what the president might do. "I recommended that you be designated director," Gray told me, "but I don't know whether those White House people will pay any attention to what I say." I gathered that he recommended me to John Ehrlichman or John Dean—the worst thing he could have done. In my dealings with the White

---

* E. Howard Hunt later admitted forging some of the material, including the "cable" about Diem, for possible political use if Edward M. Kennedy became the Democratic presidential candidate. —Editor

House leadership, I always put the interests of the FBI first and was never forgiven for it.

Certainly I would have welcomed the appointment. But uppermost in my thoughts was the state of mind at the FBI. Tension was mounting in a staff already in shock over the disclosure that Gray had destroyed Watergate evidence. Could we keep the Bureau on course? The FBI had always been a closely knit and dedicated organization. Now it was confronted by another major change and the possibility that a new outsider would be brought in. I kept thinking, "If only the president would see the light and appoint a new director from the ranks this time."

Several top officials were well qualified. My own chances should have been good since I was next in line as associate director and had been running the Bureau while Gray was learning the ropes and delivering speeches. When one of the wire services reported that I was to be named director, I thought the problem had been solved, and my secretary spent a half hour assembling photos and biographical data.

Then the rumor subsided and I was left again to sit at my desk wondering, but not for long. At 2:50 P.M., the president announced, without consulting anyone at the Bureau, that he was appointing William B. Ruckelshaus to succeed Pat Gray. Cut off from the White House, we got the news from the wire services. Now that I have carefully reviewed the White House tapes, I know there was never a possibility that Nixon would appoint anyone from the professional staff to head the FBI. He believed that the Bureau had pushed the Watergate investigation too hard. He was still looking for someone who was politically malleable to direct what had once been the "world's greatest law enforcement agency."

Nixon's feelings about me are clearly revealed in an Oval Office discussion with John Dean on February 28, 1972. Dean was briefing the president on the *Time* story that disclosed the existence of the Kissinger wiretaps.

"The other person who knows and is aware of it is Mark Felt," Dean said, "and we have talked about Mark Felt before."

"Let's face it," Nixon answered. "Suppose Felt comes out now and unwraps. What does it do to him?"

"He can't do it," Dean said.

"How about his career?" Nixon asked. "Who is going to hire him? Let's face it—the guy who goes out—he couldn't do it unless he had a guarantee from somebody like *Time* magazine who would say, 'Look, we will give you a job for *Life.*' Then what do they do? He would get a job at *Life*, and everyone would treat him like a pariah. He is in a very dangerous situation. These guys, you know—the informers. Look what it did to Chambers.* They finished him."

This was not the only Oval Office conversation about me. The general tenor was that I would not cooperate with White House schemes. I never quite made the enemies list, but I think I came pretty close. Whatever Nixon, Dean, and Ehrlichman may have thought about me, I remain proud of my FBI record as the only insider ever to climb to the top of the FBI pyramid, if only for two hours and fifty minutes.

By law, the associate director takes charge of the FBI when there is no designated director. From a practical standpoint, I made good use of the time to make new rules and abolish some of Gray's.

The most onerous of Gray's reforms grew out of the White House phobia about leaks (most of which came from the White House itself). Even the most trusted people were viewed with suspicion. Gray's response was to direct that an "accountability log" accompany each sensitive document as it made its way up and down

* Whittaker Chambers, a *Time* senior editor, was forced to resign after testifying that State Department official Alger Hiss was a Soviet espionage agent. In times of trouble, Nixon secretly drove to the Chambers farm in Maryland to seek his advice, and always professed a deep friendship for Chambers.

the various levels of authority. This sounded like a good security system but proved unworkable in the FBI.

I tried to talk Gray out of implementing this plan, but without success. He did not understand that the tremendous volume of sensitive documents circulating at FBI headquarters made the plan a bottleneck. Many secretaries, clerks, and messengers handled documents along with supervisors and other officials, and each log soon looked like a nominating petition. Gray never knew that we applied his rule only at headquarters and not in the field. When I rescinded the plan, there was a great sigh of relief. Looking back, I regret not taking greater advantage of my tenure as acting director. Ruckelshaus did not come aboard for some days, so I had plenty of time.

When we learned (again through the press) that Ruckelshaus was coming to the FBI only until a permanent director was chosen, there was consternation in the Bureau. It meant going through all the headaches and controversies of breaking in a caretaker. Ruckelshaus functioned as a security guard sent to see that the FBI did nothing to displease Nixon.

Two days after his appointment, Ruckelshaus arrived at the FBI building in his limousine, surrounded by the inevitable entourage: a personal staff to protect him from the FBI "enemy" that he had been told about by the White House and the Justice Department. His first instructions to me were to "set up a conference of all agents as soon as it can be arranged." I had a momentary vision of 8,500 FBI agents pouring in from all over the country, but I said nothing. Instead I ordered the special agents in charge of the fifty-nine field offices to report to Washington to meet their new boss on May 2, the anniversary of J. Edgar Hoover's death. For the second time in twelve months, we had to begin the education process.

In our earlier transition, I had resolved my doubts in favor of Gray and greeted him with some enthusiasm. I am afraid this was not true on the blue Monday when Ruckelshaus arrived. We gave

Gray full support and as much cooperation as he would accept. We covered his mistakes. When he did not deal fairly with us, we told ourselves that he was acting under pressure from the White House or the attorney general. If we argued vehemently with him, we nevertheless implemented his instructions to the best of our ability. But as Ruckelshaus and his entourage marched into the director's office, I had a feeling of unease—a sense that things were wrong and I should do something about it. Here was a man who would be in charge of an investigative jurisdiction covering more than a hundred laws, many requiring different approaches and different procedures. Gray at least came from the Justice Department. Ruckelshaus was fresh out of the Environmental Protection Agency. I felt like an endangered species myself.

After ten months of attempting to educate Pat Gray, we were starting all over again. And one day we would have to restart with the permanent director. "My God," my assistant, Wason Campbell, said, "we'll have to go through this twice more." This was the consensus throughout headquarters, and it contributed to a reception that was cool at best. There was no thought of insubordination or of allowing the FBI to drift off course; it was more a sense of despair.

Perhaps we should have felt sorry for Ruckelshaus, who was aware of our attitude from the beginning. The first document he saw when he took over was a telegram to the president—the unanimous declaration of fifteen top FBI officials at headquarters and all the field executives. It was written by Assistant Director Leonard M. Walters of the Inspection Division and cleared by me. We argued that "J. Edgar Hoover's precepts of careful selection of agent personnel among highly qualified candidates, rigorous training, firm discipline, and promotion solely on merit have developed within the FBI law enforcement leaders of professional stature respected worldwide." We urged the president to consider some of these highly qualified professionals as candidates for director, adding, "At this critical time it is essential that the FBI not flounder or lose direction in its service to the nation because of lack of law enforcement expertise or of other qualities essential to the FBI directorship."

Ruckelshaus read the telegram slowly without saying a word. Then he looked at me over his glasses.

"Has this been sent?" he asked.

"Yes."

"Have copies been released to the press?"

Again my answer was in the affirmative.

Ruckelshaus rose to his feet and without a word put the telegram down in front of me, then walked out of the room. He never referred to the telegram and neither did the president. We never received an answer, formal or informal, from the White House.

The telegram has been characterized as an attempt on my part to unseat Ruckelshaus and promote my own candidacy for the directorship. But there was no need to unseat someone who would barely warm the director's chair anyhow. I knew that as long as John Dean and John Ehrlichman were in the White House, I would have less chance of receiving the appointment than the man in the moon. The telegram was an attempt to serve notice on the president that the FBI could not survive another outsider. Perhaps it ultimately tilted the decision in favor of Clarence M. Kelley, who was acceptable to insiders because of his service in the FBI before he became Kansas City's chief of police. (Kelley was also active in the Society of Former FBI Agents.)

Ruckelshaus was not helped when his wife, Jill, was quoted as saying on the college lecture circuit that her husband was going to the FBI "with a clean broom." An inflamed FBI saw this as a slap in the face and an attack on our integrity. When I heard of this comment, I called Ruckelshaus and told him that I had to see him right away. As I entered the inner sanctum, I was jarred by the sight of Ruckelshaus lolling in an easy chair with his feet on what I still felt was J. Edgar Hoover's desk. Ruckelshaus let me stand there for a few minutes while he finished reading a paper he had in his hand. Finally he said, "What can I do for you?"

"Mr. Ruckelshaus, your wife is being quoted as saying that you were 'going to the FBI with a clean broom.' This is having a devastating effect on employee morale, which is already bad enough."

"She was misquoted," he said. "She didn't say that. Nothing like that at all. Nothing at all."

"Mr. Ruckelshaus, if that's the case, you should make some sort of statement to the personnel to counteract the extremely adverse effect."

Dismissing me with a wave of his hand, he answered, "I'll think it over." He never made any denial and he never brought it up again with me.

My relationship with Ruckelshaus was stormy at times. He had come to the FBI determined to protect the president at any cost, whereas I became more wary and disillusioned with every passing day. My objective was to protect the Bureau. Even more than Pat Gray, Ruckelshaus divorced himself from day-to-day operations. He reviewed only mail and material relating to Watergate and the case against Daniel Ellsberg, who was accused of leaking the Pentagon papers.

On the third day of his tenure, all the SACs reported for the conference that Ruckelshaus had ordered. I introduced him to the group. He said that he could understand the traumatic effect of the revelations about Gray's destruction of documents and his sudden resignation. He appealed to the agents in charge for their cooperation. He spoke for about ten minutes and then turned the meeting over to me and left the room. There was no applause. There were no questions, and for that matter no time for them. It was in and out, and I thought of the staggering expense of bringing fifty-nine SACs from all over the country, including Alaska and Hawaii, for this brush-off. To salvage some of the taxpayers' money, I turned the meeting into an all-day work conference. Only once before in my experience had there been a conference of all the SACs at one time—the meeting called by Gray ten months earlier.

News of this meeting leaked to the press, of course, and there were stories that we spent the day making disparaging remarks about Ruckelshaus and suggesting ways to get rid of him. In fact he was never mentioned.

My next chilling incident with the new acting director was connected with the Ellsberg case. We already knew that John Ehrlichman had met secretly with federal judge Matt Byrne, who was presiding over the Ellsberg trial in Los Angeles, and improperly discussed Byrne's possible appointment as permanent FBI director. Public notice of the meeting could well compromise the trial and lead to the reversal of a conviction by the appeals court. Then, during the closing days of the trial, the *Washington Post* alleged that the White House Plumbers had placed wiretaps on Ellsberg's phone. This led Judge Byrne to demand proof from the government that the evidence against Ellsberg had not been tainted.

Ruckelshaus immediately ordered an investigation. The wiretaps mentioned in the *Post* piece obviously referred to the Kissinger wiretaps, which had been placed at the White House's behest. Ellsberg had certainly been briefed on the subject; after all, the attorney general and the Justice Department were well aware of the situation and edgy about it. Nonetheless, we duly reported the facts to the acting director. He was told how the tapes had been made and why, that Bill Sullivan had squirreled them away in his office, and how they had ended up at the White House via Assistant Attorney General Robert Mardian. Moreover, there had never been a tap on Ellsberg's phone.

We further reported that Ellsberg had been overheard using the phone as a house guest of Morton Halperin, whose line was tapped

"For God's sake! President or not, just tell him no!"

I turned on my heels and walked out, hoping I convinced him. I had—but only until my retirement a short time later. Then Ruckelshaus ordered the list prepared and sent to the White House. It was politics all the way.

My decision to retire pleased the acting director because I frequently disagreed with what he wanted to do. After I left, he boasted to reporters that he had forced me and several old "Hooverites" out of the Bureau. It was true that we were forced out; we retired because we could not accept the politicization of the Bureau and because we did not trust him. But we left of our own free will. Perhaps he realized how we felt after he went through the Saturday Night Massacre of October 1973, in which President Nixon fired the special prosecutor in the Watergate case. William Ruckelshaus, by then serving as deputy attorney general, finally stood up to the president—and resigned.

I had remained in the FBI at considerable personal sacrifice and with the feeling that I was needed to steer the organization I had served for most of my adult life. My inclination had been to resign when Nixon appointed Ruckelshaus—and my experiences with him had convinced me that I could do little more to protect the FBI. Having decided to retire, I was primarily concerned to see that my successor would be able to run the Bureau, which is essentially what I had been doing.

I talked to Ruckelshaus about this, putting it as diplomatically as I could. "It is very important for you to select a replacement for me," I told him. "When Gray was here, he abolished two key positions—assistant to the director-administrative and assistant to the director-investigative. This means that the associate director has been functioning as chief of staff to coordinate and direct the day-to-day operations of thirteen divisions."

"But I don't want to make such a key decision when I am not

permanent," he said, evading the issue. "This decision should be left to the director who is appointed by the president and confirmed by the Senate."

"That will take weeks," I said. "How are you going to direct and control the operations of the FBI in the meantime?"

"I'll think about it," he said, which meant that he intended to do nothing. I would have stayed through a transition period, but he did not request it. The White House was anxious to get me out.

When it became clear that Ruckelshaus was not going to act on my vital recommendation, I instructed all the top FBI officials to submit their recommendations for a new associate director directly to Ruckelshaus rather than to me. They complied, and four strong candidates emerged as my logical replacement. I was encouraged and reassured, but Ruckelshaus did not respond.

Meanwhile, the White House selection process for a new director was under way. The list had been narrowed down to three contenders: Clarence M. Kelley, Henry Peterson, and William C. Sullivan. Judge Matthew Byrne of Los Angeles, a highly qualified candidate, had fallen by the wayside when his conference with John Ehrlichman about the job during the Ellsberg trial was leaked to the press; it smacked of arm twisting.

Kelley and Sullivan were the only serious candidates. Henry Peterson was on the list to show the country that other men of stature were being considered. Kelley had served as an adviser and consultant on security during the Republican National Convention in Miami and was highly regarded by law enforcement experts. Sullivan was the man the White House really wanted. He had shown himself to be a pliant tool of the Nixon staff and his thinking about the threat from the New Left matched President Nixon's.

Ruckelshaus assured me that President Nixon was giving thought to appointing a career FBI man to the job. To give credence to this, he selected two of the names that had been suggested to him for the position of associate director and sent both men to the White House to be interviewed as candidates. They were interviewed by Alexander Haig and other presidential aides. The interviews were perfunctory and intended to give the impression that insiders were being considered. It was window dressing and nothing more.

Clarence Kelley eventually received the appointment. We felt that if the new director had to come from the outside, he was a good choice. Insiders would accept him because he was respected and, having served many years in the Bureau, he was no amateur. But the front-runner, until the very last minute, was William C. Sullivan. When Ruckelshaus told me it would be Kelley, he added, "But Sullivan came *that* close to being appointed." He held up his hand, the thumb and forefinger about a sixteenth of an inch apart.

TWENTY-ONE

"YOU ARE LYING"

O N JUNE 22, 1973, I retired from the organization that had occupied most of my adult years. As I prepared to leave, I rejected the importuning of booking agents who argued that I could triple my lecture fees by attacking the Bureau. Instead, I arranged a series of lectures before college audiences intending to counteract mounting criticism of the FBI.

But I was not allowed to become a private citizen. During the last six months of 1973, the Watergate story filled newspapers and television screens to overflowing. In February 1974, I was summoned to meet with Jay Horowitz of the Office of the Special Prosecutor investigating Watergate. Francis Martin, a young aide, was also present. When I pressed for an explanation, Horowitz said, "You realize that you may have violated the law." I realized no such thing and told Horowitz so, but he would not explain further.

The questioning, in his office and later before the Watergate grand jury, was a game of cat and mouse. At issue was a statement made by L. Patrick Gray in 1973 during his Senate confirmation hearings, that FBI files held no record of the 1969–1971 Kissinger wiretaps of White House staff and journalists. That was strictly and narrowly true, since from my own inquiry at the time I knew that assistant to the director William C. Sullivan had kept all the records in his own office—not in official FBI files—before giving them to Assistant Attorney General Robert Mardian.

But Horowitz hoped to prove that Gray had committed perjury. He put before me a very faint document that appeared to be a photocopy of a carbon copy of a memorandum dated February 26, 1973, two days before Gray began his testimony before the committee. There were no initials on it, indicating that it was not an official FBI memorandum. The document briefly described each of the Kissinger wiretaps, as well as a wiretap on a navy yeoman, an aide to the navy representative on the National Security Council who was suspected of leaking sensitive information to columnist Jack Anderson.

When I told Horowitz I did not recall seeing the memorandum before, he made no attempt to conceal his anger. Very sharply, he informed me that the memorandum had been prepared in the Domestic Intelligence Division of the Bureau and that Edward S. Miller, assistant director in charge of the division, had testified he personally brought it to my office on February 26. I had no reason to doubt Miller's word and I told Horowitz so. But I saw hundreds of documents every day, not a few of which concerned wiretaps, and could not possibly recall everything I had seen.

An exasperated Horowitz would not accept this explanation. Without testimony from me, the possibility of a perjury case against Gray was remote. He wanted me to testify that I personally carried the memorandum to Gray. That was ridiculous, because if I could not remember the document, how could I possibly testify that I carried it to Gray?

Horowitz was furious. "You are lying!" he shouted.

"And you are trying to force me to commit perjury so that you can convict Gray of the same offense," I replied.

All of this was rehashed before the grand jurors, and with each repetition, Horowitz became more accusatory and more hostile, communicating his antagonism to the grand jury. Their attitudes and questions indicated that the grand jurors believed Horowitz and not me.

After two days of this dueling, Horowitz asked me to accompany him to an adjoining office. "You are lying to protect Gray," he said. "Why do you do this after the terrible damage he did to the FBI?"

"I have no reason to protect Gray," I answered, "and certainly not to the extent of putting myself in the middle. Look, I could save myself all this trouble by testifying the way you want me to but I don't remember and I won't do it!"

Very coldly, as if he had not heard me, Horowitz continued, "It is perjury to testify that you don't remember something when you really do. You leave me no choice but to have you indicted for perjury."

I refused to be intimidated and insisted, "I'll take a lie detector test."

Horowitz said scornfully, "What good would that do with an FBI agent conducting the test?"

"The FBI does not use the polygraph anymore. You can get your operator."

Horowitz rose to his feet. "I have no confidence in the polygraph, no matter who administers the test." When I insisted that I be given the test, he paid no attention.

Back in the grand jury room, he once more asked me the key questions and once more found my answers displeasing. Finally he jumped to his feet and told me I was excused. Escorting me to the door, he said in parting, "You will hear from me later."

Four months later, the special prosecutor's office was on my back again. Early in June, I received a call from the FBI. The Bureau requested an interview with me about leaks of FBI information to

the *New York Times*. On June 13, 1974, special agents Angelo Lano and
George Midler appeared at my front door. I had never met Lano but
I knew that he coordinated the Watergate investigation in the Wash-
ington field office.

Lano promptly informed me that the interview would be conducted not in my house but at a nearby Holiday Inn. This could only
mean one thing: it would be secretly recorded. I started to object but
held back because having an exact record of what was said was to
my advantage. As a former associate director, I would have expected
to be questioned in Director Kelley's office as a matter of courtesy,
but perhaps the special prosecutor thought I would be more vulnerable in strange surroundings.

Before I sat down in the motel room, Lano was advising me of
my constitutional rights. He put a form under my nose on which
my signature would acknowledge this formality and was indig-
nant when I signed without reading it. Restraining my anger, I
informed him that I had gone through this procedure with more
subjects than he would ever know. That got us off to an unpleasant start.

I asked Lano if the investigation was an internal FBI matter or
the special prosecutor's business. "Strictly internal for the Inspection
Division," he said. But when I heard his specific questions, there was
no doubt in my mind that he was working for the special prosecutor
in an attempt to prove that I had lied to the grand jury.

Donald Segretti, whom the FBI interviewed about the alleged
dirty tricks of the 1972 campaign, told agents that he had been contacted by John Crewdson, a Washington correspondent for the *New
York Times*. Crewdson, he said, had shown him a number of FBI documents, and Segretti described them in some detail. One was very
significant, a copy of the February 26 memorandum that Horowitz
tried so desperately to have me recall. I told Lano and Midler what I
had said to Horowitz and the grand jurors: I had no independent

recollection of seeing the memorandum prior to my first interview in the office of the special prosecutor.

I had taken one call about the Kissinger wiretaps from Crewdson but told him nothing that Ruckelshaus had not already made public. I never gave FBI documents to Crewdson or anyone else outside the FBI. But the intent of Lano's questioning was clear. He wanted an admission that I did in fact recall the February 26 memorandum before Horowitz showed it to me. I could then be indicted for perjury or forced to testify against Gray.

After that interview I thought the ordeal was over. But in mid-November 1974, the *Los Angeles Times* and the *Washington Post* carried front-page stories about the leaks to Crewdson and the "investigation" of W. Mark Felt. And in 1975 I was interviewed on five separate occasions by the staff of the Senate Select Committee on Intelligence Operations.

In addition, FBI agents called on me twice while investigating alleged corruption and abuse of power by high Bureau officials. I admitted that I had attended several dinners paid for by FBI funds and held in honor of the heads of England's MI-5, Israeli intelligence, and the Special Branch of the Royal Canadian Mounted Police. I also "confessed" that the Exhibits Section of the FBI had done some picture framing for me—photos of Hoover, the attorney general, and so on, which had hung in my office.

Finally I was interviewed by staff members of the House Committee on Government Operations as to the disposition of the official and confidential files that Hoover had maintained in his office. In December I testified before the whole committee, chaired by Rep. Bella Abzug. Above all, she seemed to want to dominate the scene and was more interested in juicy gossip I might have seen in FBI files—the "goodies"—than in possible file management irregularities.

Eventually the frenzy to harass and punish the intelligence community subsided. The Justice Department announced that it would not prosecute CIA personnel who opened 215,000 letters to and from the Soviet Union between 1953 and 1973. The department also declined to prosecute CIA director Richard Helms for approving a Fairfax, Virginia, break-in to investigate a suspected leak of national security information.

Nor was action taken against FBI agents who surreptitiously entered the offices of a suspected Palestinian terrorist group. This came shortly after Palestinians took Israeli hostages during the 1972 Munich Olympic Games, and the FBI wanted to learn of possible terrorist plans for the United States. The agents found the names of numerous persons in the United States suspected of being potential terrorists. Instructions were immediately sent out to interview each one, fingerprinting and photographing some of them and putting them all on notice that the FBI knew who they were. In our view, this operation ended the Palestinian threat of hijackings, massacres, and bombings in the United States (with one exception, a failed attempt to bomb three New York City targets). Convinced that the FBI was all-knowing and ever-present, terrorists refused to accept assignments in the United States.

Gray was pleased with our results and ordered an all-out FBI effort to prevent terrorism in the United States. At a meeting of special agents in charge, Gray was asked if the surreptitious entries banned by Hoover would again be used by the FBI. Gray answered yes, in urgent cases, as long as Bureau headquarters first cleared the operation. Gray now denies making such a statement.

It was clear to me that Gray intended to step up the war against terrorism. There was never any doubt about Gray's interest in the violent leftist organization known as the Weather Underground. In a July 18, 1972, note about the group, Gray wrote to me: "Hunt to exhaustion. No holds barred." I was convinced by his remarks and by that handwritten order that the use of surreptitious entries was to be resumed in domestic terrorist cases. I proceeded on that assumption.

TWENTY-TWO

THE BLACK BAG JOBS

A strict observance of the written law is doubtless *one* of
the highest duties of a good citizen, but it is not the *highest*. The laws of necessity, of self preservation, of saving
our country when it is in danger, are of higher obligation. To lose our country by a scrupulous adherence to
the written law, would be to lose law itself, with life, lib-
erty, and property and all those who are enjoying them
with us; thus sacrificing the end to the means.

THOMAS JEFFERSON, 1818

D URING THE LATE 1960s and early 1970s, the FBI found itself
enforcing the law from a dangerous middle ground—facing
attacks from both the Nixon administration in Washington and the
violence-prone New Left emerging largely from college campuses.
Dissidents talked of kidnapping Henry Kissinger and visiting heads
of state. There were plans to paralyze the nation's capital by widespread sabotage. Policemen were being ambushed and murdered.
Heroin and LSD were being supplied to our young people. Bombs
were exploding all over the country. These terrorists openly
bragged of their communist beliefs, their ties to unfriendly foreign
countries, and their intentions to bring down our government by
force and violence.

Terrorist groups were small but growing. Some represented hostile foreign governments directly, and most were getting support, financial and otherwise, from these governments, whose interests were well served by the disruptions and sabotage the radicals perpetrated. To say that I was concerned about terrorist activity would be putting it mildly.

The most threatening of these groups was the Weathermen, who took their name from a line in a Bob Dylan song, "Subterranean Homesick Blues": "You don't need a weatherman to know which way the wind blows." The Weathermen had split off from Students for a Democratic Society, a leftist group that was insufficiently violent for the crazies. When many Weathermen became fugitives and went into hiding, the group's name was changed to the Weather Underground Organization. Other WUO members remained in place and functioned as the support apparatus of the fugitives, but all referred to themselves as members of the Weather Underground.

This was nothing less than an organization of violent terrorists with strong links to foreign countries. Confirmed records show that between 1968 and 1974, members of the WUO made hundreds of visits to Russia, the People's Republic of China, Cuba, Cambodia, North Vietnam, Algeria, Lebanon (for meetings with the Palestine Liberation Organization), and Libya, which was notorious for giving sanctuary and financial support to terrorists. These were only the known foreign contacts, and WUO members were assumed to have made thousands of clandestine contacts overseas that were never detected by our intelligence agencies.

There were also credible reports that the WUO was smuggling hard drugs into the United States as a means of financing its operations, reportedly operating out of the Green Mountain commune at Richmond, Vermont. It was less than one mile from the Canadian border, easily penetrated by both drugs and fugitives. There were alleged contacts with the Mafia in Boston and Providence as well as with the notorious drug dealer of the "French connection."

Communiqué number 4 of the Weather Underground Organization, dated September 15, 1970, claimed the "honor and pleasure" of arranging the escape of Timothy Leary from the California State Prison facility at San Luis Obispo. (In his book, *Confessions of a Hope Fiend,* Dr. Leary gives full credit for his escape to the WUO and intimates that the money used to spirit him out of prison and from the United States to Algeria came from dope peddlers.) The communiqué also proclaimed:

> With the NLF [the Vietnamese National Liberation Front, commonly referred to as the Vietcong] and the North Vietnamese, the Democratic Front for the Liberation of Palestine and Al Fatah, with Rap Brown and Angela Davis, with all black and brown revolutionaries, the Soledad Brothers and all prisoners of war in Amerikan concentration camps, we know that peace is only possible with the destruction of U.S. Imperialism.

WUO leaders traveled frequently to Cuba, where hundreds of visits were confirmed between 1968 and 1974. These young radicals idolized Fidel Castro, who frequently paid their travel expenses while they received communist indoctrination and training in guerrilla warfare from the Directorate General of Intelligence, the Cuban intelligence apparatus that was dominated by the Soviet KGB. Some of the radicals were recruited for espionage and intelligence-gathering missions for the Cubans. Some were trained as "sleepers" to be activated for future espionage operations in the United States.

Frequently these visits to Cuba were followed by serious disruptions in the United States. Mark Rudinsky, alias Mark Rudd, one of the top WUO leaders, went to Cuba for indoctrination and training during the winter of 1968 and returned the following spring to organize and lead the student takeover of Columbia University, which lasted seven days. Encouraged by the unprecedented publicity, Rudd went to Chicago, where he helped organize and lead the violent antiwar demonstrations during the 1968 Democratic National Convention.

In 1969, a delegation was invited to Cuba for a meeting with representatives of North Vietnam and the Vietcong. The Vietnamese communists were concerned over the lull in antiwar activity in the United States and they prodded the radicals to protest the war more vigorously. The communists demanded action instead of talk, and their objective was to strengthen their bargaining position at the peace negotiations.

Some of the radicals had already done their part. Naomi Jaffe visited North Vietnam in the spring of 1968. On her return to the United States, she bragged that she had shot down an American fighter plane with an antiaircraft gun. Jaffe implied this was part of a training program.

WUO radicals helped organize the Days of Rage in October 1969 to protest the trial of the Chicago Seven, who led the disruption of the Democratic National Convention the previous year. Football-helmeted WUO members attacked the police following a rally in Chicago's Lincoln Park. This stepped-up opposition to the Vietnam War actually delayed the final peace agreement because it promoted North Vietnamese intransigence.

The WUO did more than consort with foreign enemies and demonstrate. Its members also were responsible for terrorist acts at home. The line between domestic terrorism and foreign subversion was razor thin in those days, and in some cases, particularly as it related to the WUO, it did not exist at all. The FBI had dealt with this kind of menace since Franklin D. Roosevelt made the Bureau responsible for the internal security of the United States. Early targets included the Nazi-financed German-American Bund, the Soviet-directed Communist Party USA, and domestic fascist groups.

In the decades after World War II, the FBI moved with equal vigor to thwart terrorism and lawlessness on the part of a broad range of militant organizations: the Minutemen, Ku Klux Klan, Black Liberation Army, and Jewish Defense League. FBI agents interviewed young members of such groups in the presence of their parents and confronted them with the Bureau's knowledge of their terrorist plans. Some of the more recalcitrant activists were taken before federal grand juries.

To those who could measure the peril, the situation in some ways was far more dangerous in the late 1960s than it had been in the late 1930s. The FBI always operates on the theory that it is better to anticipate violence, prevent it wherever possible, and contain it no matter what the source. This was the challenge that confronted me as associate director of the FBI.

The FBI therefore was breaking no new ground when it turned its attention to the WUO and allied organizations that drew inspiration from it. The WUO had acquired a national reputation for violence impressive enough to invite comparison with the PLO, the Red Brigade of Italy, and the IRA.

WUO terrorists were linked to bombings and other attacks across the nation. These incidents included a 1969 sniper attack on police headquarters in Cambridge, Massachusetts; the 1969 bombing of several Chicago police cars; a 1970 dynamite explosion at a Detroit police station, killing one officer; and the 1970 bombing of New York City police headquarters, injuring three people.

Washington was a frequent target. The WUO took credit for a 1970 bombing at the National Guard Association Building, a 1970 explosion in the Senate wing of the Capitol, and a 1972 bombing at the Pentagon. According to the General Services Administration, the 1972 Pentagon bombing was the sixty-third bomb attack on a federal building since January 1970.

The group even bombed itself. On March 6, 1970, a WUO bomb

factory in New York's Greenwich Village—a luxury townhouse—was demolished when antipersonnel bombs consisting of nails tied to sticks of dynamite exploded prematurely. Three WUO members were killed.

Who would deny that it was the FBI's responsibility to track down these criminals? Eighteen leaders of the WUO were charged with a number of the crimes listed above and the FBI had to find them. It wasn't easy. We were dealing with sophisticated revolutionaries. Some had been trained in Cuba and traded expertise and assistance with other terrorist groups. They were supported by an effective underground network, but some of the fugitives were forced to leave the country nonetheless.

Ordinarily the FBI can rely on citizens to help track down criminals. This was not so in the case of the WUO fugitives. They were protected and supported by a cadre of hardcore sympathizers, many of whom were members of the above-ground WUO apparatus. At every point we were blocked by hostility from those we felt could give us leads, including parents of the radicals. These supporters did not seem to mind the Cuban and Soviet connections of the WUO. That the fugitives were admitted bombers who adhered to Marxist-Leninist ideologies did not deter their friends.

Agents were further frustrated by tight restrictions that Hoover imposed in 1966 on effective techniques for penetrating clandestine conspiracies between persons in this country and foreign governments. In addition to drastically reducing the number of wiretaps and microphone installations, Hoover flatly prohibited the use of mail openings and surreptitious entries, defined as warrantless entries into premises without the permission or knowledge of the occupant. These also were known as "black bag jobs" because lock-picking tools and related equipment needed for a surreptitious entry were usually carried in a small black bag.

The record indicates that under pressure from the White House and the Bureau, some of the techniques that Hoover had banned were revived in 1970. In the late summer of that year, Hoover discussed terrorism in the United States with President Nixon, who wanted aggressive action taken. William C. Sullivan, who was in charge of all investigative operations in 1970 and 1971, later stated publicly that Hoover told him in the fall of 1970 to use any means necessary to locate and apprehend these dangerous fugitives. Sullivan said he conveyed these instructions to agents in the field offices who were searching for the WUO bombers.

Hoover died in 1972 and Sullivan was killed in a hunting accident in 1977. There were no witnesses to the conversation between these two men, so we will never know for sure what the instructions included. Agents subordinate to Sullivan were clearly convinced that they were acting properly on the highest authority.

As far as I was concerned, the restrictions were not lifted until Hoover died in May 1972, and L. Patrick Gray III was appointed acting director. Domestic intelligence chief Edward Miller and I sincerely believed that Gray had authorized the use of these tools. The techniques were used only in certain cases. The Department of Justice and the FBI always distinguished between investigations designed to gather intelligence and those that collected evidence for court cases against accused criminals. As I understood the standard, intelligence gathering that was not intended to result in criminal charges was not limited by the Fourth Amendment prohibition against "unreasonable searches and seizures." For this reason a different set of rules always applied. Further, as I understood it, the warrants required in routine criminal cases need not be obtained to gather intelligence on foreign agents. This was especially true when, as was the case with the WUO, the information on which an application for a warrant would be based was too sensitive to present to a magistrate. The Weather Underground of the 1960s and early 1970s was a lethal terrorist organization with dangerous foreign ties. We had to combat its activists with no holds barred.

We developed a procedure for engaging in black bag jobs. When the infrequent requests came in from the field, they would go to Miller, who would in turn consult me. If we jointly agreed that the operation was feasible and completely justified in the best interests of the United States, Miller would so advise the field office and then confirm the transaction in a memorandum to me. On occasion, I learned of the entries after they occurred. In any event, this technique was used against the WUO only a few times, as documented in FBI files.

Since Acting Director Gray had given me complete operational authority and since he was away from Washington much of the time, I authorized five black bag jobs without consulting him. I felt then, as I do now, that the actions were wise. We imposed top-level control on the practice, and it enabled us to give our country a respite from WUO atrocities.

When Attorney General Griffin Bell took office in early 1977 with the new Carter administration, he harbored the misconception that I invented the technique of surreptitious entry, even though it was known to presidents, attorneys general, and any government official with enough brains to figure out where a Communist Party membership list or data about the Mafia from "anonymous sources" really came from. Bell's prosecutors argued that the WUO was a movement of "political activists" who, because they were American citizens, must be provided the protection of the Fourth Amendment even though their goals were terrorism and subversion. Justice Department attorneys began to interview field agents involved in operations against the WUO, and it was obvious that they were laying the groundwork for a case against me.

TWENTY-THREE

"GUILTY"

WITHIN MONTHS of my retirement, I could see the investigative spotlight turning toward me. First I was singled out as a possible leaker of FBI secrets. In April 1974, Woodward and Bernstein published *All the President's Men*, revealing the existence of the high-ranking government source they called Deep Throat. Four months later, the *Washingtonian* magazine named me as the most likely possessor of that dubious nickname. At about the same time, my former colleagues in the FBI had begun grilling me about whether I had leaked documents to Crewdson, the *New York Times* reporter.

By 1975, the post-Watergate backlash against abuses of government power also disrupted my life. In the U.S. Senate, the Church Committee investigated excesses by the intelligence services, and I found myself becoming the foremost FBI witness. I was interviewed on five separate occasions by the committee staff—an exercise in futility and frustration, since most of what I said was ignored and the rest taken out of context.

I emphasized as strongly as I could that our country's complacency against domestic terrorism would lead eventually to disaster. I could agree with critics who charged that Sullivan's counterintelligence agents sometimes had gone too far. The agents had infiltrated radical groups to gather intelligence, and had unfairly defamed many of their members. I argued that the remedy was to correct the abuses, not to halt our programs to protect us from terrorists. But nothing I said could prevent the committee from recommending that domestic intelligence programs be gravely weakened—as they ultimately were.

Along came the Carter administration, elected on its promise to establish a less intrusive government. The new Justice Department leadership quickly moved to show that it could rein in the FBI. The administration pursued us with a strategy of sequential indictments. First prosecutors trained their sights on low-level employees, then used the threat of heavy prison sentences to turn these defendants into witnesses against midlevel supervisors. Moving up the FBI ladder, the Justice Department would then strike at the "top dogs," as they put it, who had authorized steps to neutralize the WUO.

It was probably in my interest to stay on the sidelines. The midlevel supervisors had hunkered down and were refusing to cooperate with prosecutors. The five-year statute of limitations on conspiracy crimes was about to expire, and when it did, no higher level official could be prosecuted. Once the legal threat had been lifted, these supervisors could emerge to exonerate the low-level employees, testifying that the underlings had obeyed legal instructions. In the end, there was a chance that none of our agents would face unjust prosecution and punishment.

But there was also a chance that some of them *would* face prison, and in the meantime they had to live with constant harassment. The Civil Rights Division attorneys threatened the agents, telephoning their wives and calling the agents themselves in the middle of the night. In the early stages of this operation, more than 125 present and former FBI agents were pursued mercilessly. Some were granted immunity from prosecution and others were left dangling for months. All were forced to hire lawyers.

I knew that many of these agents were taking the heat for me: I was one of the prosecution's chief targets. I decided I had to take a stand. When I showed up at the grand jury room unexpectedly, Brian Gettings, a lawyer representing one of the FBI agents, approached me. "What are *you* doing here?" he demanded.

"I'm going to testify today, Brian," I said. "We authorized these entries, there are memos to prove it, and I'm going to tell that to the grand jury."

Gettings urged me to hold off. The statute of limitations would expire in a little more than a year. He assured me that the defendants were not expecting me to testify now.

Thanks, I told him, but I intended to tell the full story.

I testified that thirteen memos had authorized the black bag operations—seven for the WUO and six for Palestinian suspects. I had initialed each memo, and I told the grand jury where each was filed. Since my grand jury testimony was confidential, I held a news conference and appeared on the Sunday interview show *Face the Nation* to emphasize to the broadest possible audience that I had authorized the counterintelligence operations. "You are either going to have an FBI that tries to stop violence before it happens or you are not," I said. "Personally, I think this is justified, and I'd do it again tomorrow."

I knew that I was putting my head on the block and subjecting my wife and family to prolonged anguish, but I felt honor-bound to act. I had to take the street agents off the hook in order to prevent the further laceration of the FBI and the destruction of its morale.

The *New York Times* described my statement as "the first instance in which a top executive at Bureau Headquarters has taken the responsibility for authorizing any of the burglaries that are currently the subject of criminal inquiry by the Department of Justice." It stated that I had acted on assurances by L. Patrick Gray that he would countenance the use of "surreptitious entries" to gather information "in sensitive intelligence investigations" and quoted me accurately as saying that at a meeting of special agents in charge, Gray had said that he would "approve these things" but cautioned the SACs to be "damn sure you get Bureau approval."

I was not the only former FBI official to publicly disclose involvement in the WUO entries. Edward S. Miller also made a public statement for reasons similar to mine. Both of us were flooded with letters and telegrams commending us and expressing support. The Justice Department reacted with anger and consternation. We had taken the initiative, and prosecutors could no longer harass the younger agents. A newspaper reporter told me that one Justice Department official told him, "We'll get that son of a bitch Felt." For attorneys in the Civil Rights Division of the Justice Department, the matter had become a personal vendetta.

Before the department turned its guns on me, it found what seemed to be a more vulnerable target. In April 1977, the grand jury in New York City, which had been sifting allegations of illegal behavior by the FBI, indicted former special agent John J. Kearney, who had supervised the pursuit of WUO fugitives in the New York area. Kearney, who was known for his personal courage and conviction, testified honestly and openly before the grand jury but refused to stretch the truth in what he considered an effort to pillory FBI personnel and discredit the Bureau. But what may have seemed like easy pickings for the Civil Rights Division turned into a can of worms.

FBI agents and former agents rallied to Kearney's support. More than three hundred supporters appeared on the courthouse steps at Foley Square in New York on April 14, 1977, when he appeared for arraignment. A special agents' legal fund was formed by the Society of Former FBI Agents, and contributions from agents, former agents, and supporters exceeded $1.5 million. This generous financial backing enabled Kearney to prepare a strong legal defense, and funds were also used to help pay legal expenses incurred by the many other agents and former agents caught up in the Justice Department net. Early in 1978, Attorney General Bell admitted that the Kearney indictment was a mistake and that his mail was running 300 to 1 against him.

My personal sources told me that the case was far from over, however, because Bell was being pressured by his own Civil Rights Division, as well as the liberal wing of the Carter administration. My sources proved to be correct and the Kearney case inched along for a year. On April 10, 1978, Bell succumbed to public opinion and announced that he was dropping the charges against Kearney. In the same press release, he announced the indictment of Gray, Miller, and me, explaining that in this case, "criminal prosecution should be brought to bear at the highest levels of authority and responsibility at which the evidence will support prosecution."

The indictment charged us with conspiring to abuse the rights of Weathermen relatives and acquaintances "to be secure in their homes, papers, and effects against unreasonable searches and seizures." It listed thirty-two "overt acts," including conversations between Miller and Gray, speeches by Gray to FBI officials, Gray's approval of the agenda for an in-service training course on the Weather Underground Organization, a lecture to FBI agents on how to conduct surreptitious entries in WUO cases, memorandums of conversations between Miller and me, and surreptitious entries conducted by FBI agents and reported to me by Miller. We were charged under a sixty-year-old statute used almost exclusively in the South to prosecute Ku Klux Klansmen and local authorities who beat up or otherwise harassed voters at the polls—actions having nothing to do with national security.

Gray, Miller, and I were arraigned on April 20, 1978.* It was a memorable day, partly because of the trauma but much more so because of the tremendous show of support on the steps of the U.S. Courthouse in Washington. A group of about 1,200 agents and former agents held a silent vigil in support of the defendants. There were no signs or placards, but as each defendant walked across the plaza and up the steps, our colleagues gave us loud and sustained applause.

I am not an emotional person, but tears welled up in my eyes as I walked with my wife, Audrey, through the crowd. As we paused at the entrance to the building, an agent and a former agent read brief statements expressing strong support. All I could say was, "God bless you all."

Some of those present came from as far away as Florida. Also represented were FBI agents from Richmond, Baltimore, New Haven, Boston, and Washington, D.C. Three chartered buses filled with agents from the New York office left at three o'clock in the morning for the long ride to Washington. It could not have been more impressive.

Proceedings inside the courthouse were brief. We all entered not guilty pleas and the judge announced that we were released on our personal recognizance, which simply means that we promised to appear when ordered. Then there was an unexpected development. The judge said, "You will now be turned over to the United States marshal for processing."

I knew what this meant: being taken to the marshal's office for

* Mark would have been well served to reveal his secret identity now—or at some point in the more than two years between his indictment and trial. By this time, Deep Throat had become a mythic figure, credited with bringing down Nixon and enabling the election of Carter. If Mark had acknowledged playing that role, public opinion would have swung in his favor and he might have avoided prosecution. But he kept silent. —Editor

fingerprinting and mug shots. I had thought this step would not be necessary because all three defendants' fingerprints and photographs were on file with the FBI. Many of the Watergate defendants were not put through this indignity at the time of their arraignments, but we were. There was no doubt in my mind that the Justice Department chose to humiliate us.

As I waited behind the barred door in the fingerprint and photo room and as I saw my wife standing outside with tears in her eyes, my anger grew. Yet I knew that the deputy marshals were only doing what they had been told. I was frustrated, but I had not taken leave of my senses.

Gray was fingerprinted first, and as he stepped aside I moved forward for my turn. He was standing beside me at the washbasin attempting to wash the black printer's ink from his fingers. "Pat," I said, "how many years of service have you given your country?"

"Twenty-six years. Twenty years in the navy and six years with the government," he answered.

"This is the reward that your country has for you."

Gray did not reply, but I knew he shared my feelings of anger and frustration, as did Miller, who was waiting his turn to be smeared with printer's ink.

At trial, we had to deal with a shaggy-haired prosecutor, John Nields, who personified the Watergate-inspired crusader. If we in the FBI had waged a no-holds-barred war on domestic terrorism, Nields took a no-holds-barred approach to prosecuting government officials for their abuses, real or imagined. Trial judge William Bryant and the New York City jury were a perfect audience for Nields's approach.* The prosecutor called the WUO a radical group,

---

* Bryant and eleven of the twelve jurors were African American. While antiterrorism today is not an issue that skews racially, Mark's prosecutors played to the sensibilities of the times by posturing as defenders of civil rights. —Editor

styling its members as political dissidents rather than dangerous terrorists. He cited a 1972 case, *United States v. United States District Court* (Keith), in which the Supreme Court ruled that the government requires a warrant and probable cause to conduct electronic surveillance against a member of a wholly domestic subversive group.

Nields reminded the court that we were on trial for violating the civil rights not of the subversives themselves, but of innocent friends and relatives of the WUO. Judge Bryant, denying our motion to dismiss the charges, showed that he had bought into the prosecution argument. "Suppose I had three children, and suppose during a particular political situation . . . my children break away and join a radical group," he said. "Are you telling me somebody has a right to sneak in my house and go through my effects?"

In our defense, we argued that the WUO activists were far more than political radicals. We pointed out the extensive foreign involvement of the Weather Underground Organization, demonstrating that our surreptitious entries were national security operations.* But when we introduced a motion ordering the FBI to produce files proving our case, they came out so heavily redacted—blacked out— that they were unintelligible. Hundreds of other documents were judged to be too sensitive for release in court in any form.

Prosecutors also attacked us from a different angle. They argued that only the president or attorney general could approve a warrantless search on national security grounds. Although their case was made out of thin air, Judge Bryant bought it. The prosecution called five former attorneys general—including John Mitchell and

---

* Since Mark's conviction, the Supreme Court has twice endorsed an exception to the Fourth Amendment, permitting warrantless searches in national security cases. Provisions of the Patriot Act, passed after the terrorist attacks of September 11, 2001, also permit warrantless searches, even if only a subsidiary purpose is to gather intelligence. If the FBI today conducted a warrantless search at the home of an al-Qaeda supporter in Brooklyn, it is safe to say that no federal court would object. —Editor

Richard Kleindienst—to testify that they had never approved surreptitious entries. I think they wanted to help us. Our lawyer, Brian Gettings, asked them on cross-examination if they felt the use of surreptitious entries in our case was justified and appropriate. All but Ramsey Clark, who had served as Lyndon Johnson's attorney general, said they would have approved the entries if the FBI had asked them to do so.

We conceded that we had not asked for permission from the attorney general. Our main argument was that such permission was not required until 1976, when Attorney General Edward Levi introduced that requirement—long after our operations against the WUO in 1972 and 1973. We called numerous former FBI agents and Justice lawyers, all of whom confirmed the long history of national security break-ins carried out by the Bureau and approved by the Justice Department. I took the stand, testifying that the new break-in policy approved by Gray gained momentum after the massacre of Israeli athletes at the Munich Olympics in September 1972. I added that even after the Supreme Court forced the FBI to abandon warrantless wiretapping, "I have never regarded surreptitious entry for intelligence purposes as illegal. And this is the way all people in the FBI felt."

The prosecution called Richard Nixon gingerly. Nields knew he might alienate the jury by producing the disgraced former president. But he also needed Nixon to testify—as he did—that he never specifically ordered Hoover or Gray to conduct WUO break-ins. Under questioning from our side, however, Nixon said he had seen "hard evidence" of the WUO's foreign connections, and he testified in no uncertain terms that under his administration the FBI director had authority to conduct national security break-ins. "In matters of foreign intelligence, the line of authority went directly from the president to Mr. Hoover," Nixon said.

The prosecution dropped its case against Gray, saying that there was not enough concrete evidence that he had approved the entries. I felt confident that Miller and I would be acquitted, until the judge agreed to include a prosecution instruction to the jury that said, "You may assume based on the law that if an entry did not have the express written approval of the attorney general in advance it was illegal." That all but forced the jury to find us guilty. The judge declined to sentence us to prison, ordering me to pay a $5,000 fine and Miller to pay $3,000.

The jury found us guilty on November 6, 1980, but President Ronald Reagan gave Miller and me full and unconditional pardons in March 1981. The convictions "grew out of their good-faith belief that their actions were necessary to preserve the security interests of our country," Reagan said. "The record demonstrates that they acted not with criminal intent, but in the belief that they had grants of authority reaching to the highest levels of government." In 1983 the appeals court ordered the lower court to dismiss our indictment, and the conviction was expunged from the record. The appeals court never reached our argument that we had been convicted for violating procedures that had not been established.

The years of stress were finally over, but not the pain from the constant harassment and humiliation we had endured. When I set out to write this book, I wanted to erase all of those nightmares, to portray the FBI that I had devoted my career to—the organization my countrymen revered. What stands out in my memory is the Bureau that rose above all other police agencies as a paragon of American justice. The triumphs of my career came from my place on a team that exhibited its analytical power in wartime counterespionage, its investigative expertise in solving mass murders, and its determination to bring every criminal to justice, whether he was cornered in a shootout or cowering in his mother's closet. This FBI was fair and restrained, using its police power judiciously, conscious never to exceed legislative or constitutional bounds. Above all, it was respected—by the criminals who tended to surrender simply knowing the FBI was on their trail and by American citizens who saw us as the guardian of democracy.

During my years in Washington, especially after Hoover's death, I often saw myself as standing alone against the forces working against the FBI. These struggles were frustrating, but I was determined to do what I thought was right. In retrospect, I took many risks. I did not realize that I would have a part in bringing down a president and I did not intend to. I was taking it one day at a time, trying to do what was right.

Hoover had managed to preserve the FBI's independence and integrity for a generation. But after his passing, his successors—including me—were no match for those seeking to erode the Bureau's place in our system. I fought the Nixon White House's attempt to make us a tool of the administration, and later I took on attempts by Congress and the Carter administration to portray the FBI as some sort of malevolent human rights abuser. After the passage of years I now see that my battles were essentially hopeless. By the new standards of our society, after the ructions of the 1960s and 1970s, there is no longer room for the kind of federal police agency that in today's light seems paternalistic and unchecked. It will be enough if the FBI can maintain its standards as an effective, professional crime fighter.

The nine-year legal ordeal after my retirement stole from the precious time that Audrey and I had planned to devote to our life together, time we had always promised ourselves as compensation for the rigors of a high-level FBI career. We both came out of this final odyssey weakened. But Audrey had taken the brunt of our career hardships—the constant moves, the school and job changes—all within the confines of an FBI community that demanded discipline and conformity from spouses as well as agents. If anything, the years of humiliation that followed my retirement weighed more heavily on Audrey than on me. She weakened steadily after my trial, and finally passed away on July 20, 1984. I am certain that she would be alive today were it not for the abuse she was forced to endure. I am left to salute her memory.

I

THE ARC OF Mark Felt's life, as he describes it in this book, ended in tragedy. His beloved FBI turned on him, the government he tried to save from Nixon's abuses hounded him, and his retirement devolved into depression, misery, and the suicide of his wife, Audrey (a catastrophe he has never mentioned publicly). In light of this terrible ending, we naturally search for the seeds of disaster in his earlier years. Audrey was plagued by nervous anxiety and suffered her first breakdown as Mark's career began to soar in the mid-1950s. His children endured the bruises of a nomadic life, an absentee father, and the social ructions of the 1960s. Mark's climb to the top of the FBI provided his family with pride and the adventure of having a top G-man heading the household. In retrospect, however, it is apparent that the legacy he tried so hard to build at the Bureau began to collapse with the death of his mentor, J. Edgar Hoover, in early 1972, before Watergate began to unfold. The end of his career, like the end of his marriage, was a horror story.

Mark's autobiographical writings reflect these hardest of times.

He stopped recording his story in the mid-1980s, his low point, and consequently missed the real ending—a twenty-year process of rebuilding and reconciliation that culminated on a sunny California day in May 2005, when "the guy they used to call Deep Throat" came to the open door of his suburban home, stepped forward to wave to the crowd of media and curiosity seekers, and thereby introduced himself—all of himself—for the first time. For more than thirty years Mark Felt had dreaded facing that moment, not certain how his former FBI colleagues, the courts, and other Americans would react. But the people on his doorstep cheered and applauded. When the door closed, the old man sat down, exhilarated and breathless with excitement. "I can't think of anything better than sitting here enjoying all of this with my family right here beside me," he said.

He had begun building that family nearly seventy years earlier, when he married Audrey and the young couple made their first home together in Washington. So began the greatest partnership of his life, a forty-six-year marriage that required Mark to balance his loyalty to the FBI against his devotion to a beautiful, vivacious, and needy spouse. Just as he walled off his Deep Throat identity from the rest of the world, he mentioned Audrey and his two children, Joan and Mark Jr., only in passing. Yet to understand the immense pressures on Mark Felt, we need some understanding of the joys and sorrows of his family life.

In the summer of 1938, when he and Audrey married, the capital was afire with the New Deal and debates over America's role in the growing European ferment of Stalin's Russia and Hitler's Germany. Mark was on vacation from George Washington University law school. He drove his bride to Idaho in their Chevrolet coupe to work unsuccessfully for the reelection of Democratic senator James P. Pope, Mark's employer, and then drove back to work for the winner, D. Worth Clark.

The Felts thrived in Washington. Tall, handsome, and disciplined, Mark seemed predestined to become one of Hoover's G-men. He had a glamorous wife, who had been a brilliant student at the University of Idaho and held a good job at the Internal Revenue Service. Mark and Audrey had a wide social circle and loved hosting and attending parties. Like other young people in a nation slowly emerging from the Depression, the Felts hungered for black-tie elegance despite their modest means. Audrey happily threw herself into large, convivial social gatherings. "It was hard to find time for making love with both of us working days and me going to night school," Mark wrote in notes to his family. "I didn't get home until about 8:00 P.M., and after dinner I had to at least look at a few law books. There was plenty of love, though."

Indeed there was. Mark had a courtly, gentlemanly way with women, and a passion for Audrey that lasted a lifetime. His personal writings are sprinkled with notations such as "GLORIOUS HONEYMOON!" and "Trying to get Audrey pregnant—EXCITEMENT!" Risking the wrath of the straitlaced Hoover, Mark quietly took Audrey on FBI trips to New York, San Juan, and other destinations, where their indoor recreations were intense. "Mark treated Audrey very well outside the bedroom door, and he treated her very, very well behind the bedroom door," said family friend Bea Reade Burke. Audrey's friends envied the attentiveness of her husband, who liked nothing more than painting her toenails and bringing her breakfast in bed.

Felt came to Washington in the early years after Prohibition, when government agents were fighting their sensational war to end the gangster era of bootlegging, kidnapping, and robbery. In 1933 Pretty Boy Floyd and other gunmen massacred four police officers and their prisoner in Kansas City. A year later, agents ambushed John Dillinger outside Chicago's Biograph Theater. Even as they fell, lawless villains like Dillinger, Bonnie and Clyde, Machine Gun Kelly, and Ma Barker took on mythical status. In movie houses, Jimmy Cagney's *Public Enemy* was the big hit, portraying an archvillain so ruthless that only gangsters of his own kind—not lawmen—could gun him down.

Hoover attacked the gangsters and their myth of invincibility head-on. As his agents arrested and gunned down the criminals, the Catholic Church's Legion of Decency and the International Association of Chiefs of Police demanded in 1935 that no movie or radio show glorify gangsters and threatened to boycott any studio that did. Hoover created a new national hero—the "G-man." The same Jimmy Cagney who had starred as a murderous gangster came back to the screen a year later as an incorruptible FBI agent in *G-Man*. A G-man radio series, G-man magazine, and numerous film and television exploitations followed.

Hoover cultivated the myth of his government agents as carefully as he publicized their war against violent criminals. As his power grew, only Hoover was allowed to be famous. Even the most favored agents faced big trouble if they overshadowed the director. When Chicago Special Agent in Charge Melvin Purvis won nationwide headlines for leading the ambush that killed John Dillinger, Hoover badgered him into retirement. Purvis tried to pursue a movie career until Hoover squashed that ambition, letting it be known that the FBI would withhold cooperation from any studio that employed the outcast. When Purvis committed suicide in 1960 (using the .45 automatic that fellow agents gave him when he resigned), his family blamed Hoover. In sabotaging Purvis, Hoover made the point that in the FBI, the individual agent was not the hero. Hoover presided over a new breed of incorruptible, highly educated, essentially faceless and interchangeable agents schooled in the science of crime fighting, each man a cog in the FBI system.

Mark Felt joined Hoover's system seven years after it was formally designated the Federal Bureau of Investigation, a time when the director's leadership and values were unquestioned. Mark looked the part of Hoover's idealized agent—trim, capable, taciturn. And beyond his correct demeanor he knew almost instinctively how to get on the fast track: take the big cases but keep a low profile. As he reviewed his career in correspondence with his family, his list of favorite cases—catching a Nazi spy and monitoring revolution in the Dominican Republic—were those that made Hoover and the Bureau (not Mark alone) look good.

Under Hoover's system, the FBI always had to close its cases, always had to get its man. Critics have long charged that the Bureau became a servant of this image, staying away from festering dilemmas like drug trafficking, for example, while concentrating on crimes like car theft that it could solve successfully in great numbers. But few American law enforcement officers worked as many hours (another statistic Hoover kept tabs on) or faced as much pressure to succeed as FBI agents. Felt worked ceaselessly as he climbed the hierarchy. His ambition and enthusiasm were boundless. "Much exciting work in the Espionage Section," he wrote of his 1944 assignment. "[I] actually could hardly wait to get to work each morning." But this frenetic schedule, working from early morning to late at night, often six days a week, took a toll on the Felts. Audrey was a great talker and socializer, whereas Mark, generally a quiet man like his father, would arrive home at night all talked out.

The path for any agent was straight and narrow: put in long hours, solve a prodigious number of cases, and obey rule number one: never embarrass the bureau. Just as FBI agents were essentially interchangeable in the Hoover system, so were FBI offices. A G-man was expected to move frequently, learning the geography and the local problems of all parts of the country—while finding an identical working environment in each office, be it Detroit or Des Moines. After Mark completed basic training in Virginia, the Felts were transferred to Houston, San Antonio, Washington, and Seattle—all in the first three years of his career.

Mark moved from office to office quite seamlessly. But the system often didn't work so smoothly for families who had to keep changing homes and schools. The psychological pressures were intense for the families, who were expected to behave as correctly as the agent. Often they had trouble finding trusted friends outside the Bureau cocoon. During the first three years of Mark's career, Audrey set up and broke down households repeatedly and took jobs she never held for more than a few months. In 1943, five years into their marriage, she give birth to Joan. After Mark was called back to Washington for three months in 1945, Audrey had to move to Seattle by herself and care for two-year-old Joan while staying with relatives in Idaho—a period Mark characterized succinctly as "not good."

The young family eventually found stability in Seattle, where Mark remained for nine years and where Mark Jr. was born in 1947. But again, a disproportionate share of the pressure fell on Audrey. Mark was sent back to Virginia to train as a firearms instructor and then taught and demonstrated weapons use throughout the Northwest. Though he never fired a gun during an arrest operation—a record he was proud of—his specialty led to a number of "dangerous assignments," as he characterized them. Audrey was left to care for the two young children, and she took a job at the Veteran's Administration to help pay for Joan's orthodontia. In the spring of 1954, Mark finally won the personal audience with Hoover that would ignite his career. At almost the same time, Audrey collapsed in nervous exhaustion. The family sent the children to stay with relatives and hired a maid to help out in Seattle. Day after day, Audrey stayed in bed with the lights off. People moved about the house quietly, knowing that she could not tolerate the slightest noise. After weeks of rest, Mark wrote wishfully, "all returned to normal."

That fall, it was time to pack up again and move back to Washington. Mark had won a career-advancing assignment in the Inspection Division, which served as Hoover's watchdog over the entire organization. But that turned out to be a brief stopover on the way to an assignment as assistant special agent in charge in New Orleans. He and Joan drove to their new home, Mark wrote, while "Audrey and Mark Junior stayed behind to supervise the moving, which was not complicated because we had barely started to unpack."

After more rapid-fire transfers to Los Angeles, Salt Lake City (where Mark was promoted to special agent in charge), and Kansas City, the Felts ended up back in Washington in 1962. He could have retired then after twenty years of service, which might have suited Audrey's need for stability. But his career was just beginning to heat up, and by that time his wife was as invested in his career as he was. Instead of taking a comfortable path to early retirement, the couple began to talk about the time, somewhere in the unspecified future, when they could live a more relaxed life devoted to each other.

In 1964 Mark was promoted to assistant director in the Inspections Division. That made him one of Hoover's chief enforcers—the "king of conduct," as some agents called him—and put him in the highest echelon of headquarters officials. Top inspectors not only maintained Bureau standards but were called on to solve the Bureau's most intractable cases. They were the FBI's true believers, and no one was more committed to the Bureau and its image than Mark Felt—though his elevation to what amounted to the high priesthood increased the pressure on Audrey and the rest of the family to conform. As a top supervisor, Mark could not socialize on a regular basis with field agents and headquarters officials, nor could he get too close to his underlings in Inspections. Those conditions limited the family's social circle, to the frustration of Audrey, who loved nothing more than big parties and friendly gatherings.

To a great extent, Mark also had to remove himself from the workaday world of the FBI. Ever the compartmentalizer, he concealed his soft side and sense of humor to present a strict demeanor suitable to his role as a cop of cops. He could show no signs that

Hoover might interpret as softness, for the director demanded the ruthless enforcement of FBI standards. Yet Mark tried his best to enforce the rules without ruining careers unnecessarily. His approach was to instill maximum fear throughout the organization while tending to mete out less than the maximum punishment. Nobody questioned that he got the reign of terror act right. Supervisors recalled the icy hostility of a Mark Felt grilling, or the trademark sneer he wore while striding through a local office. Even at this writing, retired FBI agents referred to the "ice water" in Mark Felt's veins and said he was "very unpopular" and "not widely liked." Such testimony shows that Mark paid a high personal price as he enforced Hoover's policies. As a retired San Francisco agent put it, "When you knew Mark Felt was in town, you stood a little straighter, you shined your shoes a little more, kept your desk a little neater."

Early in Mark's tenure as a top inspector, a senior official in Oklahoma City developed a reputation as a womanizer, taking advantage of timid young file clerks. Following their leader's example, other agents in the office fraternized improperly too. When the official went too far, dallying with a young employee at an office function in front of numerous witnesses, including wives, Mark Felt struck quickly. In one fell swoop, he disciplined not only the main offenders but anybody who knew of their behavior without reporting it. In what amounted to a scorched-earth campaign, Mark reprimanded and/or transferred forty-three of the fifty agents stationed in Oklahoma City. That ended sexual harassment anywhere in the FBI during his tenure.

If Felt worked his heart out in FBI offices around the country, in Washington he contributed his soul as well. He went to the office early and came home late virtually every day. Inevitably his family suffered from his absences. His son fell steadily behind in school. Mark Jr. got by with the help of a math tutor but found himself in trouble—mouthing off in class, getting in trouble on the bus—so often that Audrey sent him to the Wentworth Military Academy in Lexington, Missouri, for a year. He graduated from high school in Washington with a C average but won a place as an engineering major at Virginia Polytechnic Institute (thanks to his father's quiet intervention, he assumes today). Once again the son flirted with failure, ending up on academic probation after his freshman year. When he came home with dismal grades, his father took a rare Saturday off and was waiting to remind the young man that he had made a commitment to his college education. "He told me that the most important thing in life is trust," Mark Jr. recalled. "If you can't earn someone's trust, you will never amount to anything, and meeting the commitments you make is the first step toward trust." Mark Jr. pulled through, graduated with a B average, and went on to a successful air force career and later a career as an American Airlines pilot.

More vexing still were the problems that arose between Audrey and their daughter, Joan, a generational dispute that reflected cultural issues in the second half of the 1960s. Joan had it all—beauty and smarts—and as she grew up and developed, her parents doted on her. Her father predicted she would become the first woman president of the United States. He helped her with school speeches, and she remembered him as her nurturer when she was sick. Above all, he defined cool for Joan—the only father in the neighborhood who came home from work with a holstered gun under his arm. In the eyes of his daughter, he was invincible.

Audrey also loved her daughter intensely and outfitted her with bright sweaters, swirling skirts, and a dazzling fake fur coat with a red velvet lining. In college she urged her to dye her hair blond and wear padded bras. As a child, Audrey had lived in an orphanage and various foster homes and always dreamed of having a daughter for a best friend. Now she had a lovely daughter, but Joan recoiled from a mother whom she regarded as needy to a fault, not to mention domineering, assertive, and too often operating under the influence of alcohol. From Joan's perspective, her mother's probing questions never ceased: What are you thinking? What are you doing? Are you talking about me behind my back? "We have to share," Audrey would lecture her rebellious daughter. "We are a family that shares."

Her father would return from his power struggles at the Bureau to mediate power struggles at home. In a sense, Mark's wife was violating the Felt family code, drummed into him by his parents: don't complain and don't display your troubles to the world. But in family disputes, Mark inevitably stood behind Audrey. "He would never criticize her," Joan said. "He would say, 'Your mother loves you very much. She wants what's best for you. Try to get along with her. Try to be strong.' He told me after her death that it was his duty always to be loyal to her first."

School was an escape for Joan, and she marched brilliantly through her educational career. As a preteen, she showed such a talent for Spanish that her parents sent her to live with a family in a small Mexican town to perfect her skills. After graduating from high school in Kansas City with straight A's, she took the University of Kansas by storm, becoming president of her dorm, winning a seat on the student council, joining the most prestigious sorority and accepting academic awards. She transferred to Stanford in her junior year, graduated in 1965, won a Fulbright scholarship to Chile, where she worked as an actor, and came back to Stanford for a master's in Spanish and Spanish American literature. But her rebellion was not over. When she was twenty-eight years old, Joan announced that she was moving to a farm in Santa Cruz County and did not want her parents to find her. Mark sent letters to every general post office in the county; all except the one in Ben Lomond were returned, indicating that Joan had picked it up. Mark quickly tracked her down, but "she thought I had put the FBI on her trail," he wrote in family notes. "God forbid!"

He failed to negotiate a reconciliation between his daughter and his wife. A rationalist who paid little attention to religion, he now was faced with a daughter who accepted mind-expanding drugs, an alternative lifestyle, and a guru's teachings about communion with the primal divine current of love-bliss happiness. During her pre-ashram period, when Joan resided at the Ben Lomond farm, Mark's personal writings were often terse and telegraphic. He communicated his dismay at finding his daughter living in a community that, though nonpolitical, resembled a collection of Weather Underground radicals. "We were worried about Joan and decided to check out her situation," he wrote. "Because of some now forgotten disagreement, I went alone. I found Joan to be apparently well and happy. But she was a hippie and living in a commune. I took no action but I probably should have."

Later, when Joan was working for an experimental theater group in Los Angeles, Audrey called her and said, "Your father tells me you're living for happiness from moment to moment out there. But I don't believe it. Tell me it isn't true!"

"Mom, Dad's right," she answered. "It is true!"

Mark used his compartmentalization skills to wall off his family troubles from Hoover and the FBI. His career continued to soar. In 1971 he won his long power struggle with rival William Sullivan—"much intrigue at the Bureau," was all he wrote privately—and was named deputy associate director, the number three job behind Hoover and his weakening alter ego, Clyde Tolson. A year later, Hoover died, Tolson resigned, and Mark Felt launched into his career endgame, effectively running the FBI under L. Patrick Gray, including the investigation into the Watergate break-in. After Mark was passed over for the directorship again in 1973, he retired one stop from the top position that both he and his wife had sought.

He joined the college lecture circuit, became active in the Society of Former FBI Agents, and for a time he and Audrey may have seen a peaceful retirement on their horizon. In 1974, Joan gave birth to their first grandson, whom she named Ludi Kohoutek after a Herman Hesse character and the comet. (At age 8, the boy changed his name to "William Felt.") Mark and Audrey went to Ben Lomond to see the infant, a visit that almost failed when they arrived early and came upon a naked Joan breast-feeding Ludi in a field. "Was that you I saw with no clothes on?" Audrey asked. "What were you doing out there?" The parents stayed for an hour, holding the baby for pictures. But her mother remained angry, Joan recalled. "How can you live like this in a chicken coop after all the education you had?" Audrey demanded.

The power of family togetherness seemed to reassert itself when Joan visited her parents with Ludi and stayed for several months. Then Mark Jr. and his wife, Wanda, presented a second grandson, Mark III. But throughout the late 1970s, Mark's legal problems weighed on his mind. Untethered by long days with lawyers and investigators, the former Bureau disciplinarian began drinking more—as did Audrey—and grousing about unjust persecution by the government he had served. All of Washington seemed to betray him, and all of the sacrifices he made for his career came to nothing except pain for him and his family. When Mark was on the witness stand in court, his lawyer asked him if he could have avoided the trial. In fact, Mark could have. Nobody had forced him to take responsibility for the black bag jobs against Weather Underground radicals, putting the prosecutorial heat on himself. And he declined to plead guilty to a misdemeanor, refusing to admit that what hundreds of agents had done under his direction was wrong. So, yes, Mark could have avoided the trial and the devastation it brought to Audrey, Joan, and Mark Jr. After his lawyer asked the question, the steely FBI man broke down and sobbed.

Longtime friend Bea Reade Burke saw Audrey's slide from the start of Mark's trial. Nothing Mark did to relieve his wife's anxieties—from soothing talks to bubble baths—seemed to work. Audrey made it to the first day of her husband's trial, but Joan told reporters that her mother could never face the courtroom again.

By the time Mark was found guilty in November 1980, Audrey's health took a turn for the worse. Earlier that year she suffered a serious bout of pneumonia that sapped her energy permanently. During the early phases of the trial, Mark noted tersely, "Audrey extremely nervous and apprehensive—understandably so." After his conviction, "she had a flu-like condition which eventually took us to the hospital emergency room." A year later, even after the good news that President Reagan had pardoned Mark, Audrey's physical exam disclosed cardiac insufficiency, and the Felts had to put off a vacation to California and Hawaii. In December she was hospitalized again with nausea caused by a stomach inflammation.

In 1983, some family help arrived. The Felts had been living in a Virginia condo complex called Watergate at Landmark (no relation to the Washington namesake that had played such a huge role in Mark's career), and in that year Mark Jr. moved his family into a nearby apartment in the same complex. The son had a prestigious job, piloting Vice President George Bush in Air Force Two, and now lived almost next door with his wife and son. Nonetheless, Audrey continued to go downhill. "She was losing weight and was worried about her condition," Mark noted. "Side effects of medication seemed to off-set any benefit. Her mouth was dry and she felt tense."

Audrey tried to rally in 1984. Mark's decade of legal wrangling seemed to be over. In April, Audrey elected to have a blepharoplasty—an eyelid lift—which the family interpreted as a sign that her morale was improving. "But the trauma of the recovery period was more than we expected," Mark noted. One afternoon in mid-July, Mark Jr. received a call from his father asking him to come over. The son made his way past police cars and ambulances to his father's door, where a police officer took his hand and led him inside. His father was sitting down, pale and devastated, as the investigators asked questions.

"What's going on?" Mark Jr. asked. "What's going on?"

His father said simply, "Your mother has committed suicide."

Audrey had seemed fine in the morning, Mark Sr. said. He had gone out to run errands, and when he came home he found her lying in the guest bathroom, drenched in blood, with his service revolver at her side. Morgue workers took the body away, and police technicians arrived later that day to clean the bathroom's linoleum floor, walls, and fixtures. The family cleaned the room again and again after that, Mark Jr. said. But he could still see traces of his mother's blood under the floor molding.

Mark Jr. had seen gathering signs of trouble. He and his wife had played bridge with his parents only a few days earlier. He had complimented his mother on the success of her cosmetic surgery, telling her she looked "absolutely fantastic." "She took it without much show of pleasure," he said. "All night she seemed stoic and quiet—not her normal personality, which was vivacious and talkative to the point of being too talkative." After Audrey died, Mark Jr. found more than a dozen drugs in her medicine cabinet, prescribed by a number of doctors and dentists, most of them for depression.

Mark Felt immediately compartmentalized the family tragedy. Sitting with his son at a table for hours, the father decreed that the suicide would be kept a strict secret, even from Joan. Mark did not want to burden the family or the family history with the record of a suicide. The cover story would be that Audrey died of a sudden heart attack.

In the "Calendar of Events," a family chronology that Mark put together, he wrote, "Sometime during her sleep on July 20th,

Audrey passed away due to Cardiac Arrest. At least it was an easy way to go. I felt guilty that perhaps I did not take good enough care of her."

Mark made arrangements for a quiet service in a funeral home with about twenty people attending. Joan asked that the body be left in peace for a time—according to her beliefs her mother should have been allowed to settle into death gradually—but Mark had the remains cremated before his daughter could even make her way to Virginia from California. The service was not exactly Audrey's kind of party. "I don't remember anybody other than a priest or minister saying anything," Mark Jr. recalled. "I have no recollection of what was said."

It would be nearly twenty years before Mark Jr., while cleaning out some of his father's old things with his sister at her California home, first told Joan—almost casually, as she recalled—that her mother had killed herself. Joan was not surprised. "Months before her death, she had been reading the obituaries of people she knew who had died," Joan recalled. "She seemed to want some comforting or reckoning or explanation of that. I always felt she wanted me to solve some kind of underlying emotional problem. She was a drowning person desperately reaching out and pulling down other people with her."

II

In softening the violence of his wife's death, Mark Felt attempted to make Audrey's passing a loss to mourn, not a tragedy that would curse future generations. By the time his whole family learned the secret, however, Mark himself had begun to shape a very different family legacy. By that time he had built a new life, in which the elements of home and family finally came together and stayed together even as Mark's health steadily deteriorated. The story of

Deep Throat finally became the story of a man who, with love and grace, conquered the challenges of aging and of his long-held secret identity.

Mark picked up the pieces of his shattered life with the help of his daughter, his son, and their families. He found that he had the most to contribute to his daughter Joan, a single mother of three who was scratching out a living in the vicinity of her ashram in San Francisco. Joan had tough luck with men. Back at Stanford after her work in Chile, friends gave her the hallucinogenic drug mescaline, ushering her into the flower child stage of her life. She quit teaching, discarded her makeup, let her hair grow long, and moved to a farm in the Santa Cruz Mountains. She rented the chicken coop that Audrey had complained about as her new home and began living with a guitarist, James Schlesselman, who fathered Ludi. Shortly thereafter she discovered the Adidam spiritual community and its guru, Adi Da Samraj. Among practitioners of the group, which emphasizes meditation and radical self-understanding, she met the next man in her life, Rocky Jones, whom she married while pregnant with Rob. Rocky left shortly after she became pregnant with her third child, and the two reconciled briefly while Nick was an infant. Her next partner, Michael Hubbell, became a beloved surrogate father to her sons, but the family had trouble making ends meet and at times had to go on welfare.

After her mother's suicide, Joan forged a closer relationship with her father. The following summer, she brought her three boys to visit their grandfather in Virginia, and he followed them to northern California in August, taking a room at the Flamingo Hotel in Santa Rosa. For five years he continued his annual trips to the Flamingo, inviting the boys to frolic in the pool and enjoy hamburgers and fries beyond the jurisdiction of their mom and her vegetarian diet.

Back in Virginia, during this same period, Mark developed his relationship with Yvette La Garde, a striking French widow who spoke several languages and had won honors for her career at the Commerce Department. They played down their romance in front of their families, each out of respect for the memory of a departed spouse. But their love flourished nonetheless.

Over time, the pull from each side grew stronger. In Virginia, Yvette told her daughter and confidante that she and Mark were contemplating marriage. In California, Joan was diagnosed with breast cancer, had a radical mastectomy, and faced long, debilitating treatment for her cancer, which had metastasized into more than twenty lymph nodes. No one would have blamed Mark had he stayed with Yvette and continued to make his annual visits to Joan, as well as sending the occasional check. He had a large, top-floor condominium overlooking the Potomac, a substantial pension, and an elegant woman to escort about town. But none of that could match the main force in Mark's psyche: his sense of duty. His visits to Joan and her boys grew longer, and in 1991 he sold his Virginia condominium, left Yvette (who he knew would never move away from her own grandchildren in the Washington area), and made a new home at the Walnut Creek Apartment complex in Santa Rosa. (He did not ignore his duty to Yvette, writing her long, loving letters until his stroke. When Yvette later became unable to care for herself, the only items she insisted on bringing to her new assisted-living home were Mark's letters.) For the first time in his life, Mark Felt became the active, engaged head of a family.

By that time, he had joined wholeheartedly in his daughter's battle against cancer. Joan put herself on a regimen of raw foods designed to preserve healthful vitamins and enzymes. She prepared labor-intensive dishes such as cauliflower loaves (cauliflower put through a juicer, then mixed with onions, garlic, and other veggies) and mock salmon pâté (carrots, almonds, lemon, and parsley). Mark gamely joined her diet for five weeks and, says his proud daughter, cut his cholesterol from 265 to 132. Teaching himself the basics of gardening and carpentry, Mark built planting shelves behind Joan's little duplex and sowed wheat grass and buckwheat and sunflower greens. By the end of 1991 Joan was pronounced cured.

In 1992 Mark used the proceeds from his Virginia condo to buy a cozy house on a quiet street in Santa Rosa. He gave Joan the master bedroom and took a smaller upstairs bedroom for himself. He shuttled his grandsons to their games and got to know their friends, luxuries he had never experienced with his own son. He contributed his own style to the life of the household. He looked the other way when the boys violated Joan's strict health food regimen but gently corrected another aspect of her Northern California countercultural style—the almost total absence of behavioral rules. "We were brought up by a hippie mom," said Joan's youngest son, Nick, a Stanford graduate and Hastings College law student. "There weren't any rules." But when Grandpa was around, Nick added, "you knew you had to clean up after yourself, have your stuff in order, be responsible." Most important, perhaps, Mark taught the boys his ethic of consideration for others. At the supermarket, they would see him yield to other drivers in the parking lot, make way for other shoppers at the checkout line, and leave the cashier giggling from his barrage of compliments.

Gradually the trips to the supermarket and the joyrides in Mark's Buick Skylark became less frequent. As he advanced into his eighties, Mark's mental function gradually deteriorated. He still had good days when he could recall his battles against the Nixon administration, but increasingly he had bad days, when he had trouble remembering the outlines of his FBI life. Hardwired into Mark's psyche was the idea that his role as Deep Throat must stay in the closet in disgrace. It took many intimate family chats and relaxed conversations to change his mind. He made his decision to go public hesitantly and reluctantly. Finally, the decision made, he accepted it peacefully. As a *Vanity Fair* photographer posed him for photos in

April 2005, Mark turned to Joan and said, "People used to think that Deep Throat was some kind of a criminal, but now I guess they think he's a hero."

As Mark opened the letters and packages that arrived after our announcement—from ladies in New York and Texas, from grade school children in Michigan, from a retired army officer in Florida—he was ecstatic about the outpouring of thanks and praise. His family, his caregiver, Bola, and I were delighted to see him accept his full identity, to proudly acknowledge every aspect of his career. Mark Felt had at last let go of his secret, had opened the one compartment that he had vowed to keep sealed until death. It was a day that made him a new man. "It's very cool to see this person of infinite guile become open, spontaneous, completely in the moment," said Nick. He was even more amazed to see his ever rational grandfather begin to welcome religiosity into his life. One day Mark and his buddy Bola watched television, Mark sitting in his favorite chair beneath a large oil painting of a radiant Audrey. A preacher on the screen talked of God's constant, tenacious pull on each soul. "This is one heck of a sermon, isn't it, Nick?" Mark said.

Taking in the happy scene, observing his grandfather absorbing the sermon without his lifelong filters of rationality and reserve, Nick responded, "Yeah, Grandpa. Seems like a pretty cool sermon to me."

Joan discovered that her philosophical and lifestyle differences with her father no longer seemed so irreconcilable. Though she never would have predicted it during her hippie days, she developed a strong interest in her father's world and came to respect his ideals of democracy, constitutional checks and balances, and effective government. At the same time, Joan's desire to realize true and abiding happiness—moment to moment—became a natural priority in Mark's life, though he would still prefer to call it "good, common sense" rather than "religion."

As father and daughter were sitting by the pool appreciating a shared silence, Mark said, "Why didn't we know about this before?"

"Know about what, Dad?"

"This . . . love."

"What do you think?"

"I guess we were just too busy."

"Well, we know about it now, don't we?"

"Oh my, yes! We certainly do!"

Mark Felt entered the last chapter of his life with most of his extended family by his side. He had moved to California to care for his daughter; now she and her sons devoted much of their lives to caring for him. His health took a turn for the worse in 1996 but improved when doctors inserted a stent to improve blood flow to his heart. Three years later, after surgery to clear the carotid arteries in his neck, he suffered his first stroke, which temporarily paralyzed his right side. When he returned home from the hospital, he had trouble keeping his balance and suffered two serious falls. Going out to get the newspapers one morning, he fell and broke both arms. Joan managed the intensive care he required during recuperation and had the garage remodeled into a ground-floor apartment. But then he fell through a gap in the rear deck of the house, severely injuring his leg, and a few months later he suffered a second stroke.

This time his doctors sent him from the hospital to a convalescent home, where Mark sank into a deep gloom, telling Joan that nobody could live there. Joan moved him into a board and care home for the elderly, but that provided scant improvement. The Thai accent of the owner and her assistants was hard for Mark to understand, even disorienting, and he kept forgetting to comply with the restrictive rules. The owner complained that Mark would awaken at night hallucinating, making his way from room to room demanding that someone let him call the FBI to rescue him and bring him home.

Joan didn't need the FBI to decide. Against doctors' recommendations, she brought her father back to his apartment in the garage. She worked as a college Spanish teacher, squeezed her budget, and took in student boarders. She engaged Fijian caregivers, who have a wonderful way with the elderly. They see the aging process as natural, humorous, and endearing, to be handled with music and laughter. As her father gradually realized that he was home to stay, and as he was weaned off the antipsychotic drugs administered at the board and care facility, his health rebounded dramatically.

Mark began to move around and happily joined the life of a household that included his daughter and various combinations of grandsons, students, and caregivers. Although his dementia continued to deepen, he did not suffer from Alzheimer's disease with its attendant nervousness and restlessness. To the contrary, as his physical problems multiplied—in later years his kidneys began to fail—Mark Felt grew steadily happier. Joan had worked in nursing homes and believed that as age advances, a person's true character emerges. She saw many elderly patients grow bitter and vindictive in their isolation. But she saw her father grow sweeter and gentler. "He used to say, 'I feel old,' or 'This is difficult,' but he has passed through that," Joan said. "He has surrendered to his situation, which is quite extraordinary. He gets out for rides, goes to the neighbor's house in his wheelchair, takes drives for visits to Sacramento. When I ask him how his day has gone, he'll say, 'I had a lot of fun.'"

When her father was more mobile, Joan would routinely take him on errands—to get a haircut, to fill the car with gas. At the supermarket, Mark would push the cart while his daughter filled it. Joan noticed other shoppers staring at them and realized that she and her father were indeed an oddity. "People aren't used to seeing someone that old out and about," she said. "Most of our elders get shut away in nursing homes where nobody sees them." In Joan's home, the resident nonagenarian contributes to the life of the family. His grandsons care for their grandfather's every need, including personal hygiene. The first time Nick helped his grandfather in the bathroom, he "went through that process of revulsion and fear back into intimacy and love," Joan said. "It was really an important experience for him, having old age become a normal and actual thing."

When the time comes, Mark's family plans to honor him with a funeral service at home, including a casket painted by his grandson Rob. Joan will allow plenty of time after her father's heart stops beating to let his life leave at its own pace, as she put it, "to let him feel guided and loved through the process. . . . Even though he is enjoying his life, he deserves a rest too. He has fought long and hard for his principles and his family, and he deserves a rest."

Mark Felt was part of a generation of Americans who fought the Nazis and communism as a matter of duty to God and country, no questions asked. Grandson Nick now reflects that his mother's generation and his own have adopted a different set of values. Americans today believe in openness, honesty, and transparency, not blind loyalty. They demand government accountability and they ask questions. History books trace these attitudes to the tumultuous scandals of Watergate. And these strong new ideas were influenced in no small part by the courage of Bob Woodward's mysterious source, the man who demanded that questions be asked. How ironic that for most of his life, Deep Throat himself shied away from the standards of openness he helped introduce. And how fitting that at the end of his life, Mark Felt has opened the door to acknowledge his gift to his country.

ACKNOWLEDGMENTS

We first acknowledge the San Francisco law firm of Howard, Rice, Nemerovski, Canady, Falk and Rabkin, without whose support this book, Mark's intitial revelation, and his accompanying recognition would not have been possible. The Howard Rice firm reflects the best of the American legal tradition, as it is so well applied in San Francisco, offering the profession's legal talents not only for the financial success of its clientele, but also for generous assistance to a wide variety of civic and charitable causes, with this contribution to history but one of many proud examples. Many individuals at Howard Rice contributed to this effort, chief among them nonpareil paralegal Will Rehling, the estimable lawyer/physician Dr. Duane Nash, legal assistants Marie Leahy, Liz Carmichael, and Kasa Cotugno, and intellectual property experts Simon Frankel and Tom Magnani. And there is no finer or more thorough research assistant than Michael Ginsborg. The encouragement of firm management and directors made this all a reality.

The amazingly energetic Joan Felt first sensitized us to the need for more caring approaches to our elderly, and Sister Susan Dinnin has enlightened us even further through the work of A Caring Place, her stellar, charitably supported program for the elderly in Indianapolis, Indiana.

Insightful agent and friend David Kuhn served us exceedingly well as a reassuring guide to the literary world. In Mark's initial revelation, the value of *Vanity Fair* editor David Friend's journalistic mentoring was incalculable.

Finally, we thank our editors and publishing staff at PublicAffairs, the visionary former Watergate and Vietnam reporter, now editor-at-large, Peter Osnos, and the brilliant editor-cum-writer Steven Strasser, who helped us condense our encyclopaedic ambitions into one book.

INDEX

310 INDEX

Felt, W. Mark (*cont.*)
  Reagan's pardoning of, 278, 293
  retirement of, 251, 254, 269
  Ruckelshaus relating to, 247–250
  Sullivan relating to, 97, 118–121, 270
  as "Three-Hour Felt," 239–253
  Tolson working with, 26, 127–129
  trial of, 275–278
  Wallace relating to, 185–187
  wiretaps relating to, 97–100, 121
Felt, W. Mark, assignments of
  associate director, 243–244
  chief inspector, 65–67
  deputy associate director, 117–118, 126
  in Houston, TX, 13–14, 285
  Inspection Division, as head of, 65, 66, 87, 99, 127, 286
  ITT memorandum, 137–144
  in Kansas City, MO, 43
  in Los Angeles, CA, 34
  in New Orleans, LA, 27–34, 287
  in Salt Lake City, UT, 34–43
  in San Antonio, TX, 15, 285
  in Seattle, WA, 23–26, 285, 286
  in Washington, D.C., 15, 16, 27, 285, 286–287
  Watergate investigation, 193, 195–196, 198, 201–202, 214
Felt, W. Mark, III, 292
Felt, W. Mark, Jr., 282, 286–295
Felt, Wanda, 292
Female agents, in FBI, 179–180
Fields, Annie, 149–150
Files. *See also* Secret files, Gray relating to
  of Hunt, 234, 237, 239–241
  Watergate, 230, 233
Finch, Robert H., 121

Fiorini, Frank Anthony, 195, 211
Floyd, Pretty Boy, 283
Fourth Amendment, 267, 268, 276
Fraley, Geneva, 59
Freedom of Information Act, 164
FTC (Federal Trade Commission), 9

Gale, James H., 64–65
Gandy, Helen, 73, 80, 127, 155–158, 174
  Hoover's death relating to, 146, 147, 150, 151
General Accounting Office, 201
General Investigative Division, of FBI, 119, 195
German espionage, 16–20
German-American Bund, 17, 264
Gettings, Brian, 271, 277
Gillette, Faye, 39
G-Man, 284
Gold, Helmut, 21–22
Gonzales, Virgilio R., 195, 211
Gray, Bea, 153
Gray, Fred, 54–55
Gray, L. Patrick, III, 69, 74, 122
  as acting FBI director, 152–154, 159, 173–184, 187–192, 227, 245, 259–260, 267, 268
  case dropped against, 277
  Dean relating to, 205–207, 231, 234, 235, 236, 237
  Ehrlichman relating to, 228, 234–235
  as FBI director, Nixon's appointment of, 228–238, 241
  for FBI director, senate confirmation hearings of, 228–238, 241, 254
  Felt relating to, 152–159, 176, 178–179, 181, 182–184, 187–188, 190, 241, 272, 291

PublicAffairs is a publishing house founded in 1997. It is a tribute to the standards, values, and flair of three persons who have served as mentors to countless reporters, writers, editors, and book people of all kinds, including me.

I.F. STONE, proprietor of *I. F. Stone's Weekly*, combined a commitment to the First Amendment with entrepreneurial zeal and reporting skill and became one of the great independent journalists in American history. At the age of eighty, Izzy published *The Trial of Socrates,* which was a national bestseller. He wrote the book after he taught himself ancient Greek.

BENJAMIN C. BRADLEE was for nearly thirty years the charismatic editorial leader of *The Washington Post*. It was Ben who gave the *Post* the range and courage to pursue such historic issues as Watergate. He supported his reporters with a tenacity that made them fearless and it is no accident that so many became authors of influential, best-selling books.

ROBERT L. BERNSTEIN, the chief executive of Random House for more than a quarter century, guided one of the nation's premier publishing houses. Bob was personally responsible for many books of political dissent and argument that challenged tyranny around the globe. He is also the founder and longtime chair of Human Rights Watch, one of the most respected human rights organizations in the world.

For fifty years, the banner of Public Affairs Press was carried by its owner Morris B. Schnapper, who published Gandhi, Nasser, Toynbee, Truman, and about 1,500 other authors. In 1983, Schnapper was described by *The Washington Post* as "a redoubtable gadfly." His legacy will endure in the books to come.

Peter Osnos, *Founder and Editor-at-Large*